9-3100

Travel on
Southern Antebellum
Railroads

Travel on Southern Antebellum Railroads, 1828–1860

Eugene
Alvarez

The University of Alabama Press
University, Alabama

Copyright © 1974 by
The University of Alabama Press
ISBN 0–8173–5213–7
Library of Congress Catalog Card Number: 74–2820
ALL RIGHTS RESERVED
Manufactured in the United States of America

Motif on chapter openings courtesy of
Southern Railway Company.

To
Mother and Father

Contents

Preface   viii
1 The Introduction of the Railroad   1
2 The Railroad Mania Continues to Grow   14
3 Engines of Smoke, Fire, and Cinders   26
4 The Railroad Passenger Car   47
5 The Hazardous Roadway   68
6 The Perils of the Road   81
7 The Railroad Station   107
8 Society in the Cars   126
9 Traveling Through the South   150
    Epilogue   164
    Appendix   168
    Notes   176
    Bibliography   203
    Index   215

Preface

The antebellum railroad in the South, as well as in all of America, was a phenomenon which provided a moving, restless population with the mixed blessings of much-needed speed and dirty discomfort. To many people it was retrograde, a step backward rather than forward. Citizens frequently complained that the wood-burning engines frightened their horses, set fire to their silos, and produced an awesome death rate unmatched anywhere in the world. However, despite the hazards, most Americans welcomed the "iron horse" as a means to prosperity for rural and urban communities alike. Steel rails, they reckoned, would connect isolated plantations with ports of trade, bringing affluence to all concerned. In fact, the first significant railroads were built from coastal cities to the hinterland in order to capture the inland trade; that is, to deliver cotton and other agricultural commodities to a world market which meant dollars in Southern pocketbooks.

Although passenger travel was of secondary importance in antebellum railroading, many travelers, particularly those from abroad, were drawn to the South for several reasons: slavery, a highly controversial topic; the reputation of Southerners as genteel, aristocratic hosts, particularly open-hearted to Western Europeans; and of course the natural beauty and salubrious climate of the region. However, because of the emotional impact of these factors, and a not infrequent personal prejudice on the part of travelers, both domestic and foreign, their accounts are not always to be accepted without reservations.

The American of the first half of the last century took great pride in his railroads. Fiercely nationalistic, he viewed the spreading network of rails throughout his new and growing country as concrete evidence of power, of prestige, of economic prowess in world economy. Even more important perhaps, at least socially, was the ever-surging spirit of democracy rampant on the railroads. There, no class structure, no social caste applied—only pure, raw, down-to-earth democracy was evident. The rail car was one of America's greatest economic and social levellers. Foreigners were always amazed at the absence of class distinctions in the new nation and frequently marvelled at the crudeness, coarseness, even vulgarity, expressed by Americans in their manners and particularly in their habits of travel. As one shocked English traveler put it, these "sons of the New World" were a sight to behold. But behind all their bravado and boastfulness and lack of refinement, astute foreigners saw the seeds of greatness in the democracy of American life.

Although numerous books and articles have been published about early railroads in the United States, they chiefly concern the history of research, construction, and development—the routes, the costs, the mechanics of machines, the use of rails in war times, and the like. So far as I know, no single study heretofore has dealt primarily with the societal aspects of railroad travel in the South before the War Between the States.

Largely through the use of eyewitness accounts and contemporary opinions, I present an insight into the actual day-by-day reactions of railroad travelers in the antebellum South, the hardships they endured, their non-professional observations, and their ultimate reception of the most innovative mode of transportation the world of their time had ever known. Alternate titles for the book might well be "Railroads in the Old South: A Social History" or "The Democracy of Antebellum Southern Railroading" or even

"The Railroad in Southern Society, 1828–1860." In any event, the traveler tells his own story—what he saw, believed, heard, tasted, felt, and smelt on the "iron horse"—as he moved about America in that point of time known as the Jacksonian Period.

Travel on Southern Antebellum Railroads could not have been completed without the valuable assistance of several persons. Professor John Hebron Moore of the University of Mississippi first suggested the desirability of my study. Professor Horace Montgomery of the University of Georgia labored with me in developing the manuscript. I am also indebted to Professors J. Allen Cabaniss, University of Mississippi, J. Chal Vinson, Lee Boone Kennett, and Richard Murdoch of the University of Georgia, each of whom assisted materially in preparing the book. To Mrs. Eugenia Butler and especially to Dr. Florence Jean Christy, I am grateful for valuable suggestions in revising and proofreading the manuscript. And last but by no means least, my gratitude goes out to the many librarians of special collections in the libraries of the University of Kentucky, Duke University, and the University of Mississippi for their altruistic guidance and assistance.

Needless to add, any errors (whether of omission or commission) are mine, and mine alone.

EUGENE ALVAREZ

Travel on
Southern Antebellum
Railroads

Stone Mountain

1

The Introduction
of the Railroad

During the 1830's strange, noisy little machines, followed by clouds of smoke, shattered the peaceful seclusion of the countryside and announced to America that it had entered the age of steam. Never again would the landscape or the outlook of the nation be the same, for the advent of the railroad signaled the beginning of an amazing surge of expansive growth, which by 1869 connected the nation from sea to sea by rail. Within the century, by sheer determination and ingenuity, a richly endowed nation built railroads across valleys, over and through mountains, across swamps and rivers, and through cities, hamlets, and towns. Before the birth of the twentieth century, overpowering locomotives conquered a continent, closed a frontier, and manifestly contributed to the defeat and subjection of that indigenous race, the American Indian, which fell victim to white men and steam.

During this amazing era of growth and influence of the American railroad as a national institution, perhaps no period of development was more significant than the formative years preceding the Civil War. In their first three decades of experimentation, pioneer railroad inventors and engineers improved rails and roadbeds, learned to build locomotives capable of attaining twentieth century speeds, and attempted to better passenger comfort and service through the innovation of such devices as ventilating systems and sleeping cars. In a vast country, favored by an abundance of cheap and accessible land, unhampered by customs and political barriers, the railroad wedded the town and country, accelerated the settlement and defense of distant territories, and opened the possibility of inviting commercial ventures as far away as California, Oregon, and even the Far East.[1]

Following the near disaster of 1812, and during the significant years between the Treaty of Ghent and the attack on Fort Sumter, few aspects of the nation's phenomenal growth were more spectacular than the transportation revolution. Among the more celebrated achievements were the completion of the Erie Canal in 1825, the first successful trans-Atlantic voyage under steam and sail by the S. S. *Savannah* in 1819, and the growth of a dynamic rail system which boasted more miles of track than the rest of the nations of the world combined.[2] Indeed, it is not surprising that Americans were sometimes described by visiting foreigners as "haughty with hope of endless progress and irresistible power," and "essentially a locomotive people" who were continually on the move.[3]

Two decades before the nation succumbed to the locomotive craze of the 1840's and 1850's, however, the heart of the transportation revolution had centered primarily on riverboats and especially inland canals.[4] The more advanced steamboat had operated on American waters as early as 1807, when Robert Fulton's *Clermont* churned up the Hudson River from New York to Albany and back in only thirty-two hours. By 1809 regular passenger service commenced and a new era in water transportation began. But the heyday of the river steamer was yet to come.

In the interim, Americans turned to canals, and for approximately twenty years an elaborate construction program was underway, highlighted by the completion in 1825 of New York's Erie Canal. The seriousness of other such ventures is reflected by the determined efforts to surmount the numerous difficulties encountered during construction, and by the large increases soon evident in canal mileage. The building of these canals, it must be remembered, was all the more remarkable since the builders had only human and horse power to remove soil, only black powder for blasting, and holes for blasting had to be drilled in rock with nothing more than hand drills. Nevertheless, from a scant one hundred miles in 1816, canals claimed more than three thousand miles by 1840. But despite differing opinions on the superiority of the railroad over canals, the promise of the prosperous twenties gradually faded away, and the short-lived "canal craze" was over. In fact, even as early as the 1830's, more than three miles of rail were constructed for every two miles of canal. In the succeeding decade, less than four hundred miles of canals were built; and by 1850, 123 miles of canals fell victim to railroads, as abandonments began exceeding new construction.[5] Eventually only the most necessary water systems were capable of surviving the onslaught of the steam locomotive.[6]

To the more alert and well read speculators of the antebellum years, the fate of canals was possibly detectible as early as 1825. From England reputable periodicals reported that canals had served well in the past, "but we have now got something that will do better."[7] Two years later another sign of the changing times was printed in the *North American Review*, which wrote that the substitution of railroads for canals, then occurring in England, would also be likely to occur in the favorable conditions and climate of the United States. In 1828 and 1830 *Niles' Weekly Register* reported that transportation by rail would reduce by two-thirds the costs suffered on regular roads, and predicted that within twenty years "the many hundred miles of canals made, and now making in the United States, at an expense of about thirty millions of dollars, will be all filled up or drained, to make foundations for rail roads."[8] Warnings appeared: "The public mind is every day more and more settling into a belief that rail roads will supercede canals."[9]

The demise of canals was also noted by native and foreign travelers. One of the most attentive was the celebrated French economist Michel Chevalier. While traveling in America as a representative of the French Ministry of the Interior to study railroads and other public works, Chevalier reported between 1833 and 1835 that canals around Charleston had deteriorated to such a state of obsolescence that they were of minor importance, and were also too difficult to construct in the muddy soil of the lower Mississippi River.[10] Among numerous other travelers who detected the creeping influence of railroads at the expense of stage routes and canals were James D. Davidson and John Lee Williams. Davidson gloomily predicted the demise of stage lines because of the attraction and advantages of railroads,[11] whereas Williams observed, during a journey in the 1830's into the Florida territory, that canals were being superseded by railroads, which were cheaper, more expeditious, and more permanent.[12]

Among other reasons for the abandonment of canals was the fact that their usefulness for long distance hauling was terminated once canals attained their natural limits. But with railroad tracks long hauls could continue indefinitely, since lines were operable year round, and were seldom affected by frozen rivers and hindrances caused by floods and droughts. Other serious disadvantages of canals were that frequent reloadings were necessary for barges to reach landlocked destinations that could be more easily gained by rail. Passengers often remarked that water routes, though pleasing, were slow, unhealthy, and not as safe as the way taken by trains, so it was not surprising that by mid-century

Americans preferred the faster and more versatile locomotive to the slower and less adaptable canal.[13]

To England must go the credit for first applying steam power to locomotion on land, when in 1801 Richard Trevithick mounted an engine on wheels that could be run on a road.[14] American interest in steam took a significant step forward eleven years later, when John Stevens of Hoboken, New Jersey, proposed a steam railway between Albany and Lake Erie. Although it was not until 1828 that the United States seriously began building railroads, some citizens in coastal cities began to express an interest concerning their possibilities even before they were in operation. For instance, in 1825 the *Museum of Foreign Literature and Science* reported as follows:

> Rail-roads have already excited the strongest feelings of interest in America, that theatre where every faculty of human nature and every discovery in art and science is developed with such miraculous energy. They are undergoing discussion at the seat of government, and letters from Washington are full of inquiries concerning them.[15]

In later years the early zeal of pioneer builders was recalled in 1850 by the railroad expert Dionysius Lardner, who wrote that no sooner had England developed her first roads, "than the Americans, with their usual ardor, resolved to import this great improvement; and projects of passenger railways, on the vast scale which characterizes all their enterprises, were immediately put forth."[16]

Although it may be argued that some of the first railroads in America were conceived for use primarily by passengers, for the most part the early companies were built to further the expanding inland trade of seaboard merchants and coastal ports.[17] As an alternative to canals, two pioneer lines built for this purpose to serve parts of the South were Maryland's Baltimore & Ohio Railroad and South Carolina's Charleston & Hamburg Railroad.

The objective of the Baltimore & Ohio Railroad, chartered in 1827, was to compete with the Erie Canal, and siphon off portions of trade for Baltimore from New York and Philadelphia. The citizens of Maryland were all agog over the prospects of a railroad and enthusiastically endorsed the line as a means of capturing the much sought-after trade of the West. According to Samuel A. Mitchell's guidebook of the day,

> [The railroad was] by far the most stupendous national work of the kind ever undertaken in this or any other country. The entire distance will exceed 300 miles; on this road every mode of passage, by horse car power and locomotive steam car power, and wind power by sails, has been adopted. The route of this great undertaking is through a country abounding in every variety of splendid scenery that mountains, valleys, cascades, rivers, forests, and the wildness of nature in her mountainous retreats, can furnish. Various other works of the same kind are in contemplation. When these shall be completed, Maryland will probably come in for her full share of the trade of the west.[18]

From the very beginning the railroad was a major attraction of the city, and for one to visit Baltimore and not ride the horse-drawn trains was to have missed completely one of the major attractions of the town.[19] Even during the initial construction of thirteen miles of track between Baltimore and Ellicott's Mills, the progress of the great national work excited curious citizens and daily attracted large numbers of persons to view the progress of the workmen.[20] Curious members of Congress from nearby Washington were also dazzled by the railroad. For the modest fare of nine cents members of the august assembly frequently rode in the horse-pulled cars, which attained amazing speeds of eight to fifteen miles per hour, depending on the number of animals used and the passenger load aboard.[21] To Henry Tudor, an Englishman, who in 1831 and 1832 came to behold the wonders of the New World, the impressive affair was "the most prodigious work at present carrying on in the United States ... and will be travelled with the greatest possible ease."[22] A similar assessment was expressed by Francesco Arese, visiting from Italy in 1837 and 1838.[23]

The Maryland railroad may lay claim to beginning the foremost passenger service in the United States, but it did not run the first steam powered passenger trains. This distinction belongs to the Charleston & Hamburg Railroad, of South Carolina, which, like the Baltimore & Ohio, was formed to capture the rich trade of the Piedmont then being lost to the Savannah River. Hoping to rectify the loss, a band of progressive Charlestonians turned to railroads and founded a line in May, 1828. The road was planned to emanate from Charleston, running west to the small hamlet of Hamburg, across the Savannah River from Augusta.[24] Almost immediately the South Carolina company seemed destined for success. Besides being the first major American railroad equipped with steam engines, the Charleston & Hamburg was also the first to carry mail.[25] Among its other laurels was the dubious honor of claiming the first locomotive explosion in the history of American railroads in 1831, and by 1833 it was the longest railroad in the world with 136 miles of track.[26]

Magazine columns and the reports of travelers reveal the enthusiasm for the acceptance of these two railroads, and the records of their first years of operations seem to have substantiated the great expectations of their promoters. According to *Niles' Weekly Register,* in 1828 the activity and laborious industry taking place on the Maryland line indicated the railroad would yield large revenues from "pleasure carriages" and the transportation of heavy goods.[27] So rapid was the Maryland company's growth that by 1832 the scientist Charles J. Latrobe reported that, although the company was still in its infancy, when compared to the first time he traveled on its tracks, the progress of the railroad was something to behold. Most of the surrounding area had been transformed from a few rude and shabby shacks into towns with hotels and warehouses, while an incessant amount of traffic conveyed the natural resources of the country to demanding cities and towns.[28] Several examples of the lines' financial success, as indicated in *Niles' Weekly Register,* reveal that in the last six months of 1832 the total income of the Maryland line amounted to $78,160.44, although the operating expenditures were but $41,414.29. The following six months, in 1833, the company spent for operations $41,534.35 but showed receipts of $92,556.86.

In South Carolina substantial profits were enjoyed by the Charleston & Hamburg Railroad as well. In April, 1835, the *Register* carried in its columns a statement revealing this fact:

> The increasing travel and transportation on our railroad, since the commencement of the present year, have exceeded the most sanguine expectations of its projectors and those who have been its steady friends through good and evil report.[29]

By 1847, because of the railroad, the once quiet town of Hamburg, South Carolina had become a leading market center of the state and was handling as much as 900 bales of cotton, 3,000 bushels of corn and wheat, 50,000 pounds of Tennessee bacon, and 600 bales of yarn in one day.[30]

While Englishmen were often content to sit back and complacently admire the several outstanding lines of their country, American enthusiasm for steam transportation had become overwhelming by mid-century. With a mania for size and a frequent disregard for safety, the "enthusiasm was not far short of hysterical." London businessman Joseph Biggs, visiting the United States during the Panic of 1837, was aware of the American zeal for size and said the nation had "many hundreds of miles of railways."[31] The geologist and lecturer Charles Lyell witnessed similar findings in 1845 and 1846. But to him the people had displayed prudence and economy in building their railroads, and had provided service for the greater part of the population.[32] A decade earlier, *Niles' Weekly Register* commented on the craze for railroads and declared, "It may doubtless be said without exaggeration, that rail roads are now projected in this country on a more extensive scale than in all other parts of the globe."[33] The craze for railroads was noted by other observers. By 1839 Grenville Mellen wrote that the number of railroads throughout the nation had increased so rapidly that even the most careful reader of daily newspapers could scarcely retain them in his recollection.[34] Additional testimony was recorded by *Hunt's Merchants Magazine* in 1843 and 1845. According to this publication the history of American rail-roads had presented one of the most remarkable instances of progress ever recorded:

A few years since, the advocates of railroads were ranked among visionaries and schemers; but so rapid has been the growth of the system among us, that the small beginning and its recent date are generally forgotten.

So universally was the importance of railroads recognized in other nations that *Hunt's* magazine stated that even Czars in Russia risked their power and influence to the spread of democracy "for the immense commercial advantages they [railroads] hold out."[35] But perhaps *DeBow's Review* best explained the omnipresent railroad fever sweeping the nation with the following comment in 1854: "In the railroad movements of the country at large, all is animation; 'progress' is the order of the day; stagnation is a thing unknown; and among the people 'there is no such word as fail.'"

The fact of the new railroad mania was amply supported by the impressive amount of track in operation by 1860. Although antebellum statistics are sometimes conflicting, in 1844 *DeBow's Review* reported that with only fifteen years of railroading behind it, America led the world in rails with

3,688 miles. Great Britain was second with 2,069 miles, followed by Germany with 1,997 miles, and France and Belgium with 552 and 343 miles respectively. Americans had been so industrious that by 1855 the magazine stated that the number of miles in the United States exceeded the rest of the world by 2,712.[36] On the eve of the Civil War the United States claimed 30,626 miles of track, placing it well ahead of the other nations of the world.[37]

Although railroads were more numerous in the North by the Civil War, the distinct advantages of the Southern physiography over other sections meant that construction problems were more easily solved on the generally flat terrain, and the rich Southern forests provided a source of wealth in raw materials for making ties and track. In fact, some speculators predicted great things in store for railroads in the South. Michel Chevalier was moved by the potential for railroads in the South while traveling from Blakely to Charleston in South Carolina, and commented that no region in the world was more favorably endowed to accommodate a railroad network than the "Palmetto State." Here, he observed, "the surface has been graded by nature and the vast forests which cover it will furnish the wood of which the railroad will be made." A similar opinion was offered concerning the Petersburg, Virginia area.[38]

The eagerness with which some Southern railroad promoters accepted the opinions of the more optimistic is revealed in various editions of *DeBow's Review*.[39] Especially during the 1850's the publication lauded the railroads and the mileage additions of the more industrious companies, reporting in 1853, "The tide of railroad enterprise seems now to be tending strongly towards the South. The progress that railroads are now making in the South is truly wonderful." The report continued, "The spirit for railroad improvements seems now to be thoroughly infused into the whole South, and we hear of movements being made for new roads almost weekly." Seven years later, the *Review* stated on the eve of Fort Sumter, "Nothing can give a more forcible idea of the growing importance of the Southern States of the Union, than a survey of their immense railroad system." And reflecting a sensitivity to Northern criticism of slavery in the South the magazine added that her railroads were "a standing refutation of all such misconceptions."[40] Indeed, by 1860 the future seemed promising for the infant and older lines of the South, which were urged onward by railroad promoters throughout the entire nation.

Yet despite its rapid progress in the 1850's, the South lagged behind the North in road construction, mechanics, engineers, and other positions related to railroading. Although many Northern companies often relied on rich Southern forests for ties, track runners, and fuel, by 1860 the Southern states could claim only one-fifth of the railroad personnel in the nation, though nearly one-third of the country's track lay within Southern boundaries.[41] But even though Southern lines placed second to those in the North in mileage, the Southern enthusiasm for railroads was enormous and vital. By 1859 Virginia boasted 1,525 miles, Georgia 1,241 miles, and Tennessee had 1,062 miles. The total mileage of the Southern states (including Missouri and Kentucky) was 8,794 miles, according to *DeBow's Review*, exceeding Great Britain's total by more than 745 miles.[42]

The astounding growth and mania for railroads was not confined to the interests of Americans, North and South; it also aroused the concern and curiosity of foreign promoters and economists. Michel Chevalier was surprised to discover that no sooner had he boarded his ship for the United States than the word "railroad" was heard at least every ten minutes in the conversation of the passengers aboard. The Frenchman reported that Americans seemed to have "a perfect passion for railroads" and loved them "as a lover loves his mistress." He discovered too that Americans were so railroad conscious that they wanted to apply steam everywhere and to everything. Railroads were discovered in prisons and coal mines, in tobacco manufactories, in the water, the "bowels of the earth," and even on bridges and viaducts high in the air. Chevalier best expressed the zeal he found in the following statement:

> The old story has often occurred to my mind since I have been in the United States and I have often said to myself, if Aesop's boys had been Americans, instead of having been subjects of King Nectanebus, they would have demanded materials, not for building a city, but for constructing a railroad.[43]

Henry Tudor, who came to the United States for health purposes in 1831, referred to the Baltimore & Ohio project as "truly a vast undertaking." The proverb of "nothing venture, nothing have," was never better exemplified to the Englishman than what he saw in America during his tour.[44] For Charles Latrobe the spirit of the Americans was "worthy of great admiration,"[45] while the practical Italian Count Francesco Arese went so far as to remark in his *Trip to the Praries* that it would be fortunate if his country could exchange some of its art treasures for a few leagues of American rails.[46]

Among other travelers who were struck by the American railroad mania was the famous English tragedienne Frances Anne Kemble. While journeying from Philadelphia to her American husband's plantation in South Georgia, this aristocratic and highly critical actress compared her observations of the zeal of Americans for railroads to that of impatient children trying out a new, incomplete, perilous, and hazardous thing.[47] Similar criticism was voiced by Léon Beauvallet, a member of Rachel Felix's opera troupe which toured the United States in 1855–56. This often humorous and keenly critical Frenchman jibed that the Americans were quick and proud to boast of their "nine hundred thousand leagues of railroads," and that by placing them together "there would be enough to make a girdle for the terrestrial globe!" After denouncing the nation's railroads as "a miracle of headlong carelessness," Beauvallet added, "My God! had they more than enough to make a road to the moon, that would not make them any better."[48]

Foreign critics notwithstanding, Americans by 1850 were quite pleased with the achievements they had made in railroading and the railroad mania continued to grow. As the practicality of steam power became more apparent, agriculture and industry expanded across mountainous barriers, virgin forests, and great plains. For the nation's unemployed and immigrant class, I. W. Warner noted (p. 97) in his *Immigrant's Guide,* which was published in New York in 1848, that the entire population of the country might find employment for years completing the railroads which were then under construction. But perhaps the attraction of Americans to steam and railroading was best expressed by an anonymous writer of the 1830's:

> We are born in haste . . . we take our education on the run; we marry on the wind; we make a fortune at a stroke and lose it in the same manner, to make and lose it again ten times over in the twinkling of an eye. Our body is a locomotive going at the rate of twenty-five miles an hour; our soul, a high pressure engine; our life is like a shooting star, and death overtakes us at last like a flash of lightning.[49]

Indeed, it is not surprising that in 1858 *DeBow's Review* wrote that "Americans are born, not with silver spoons, but with iron rails in their mouths."[50]

2

The Railroad Mania Continues to Grow

Although the prosperity accompanying railroads was often elusive to some towns, the coming of the "iron horse" to other Southern communities brought hopes for the dawn of a new day. Always a friend of the railroad, J. D. B. DeBow optimistically reported in 1853 that in localities where railroads had been most freely used the general wealth of the area had increased far beyond the initial cost.[1] New Orleans was a case in point. Long favored by her natural and strategic location on the Mississippi River, the city seemed assured of an even brighter future because of her newly acquired railroad facilities. Teacher Joseph Ingraham from Maine was one who noted the impact of the railroads around the port city and described the advantages resulting from the Lake Pontchartrain Railroad as "incalculable" and as an "avenue of wealth." Besides its financial rewards, the line provided passengers smoother rides than horse-carriages, traveling in and out of the town, and spawned a tourist trade to nearby Lake Pontchartrain as well.[2] In neighboring Carrollton, railroad prosperity was revealed by the construction of a new hotel, a terminal building, and several small shops.[3] The building of the New Orleans & Great Northern Railroad brought in more money and stimulated the local tourist trade and excursions by rail to the adjacent lakes and woods.[4]

Successful ventures that were apparent in other parts of the South were recorded during visits in 1853 and 1854 by the New England abolitionist Philo Tower. Tower praised the importance of the railroad to the city of Wilmington, North Carolina, observing that "its population and business elements have been greatly increased by the construction of the Wilmington & Raleigh railroad, which forms a part of the great highway of travel north and south."[5] In Virginia, Amelia Matilda Murray commenting that Petersburg was a growing town, predicted that because of the many railroads traversing the state, Virginians would soon exploit its capabilities and render it one of the most prosperous in the United States.[6]

The impact of railroads was pronounced in Mississippi, where slaves and livestock were driven over the Natchez Trace and other roads, or shipped south by riverboats from Pittsburgh, Cincinnati, and Louisville. But once a system of railroads began to spread over the state, deliveries were more reliable and prompt, and the expediting of purchases increased the profits of the traders. Other advantages brought by rails were graphically illustrated by the cotton trade between Jackson and Vicksburg. On deplorable roads between these two commercial centers, oxen were often broken by loads up to 3,000 pounds and died of exhaustion along the slow, difficult, and tortuous route. One wag reported that so many of the animals had perished under these burdensome loads that one might walk on dead animals all of the way.[7] Eagerly consumed accounts that glorified the projects and economic benefits of railroads informed readers that freight cars could inexpensively transport cotton to the coast and return with manufactured goods, groceries, immigrants, and the mails.[8] One Col.

Tarpley, writing in the *Mississippian*, stated that railroads in Central Mississippi would save as much as $300,000 yearly in cotton shipments and in the expenses of imports to the state. He also added that railroads would improve land values and make profits more attractive in lumber, tar, pitch, cordwood, and beef cattle.[9] Similar reasoning was offered by the honorable J. M. Niles in 1846. It was reiterated that railroads facilitated the construction of manufacturing plants far from rivers and bays, and that western provisions such as flour, hay, milk, fruit, and vegetables, through the railroads' rapid transit could now be shipped great distances without spoilage.[10]

Commercial value aside, the railroads were also hailed for their health and educational benefits and their unifying influence. In 1858 the *Atlantic Monthly* reported that railroads enabled people to live away from unhealthy and densely populated cities, yet still made it possible for businessmen to go to the city and carry on business therein.[11] Thomas Cather, an Englishman who visited America in 1836, to relieve boredom and have adventures, saw the railroad as affording to the union a powerful bond. Were it not for this cementing influence, Cather argued, the "distant states would soon become estranged," and the "people of the extreme South in a few generations would know as little of the Northerners as the Spaniards do of the Russians."[12] Agreement with Cather's judgment appeared twelve years later in *Hunt's Merchants Magazine*, which added that much of the ill will, ignorance, and jealousies of the past had been the result of a lack of social intercourse among peoples, and that through the avenues of transportation men could learn to live harmoniously together and be capable of great achievements. "Such is the general effect of the introduction of steamboats and railroad locomotives."[13]

Although the railroad transformed Southern towns such as Chattanooga, Corinth, and Atlanta into teeming centers of trade, scores of other communities did not fare equally well. Overspeculation, wildcat banking, and severe panics in 1837 and 1857 were partly to blame. Undoubtedly, many of the bankruptcies and plights of stockholders brought about waves of criticism that were heaped on various railroad lines. One of the gravest problems contributing to failing lines was the ease with which new companies could be formed. Dionsyius Lardner, who claimed to have traveled over twenty-thousand miles on railroads, expressed concern, adding that since companies were so simple and cheap to open it was a small wonder that many more of them did not fail.[14] Travelers particularly criticised an unimpressive Kentucky line that offered subservice between Frankfort and Lexington. Author and educator Frederick Hall in 1838 expressed wonder at how the expenses of the company could be justified, since it was operating but one horse-drawn car whose seats were rarely filled.[15] Traveling on this line in 1840, the English reformer and world traveler James Silk Buckingham remarked that "the railroad hardly deserves the name, and might be advantageously and agreeably superseded by an ordinary turnpike."[16]

Several railroads in North Carolina and Georgia received criticism. Of the Weldon to Wilmington railroad in North Carolina, Charles Lyell remarked in the mid-1840's that it had not been improved in three years and was being replaced by another more favorable route. Bishop Henry Whipple expressed sympathy for the small investors in Georgia. Here farmers who had unwisely invested their money in a Macon line which Whipple called a "pest to all travelers but a greater curse to the poor farmers who took stock" in the company, were not only financially ruined, but also had to liquidate the remaining debts of the railroad which had made them so miserably poor.[17] Indeed, these two gentlemen must have expressed a sense of wonderment at an article in an 1853 *American Railroad Journal* which proclaimed that as a general rule, "which is fully borne out by the facts," railroads in the South were as well managed and as profitable as those of any other section of the United States.[18]

Most Americans were enthusiastic and eager to accept the new mode of transportation, but because of the many financial problems and operating hazards that accompanied them strong opposition was not infrequently heard. For instance, vested interests often protested that the railroads were responsible for obliterating stage lines and canal companies, and for the tavern keeper unfortunate enough to be off the line the results were indeed ruinous. Urban dwellers who opposed railroads and favored other modes of transport objected most to the noisy, wood-burning engines that frightened their horses. Serious injuries were sometimes caused by the commotion when a bolting animal could not be restrained. Traveling by train between Charleston and Augusta in the 1830's, David Crockett witnessed such an incident when a team of frightened horses overturned a wagon and smashed the owner's combustibles to bits. Crockett recorded that the harassed wagon-driver escaped apparent injury and ran to a nearby house for help. On being asked what had alarmed the animals so, the frightened man replied "he did not jist know, but it must be hell in harness."[19]

Citizens of Charleston objected in 1837 to locomotives entering their city and regarded the steam engine as an unwelcome nuisance. In other parts of South Carolina it was feared the machines would run over cattle and slaves, and that the blowing of whistles and ringing of bells would constitute an intolerable nuisance. So vehemently opposed to railroads and their attendant noise was one Colonel Barney Brown, a large landholder in Barnwell, South Carolina, that he refused to grant a right of way to a railroad, causing the company to run its line through Blackville ten miles away.[20]

Frightening to city-dwellers also was the alarming fre-
quency with which locomotives ran over pedestrians at unprotected crossings. Lacking such warning systems as those
used by modern lines, locomotives often collided at crossings with wagons, bringing injury or death to the unfortunate and careless occupants.

In rural areas farmers accused railroads of running over
their livestock. S. H. Burford recalled the first trains of the
Tuscumbia & Decatur Railroad passing his father's farm in
Lawrence County, Alabama, and remembered that nine
horses bolted and ran away with their plows.[21] Other
justifiable complaints were that engines set fire to barns and
silage, and that the noise of the machines frightened hens
so badly they refused to lay. One farmer in Florida even
asserted that fragile eggs transported by wagons were destroyed because rails were raised so high above the surface
of many roads.[22] Small wonder that locomotives and their
trains were often referred to as "hell in harness" and "mad
dragons."

Dangers that dulled the appetite of many for railroads
included the large number of boiler explosions that
brought injury and death by scalding steam. Psychopaths
and inebriates sometimes sought the locomotive as a de-
liverance from an insecure and sick life. One such incident
occurred during the tour of Amelia Murray in 1854 and
1855. "Either from intoxication or insanity, a fine-looking
young man" approximately twenty-three years old had
placed himself on the tracks at a point where the railroad
curved and was out of the view of the engineer. As the
locomotive rounded the curve the operator did not have
adequate warning to stop his machine and the "poor wretch
was cut in two."[23]

Noise and hazards explain the opposition of some citizens to railroads, but others voiced a protest against the
operation of trains on the Lord's day. In South Carolina,
the *Camden Journal* asked what right stockholders of rail-

roads had to operate their cars on the Sabbath, when farmers and other persons were forbidden to employ their hands and teams. The complaint was reviewed and answered by the railroad, which ceased the operation of Sunday trains except in cases of necessity. Other arguments leveled against railroads were also more of a religious nature than an economic one. The Reverend Dr. Whitefoord Smith complained in 1853:

the profanation of the Sabbath is a violation of the express law of God, not confined to one dispensation or to one people, but a law of universal obligation, whose sanction is found everywhere in the constitution and necessities of our nature—a law never violated with impunity—and against the infraction of which the strongest denunciations of an offended God have repeatedly uttered and faithfully executed.

Because of this pressure from the clergy the railroad instructed officials to discontinue all Sunday trains except for those carrying the mail.[24]

Ignorance and lack of foresight brought many reluctant communities economic stagnation, and opposition to railroads was at times irrational—nothing more than a protest against change. Their attitude is understandable since the new machines did indeed create a myriad of social problems to a predominately rural citizenry unaccustomed to machines. Only the passing of time and a journey in the cars convinced the skeptics that America's future lay with steam and rail. But once the momentous decision was made, railroad mania took hold, and most communities held gala celebrations to launch their dreams for prosperity and happy days. A program for one of these festive affairs might include band concerts, political orations, with inspection tours and rides in the equipment on hand. Almost always the celebration included a solemn ritual of some kind, followed by picnics occasionally accompanied by strong drinks for the men. Nothing seemed too good for the ambitious new companies, large and small, who built their railroads and ushered in the age of steam.

Perhaps one of the most impressive ceremonies attending the opening of a new railroad was that of the Baltimore & Ohio company during the summer of 1828. Several weeks before the festive occasion newspapers and journals heralded the forthcoming event to be celebrated by the citizenry of the city including members of learned professions, masonic bodies, and other groups that would carry appropriate banners to mark the historic day.

After weeks of excitement the inhabitants of the city assembled on July 4, 1828 for the ground-breaking that marked the birth of one of America's most historic lines. On that bright and cool morning the more solemn parts of the program came first, with the offering of prayers, and speeches by visiting dignitaries. Among the most important persons present were the Speaker of the House of Representatives, and other congressmen, Governor Coles of Indiana, the Mayor and city council of Baltimore, soldiers of the American Revolution, and the president and engineers of the railroad. But the highlight of the day was the ground-breaking ceremony executed by Charles Carroll of Carrollton, the last surviving signer of the Declaration of Independence. According to *Niles' Weekly Register,* Mr. Carroll was the most suitable American to commence construction on the railroad that hopefully would more firmly unite the bonds of the union, "and dispense unnumbered blessings, not only to the citizens of Baltimore, but to millions of hardy freemen who till the soil."[25]

On the very same day that Charles Carroll laid the cornerstone for the Baltimore & Ohio Railroad, President John Quincy Adams broke the ground, with some difficulty, for the Chesapeake & Ohio Canal.

> Attending this action was an incident which produced a greater sensation than any other that occurred during the day. The spade which the president held struck a root,

which prevented its penetrating the earth. Not deterred by trifling obstacles from doing what he had deliberately resolved to perform, Mr. Adams tried it again, with no better success. Thus foiled, he threw down the spade, hastily stripped off and laid aside his coat, and went seriously *to work*. The multitude around, and on the hills and trees, who could not *hear*, because of their distance from the open space, but could *see* and understand, observing this action, raised a loud and unanimous cheering, which continued for sometime after Mr. Adams had mastered the difficulty.

Only time was to show that the President had backed "the wrong horse."[26]

Upon completion of the Baltimore & Ohio ceremony, a glass cylinder containing a copy of the railroad's charter was placed in a cavity of the cornerstone, artillery salutes were fired, and dignitaries exchanged gifts. A great parade was held, and at some places along the route "heads were arranged eight or ten deep, and bodies placed as closely as they could be stowed." The impressive ceremonies were witnessed by an aggregate of spectators estimated by some to exceed 70,000 persons, the only mishap being that two children were lost.[27] Thus ended what *Niles' Weekly Register* described as perhaps the most "splendid civic procession" that Americans had ever seen.

In South Carolina ceremonies were also held to mark the ground-breaking and beginning of operations for the Charleston & Hamburg line. To promote interest in this railroad, the company at times conducted a series of demonstration runs in May, 1833, intended for the enlightenment of the citizens of Hamburg and Augusta, the western ten miles of the line. Amidst the sounds of cannon fire, the ringing of bells, and "loud huzzas" from the assembly witnessing the show, hand cars were used to familiarize the curious with transportation by rail. All along the route the track was crowded with spectators, and refreshment stands were erected to accommodate the appetite of the crowds.

Even into the night the little cars ran up and down the road, with persons drawing lots, and then patiently waiting until it was their turn to ride on the train.[28]

At other ceremonies sponsored by the line the sectional animosity of the 1830's raised its ugly head. Yet in the opinion of *Niles' Weekly Register* the opening of the railroad would hopefully place the people of South Carolina in step with the rest of the union's views.[29] Reflecting the nullification crisis of the 1830's, the *Register* went on to say that the majority of Southerners knew the "real state of things" in New England about as well as a Highlander would have known how to use a kneebuckle two centuries ago. In later years, during a ceremony opening the Charleston & Memphis Railroad in 1857, sectional bitterness was even more pronounced. Charleston's Mayor, William P. Miles, in his speech charged that the South could not conciliate the North:

> their settled purpose and eager desire is to destroy us. . . .
> Our only hope is in union among ourselves, and a settled
> determination, in forming an unbroken phalanx, to dispute
> each step and fight every inch of ground. . . . We cannot cry,
> "peace, peace," when there is no peace. The war has actually
> begun.[30]

Besides the speech of Mayor Miles, the joyous occasion included the firing of guns, and a parade witnessed by 15,000 that passed under a "triumphal arch, decked with flowers," which adorned one of the streets.[31]

Other less war-like ceremonies included the inauguration of the main line of the Wilmington & Weldon Railroad on March 9, 1840. Boasting of the longest continuous railroad in the world, operations on the 161 miles of track began with the driving of a gold spike. The event was witnessed in all by about 550 spectators from North Carolina, South Carolina and Virginia, and was highlighted by a barbecue at the Wilmington depot and the firing of a

161 gun salute.[32] On the opening of a stretch of the Louisville & Nashville Railroad from Nashville, Tennessee to
Bowling Green, Kentucky, a great barbecue was held in
Nashville on August 10, 1850 which attracted about 10,000
people, with speeches and entertainment as a "carnival
spirit prevailed throughout the city."[33] Among many other
celebrations announcing the opening of new lines were
those of the Louisville to Frankfort railroad and the Montgomery & West Point, Alabama line.[34] But perhaps the
most popularly acclaimed opening of a railroad was the
celebration of the Mississippi Central, which began business
with 228 bottles of champagne, "besides several barrels of
other drink."[35]

Although the significance of the railroad in the antebellum South has been argued by historians, there is no question of its superiority over the other existing means of
transportation before the Civil War.[36] The steam engine
was faster and more reliable than boats or horses, it could
penetrate almost any section of the country where men
were willing to lay tracks, and socially the locomotive facilitated communications and contributed to spreading news
and opinions and the custom of visiting cousins throughout
the South during its most crucial years.[37]

But there were great gaps that existed in the railroad
network of the South in 1860—gaps that were not truly
revealed until the Confederacy attempted to establish its
independence during the Civil War. What had previously
appeared to be a well developed system soon dissolved into
mere fragments in the crisis of war. At the time Jefferson
Davis took charge of the new government in Montgomery,
the railroads of the South stretched toward one another but
seldom joined. At the outbreak of the war, the only route
from the Atlantic to the Mississippi River embraced the
lines of seven companies. To the North, the only junction in
operation was at Bowling Green, Kentucky, and this quickly
fell into Union hands. Consequently, at a time when the

South badly needed an adequate transportation system to forward men and supplies to the various theaters of the war, it could only fall back on facilities that had been built for the more limited purpose of speeding bales of cotton to rivers and on to northern mills. The mistake was a costly one and ultimately contributed to the defeat of the South.

But before the South learned to fear the names of Sherman, Sheridan, and Grant, the section enjoyed a period of prosperous years that has often been obscured by the hateful memory of reconstruction. And whether a railroad was initiated by a barbecue, a train ride, or a picnic, gay and optimistic celebrations were an auspicious introduction to experiences Southerners would encounter while riding the trains in an era long gone by.

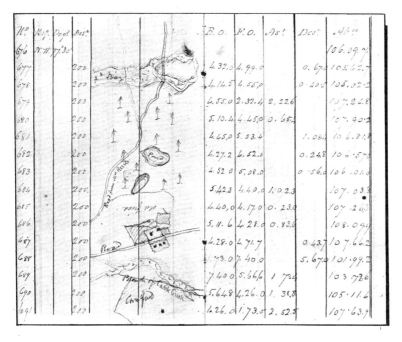

Engineer's Notebook Page

3

Engines of Smoke, Fire, and Cinders

The earliest Southern railroads were directed solely at commercial markets; from the very beginning, however, there seems to have been little doubt that trains could be used successfully for passenger transport as well. But before the newly formed companies could carry travelers at respectable speeds, many had to transform their vehicles from other sources of power to steam.

Before the adoption of steam made railroad travel at once more exciting and more hazardous, it was not uncommon for the traveler journeying by rail to be introduced to the rigors of the road via the horse-drawn coach. The speeds attained by these modified carriages were anything but remarkable; the usual range, from about four to ten miles per hour, was determined by the number of animals used to pull the car. But if such slow performances evoke little praise from twentieth century travelers, they were amazing indeed to railroad-minded Americans of the 1830's. Rail transport via horse-drawn coaches was lauded by the editors of *Niles' Weekly Register,* who called it marvelous that Baltimore newspapers could reach the hands of readers in Cincinnati only 130 hours after publication. It was added hopefully that the time would some day come when only thirty-six hours would be required.[1] Six months later in 1830, the magazine expressed similar wonderment concerning the Baltimore & Ohio's horse-drawn passenger runs. It was reported that each of the passenger wagons was to carry between twenty-five and thirty occupants, and, to insure the progress of the cars, horses were to be changed in about half a minute at midway. The thirteen-mile journey between Baltimore and Ellicott Mills was to be spanned at ten miles an hour, with "every minute presenting something new to be admired by strangers on the road." Other reports from the line recorded that on January 4, 1830 one horse pulled eighty persons, the weight being more than eight tons, at eight miles an hour. "Like incidents are now of daily occurrence."[2] Yet these reports were seen as overly optimistic by other passengers, who recorded the route was actually traveled by one horse at a less than enviable speed of four miles an hour.[3]

Horse-drawn carriages were the only means of land locomotion before the advent of steam, but even after the new engines were acquired, passengers found that horses were still frequently retained. As late as the Civil War, draft animals were used on many lines for short distance runs and emergencies such as mechanical failures, as well as for hauling lighter loads. One of their most useful services was to pull railroad coaches quietly through cities and towns.[4] During this operation, intended to lessen the hazards and noise attending steam locomotives, engines surrendered their cars to horses on the out-skirts of a town. At this point the cars were quietly towed to a second station across town where another locomotive was attached to the train. Pulled by the second engine, the train resumed the journey. Dionysius Lardner described one such operation in the following way:

> In several of the principal American cities, the railways are continued to the very centre of the town. . . . The locomotive station is, however, always in the suburbs. Having arrived

there, the engine is detached from the train, and horses are yoked to the carriages, by which they are drawn to the passenger depot, usually established at some central situation. Four horses are attached to each of these oblong carriages.[5]

The transfer of cars by horses certainly diminished the speed of the trains and helped lessen the number of complaints from inhabitants. Nevertheless, in the more adamant communities citizens continued to deny the penetration of steam engines to urban areas at all.[6]

Cars pulled on rails were a great improvement over conventional carriages, but they were still a far cry from satisfying the ambitious demands of commercial interests for a faster and more reliable mode of transportation to capture the profits of the inland trade. Consequently, before the final marriage of steam engines and rails, numerous power sources were tried on an experimental basis. One idea, "a car with a moving floor," involved propelling a carriage by a horse stationed on an endless tread or belt. According to an observer writing in 1831, an animal on one of these cars walked at two and a half miles per hour, but because of gears and the endless belt the car moved at fifteen. It was said that animals could operate these cars with "as little fatigue as horses experience in ploughing, or travelling with a wagon conveying a moderate load."[7] To lessen discomfort, the passengers sat around the horse and along the sides with the animal and tread belt to their backs.

For his idea, the inventor of the tread belt car was awarded $500 by the Charleston & Hamburg Railroad. Yet there were serious flaws. Most important was the fact that even though these tread-mill carriages were capable of transporting a dozen passengers in one car at speeds up to twelve miles an hour, the velocity of the machine diminished when the horse started to tire. When the animal was completely exhausted, the train simply came to a halt.[8]

Another railroad ingeniously planned to power a train by placing horses between the cars rather than in front of the train. The animals were restrained from flanking by installing poles along their sides. To prevent their falling underneath the wheels, a broad leather belt was suspended across their undersides. The shafts connecting the cars rested on a pivot that enabled the train and horses to navigate curves; to keep the horses from rearing upward, two bows of iron were suspended from shafts that rested over the horses' back.[9]

The Carolina road tried another unsuccessful experiment which was an attempt to propel a train by sails. In 1829 one of these sailing-cars, with fifteen passengers aboard, actually attained a speed of twelve miles an hour. But the reliance on wind power presented obvious drawbacks. Stiff breezes could swing the boom so completely about that the crew and passengers were constantly in danger of being knocked off the car. Nor was it rare for these engines to be completely toppled, with passengers and crew, if they survived, having to upright the machine and set it back on the track. But the most serious disadvantage was the uncertainty of there being a wind to drive the vehicle over the tracks. In this event passengers were forced to walk, or stand patiently by their immobile car and wait for nature to come to their aid.[10] Such experiments were amusing to some observers, but to other spectators they "went to show that, with a large sail and a fresh breeze, carriages may be propelled with great velocity."[11]

Even more bizarre experiments than the sailing engine were attempted: one strange device involved an explosion-proof engine operated by springs. Its designers estimated the "spring power locomotive" could attain speeds of seventy to one hundred miles per hour by use of its five hundred springs.[12] Probably the oddest experiment of all, however, was the employment of two dogs to pull six persons in a car. *Niles' Weekly Register* appropriately commented that, "Those who have not seen [it], can hardly believe such things; but they are true."[13]

When one considers all these strange and sundry plans, it is not surprising that railroad engineers quickly realized the impracticality of wind power and springs and turned to perfecting more reliable power plants.[14] The need for a power source which could be mounted on carriages to attain constant, safe, and fast speeds could be most successfully met, they finally realized, by the use of the steam engine.

The first steam engines of the 1830's must have seemed marvelous contraptions to Americans seeing them for the very first time. As these small, colorful, and noisy "demons" shattered the serenity of isolated hamlets and towns, many spectators and travelers probably experienced a thrill similar to that of future Americans upon taking their first automobile or jet plane rides.[15] The celebrated author Charles Dickens, during his tour of America in the 1840's, vividly described, amidst somewhat confusing circumstances, one town's impression and its introduction to the age of steam:

> There—with mechanics working at their trades, and people leaning from their doors and windows, and boys flying kites and playing marbles, and men smoking, and women talking, and children crawling, and pigs burrowing, and unaccustomed horses plunging and rearing, close to the very rails—there—on, on, on—tears the mad dragon of an engine with its train of cars; scattering in all directions a shower of burning sparks from its wood fire; screeching, hissing, yelling, panting, until at last the thirsty monster stops beneath a covered way to drink, the people cluster round, and you have time to breathe again.[16]

The "thirsty monster" was seen by various travelers in many different moods and forms. To some the steam engine was an object of humor, while to others it took on the

characteristics of a living being. Charles Weld, an Englishman of some repute in law and science, and an authority on
Polar expeditions, once described an American locomotive
as an "uncouth-looking machine," having a "prodigious
bottlenose chimney." Noting several dissimilarities between
American and foreign engines, Weld further commented
that the two models even sounded different. His explanation for this phenomenon was that English locomotives
were fueled with coal, whereas most American engines still
burned wood. This, Weld observed, possibly accounted for
their unearthly sound, "comparable only to the simulta-
neous braying of a dozen donkeys labouring under oppres-
sive asthma."[17]

American locomotives were also depicted in vivid terms
by Carlton H. Rogers and Joseph Ingraham. Rogers, on the
way to Charleston, South Carolina, accused his "asthmatic,
rickety old concern" of giving up evidence of a want of
vitality, when after "several spasmodic efforts at locomotion, it stopped moving, gave a few convulsive shrieks, and
yielded up the ghost." Later, he and his fellow passengers
were rescued by a freight train which "like a wounded
snake, dragged its slow length along, 'and propelled us to
the next station ... some ten or twelve hours behind
time.' "[18] Joseph Ingraham, on the way to New Orleans in
the 1830's, referred to one of the engines pulling his train as
"our fiery leader," which, "smoking like a race-horse," puf-
fed and coughed "like a bustling little man in a crowd."[19]

Interested travelers also noted a similarity to animals in
the new machines. One observer in the 1840's described an
engine he saw as a "gruff" and puffing old steam
machine.[20] The performance of an engine encountered by
Abraham Hall while traveling in Louisiana on the Lake
Pontchartrain line was evidently less than spectacular, since
the New York journalist sardonically described the vehicle
as having "one thousand mosquito power."[21] Philo Tower
and David Crockett also recorded vivid impressions of

American locomotives in the antebellum years. According to Tower, his train departed the depot with a "purr and a snort." The engine was likened to a "prancing fire-eating horse." Yet the abolitionist did not appear too disgruntled with the machine, which achieved speeds of thirty miles per hour.[22] More renowned for killing bears than riding trains, the famous pioneer-statesman described one of the first steam engines he saw as chugging along with a wheezing sound "as if she had the tizzick." Taking "short breaths" as it gathered speed, Crockett recorded that the engine surged forward, and "away we went with a blue streak after us."[23]

Some locomotives were described in periodicals and newspapers as sporting monsters that might at any moment devour the roadway and rails. *Harper's Monthly*, for instance, described a locomotive in 1851 as "tearing and wheezing, and panting away," and as a "great brassy monster at the head of the train."[24] In another magazine, the *New York Monthly*, an account read: "The iron horse pants and puffs, as if struggling to free himself of the lengthy train to which he is bound."[25] But in 1838 the editor of the *Mississippi Free Trader* outdid all the rest in his colorful personification of the wonderful new engine. While anticipating the operation of an engine on the Natchez & Jackson line, the *Trader* recorded its appearance as follows:

> [the machine] looks out from its house toward Washington, coughs, snorts fire, sometimes yawns, and stretches its legs toward the race track, like an old racer who expects sport soon. It has a perfect contempt for horned cattle, and despises wagoning in the mud, and cares not a fig for a rainy day.[26]

The first of these locomotives built in the United States for service on American roads were products of the West Point Foundry Works of New York. The initial two machines were purchased by South Carolina's Charleston & Hamburg line and had the distinction of pulling the first real passenger trains in the United States. Engine No. 1, built in 1830, was named the *Best Friend* and served the line until its untimely explosion in 1831. Engine No. 2, christened the *West Point,* was built in 1831.

Each of these locomotives was small by present standards, weighing between three and five tons. Their miniature size is illustrated by the fact that the weight of one twentieth century giant equalled that of twenty-five engines of the first West Point Foundry machines. Their size and weight is more dramatized when they are compared with the 200,000 to 500,000 pound engines of the 1920's.[27] Yet this is not to say that American foundries and engineers were unable to produce larger and more powerful engines, since by 1860 some locomotives on American roads weighed as much as 50,000 pounds and were capable of pulling as many as one hundred loaded cars.[28] Rather, smaller machines were favored since they were less prone to operating wear and tear, and savings derived from purchasing smaller units enabled companies to buy more machines.[29]

Besides the use of wood for fuel instead of coal, the weight and cost were two distinguishing features between American and foreign engines, the latter the more expensive to buy. According to 1850 figures listed in the *American Railroad Journal,* the comparative costs of American and English locomotives were approximately $8,300 for the American machines to $9,360 for those produced abroad. The differential for larger models ran as high as $2,000 per machine.[30]

Other dissimilarities involved maneuverability. In mountainous locales American locomotives were more capable of ascending difficult inclines and more agile on curves. Michel Chevalier noted that railroads in America had sharper curves, and that on "most of the American railroads, the inclinations are much greater than what in Europe are usually considered the *maxima.*"[31] In fact, so adept had some companies become in producing steam engines and cars, and so quickly had improvements in steam locomotives surpassed almost all other branches of mechanical science in America, that by the 1840's the United States was exporting engines to foreign nations. In February, 1849, the *American Railroad Journal* commented on the newly emerging industrial might and reported that the United States no longer imported engines for her railroads, but was now exporting them to Canada, Cuba, and Europe. The following June the *Journal* praised domestic foundries by announcing, "America is distinguished for the superiority of her locomotives."[32]

Critical foreigners often belabored the fact that American trains could not safely attain European speeds.[33] Even allowing for natural caution on the part of the engineer, average speeds for pioneer engines of the 1830's were seldom more than eight to fifteen miles an hour when the engines were coupled to a train of cars. Faster speeds were possible, however, as shown by the trial run of the celebrated *Best Friend*. This four-ton engine ran as fast as thirty to thirty-five miles an hour without the cars, but attached to several coaches with forty to fifty passengers aboard, the top speed was reduced to between sixteen and twenty-one miles an hour.[34] By 1860 improved engines such as the Baltimore & Ohio's *Mercury* could run as fast as sixty miles an hour, but for safety purposes these fleeter engines were required to maintain slower speeds. In general most engineers were required to run their locomotives no faster than twenty miles an hour in the antebellum years.[35] Yet there were exceptions, such as express trains and the conveyance of presidential messages, when trains traveled as fast as forty-five miles an hour.[36]

Naturally, on a normal passenger run, a multitude of circumstances often caused lesser speeds, to the accompaniment of complaints from the passengers. Cars were often delayed by obstacles like livestock and disabled wagons blocking the road, while washed-out bridges and broken tracks caused a loss of time and were, in addition, serious safety hazards.

It could be argued that most often one's progress was determined simply by luck and the unlikely prospect that the companies' roads were well managed and properly maintained. While traveling between Washington and Baltimore in the mid-1830's, Charles Murray used a railroad whose track was as rough and as "ill-constructed" as any he had ever seen. Four hours were required for a trip of forty-five miles.[37] Further South, on a railroad operating between Charleston and Columbia, South Carolina, Philo Tower, while not mentioning any specific road problems, did record that the train went 140 miles at approximately eleven miles an hour.[38] Other variations in speed were reported by Francis and Theresa Pulszky and Frederick Law Olmsted. Accompanying Louis Kossuth on his much heralded visit to the United States in 1851, the Pulszkys noted that American railroads generally averaged about twenty miles an hour, and up to forty-five miles an hour for express and mail runs.[39] But during the well known travels of Olmsted in 1852, one Virginia train was recorded as running twenty miles in an hour and thirty minutes. Olmsted, apparently dismayed by the pace, commented that the train had been advertised as *fast*[40]

Passenger accounts support the idea that Southern trains were slower than Northern ones. Included among the many observations of Michel Chevalier, made during his travels from 1833 to 1835, was a mention of this regional variation and some praise for the fleet engines on the Boston & Lowell Railroad. While using the services of this line, his train ran at about twenty-five miles an hour, but when he traveled in the South, a Charleston & Hamburg locomotive attained only twelve miles an hour, and a Baltimore & Ohio engine was even slower.[41]

One other interesting aspect of locomotive speed to some passengers concerned trains carrying freight and other goods. Solon Robinson, who criticized farmers for ignoring the great opportunities that railroads afforded them, marveled at the ability of trains to transport fresh milk from the country to cities by night. But the impact of rail travel and its changing influences through speed was best recorded in 1836 by the Virginia lawyer James Davidson:

> If my great grand father had have been told that his great grand son, at this day, would dine at one in the evening and go to bed the same evening 120 miles distant, he would have called the Prophet a fool.[42]

Although speeds on American roads sometimes varied greatly, perhaps they can best be deduced from the accounts of two other travelers, David Stevenson and William Chambers. Stevenson, traveling in the country in 1837, reported that most American trains seldom exceeded fifteen miles an hour.[43] But with the improvements of the 1840's, Chambers observed that the average speed for trains was between twenty and thirty miles an hour, a figure which seemed to prevail until the Civil War.[44]

American and foreign locomotives also differed in their source of fuel. In spite of the ready availability of coal in many areas, firewood was the main source of fuel for American engines, and was so available in certain areas that firewood lay rotting on the ground.[45] Joseph Biggs mentioned in 1837 that he occasionally saw coal used in American machines, but the practice was not general until after the Civil War. One explanation for this was that even though anthracite coal was cheaper and more efficient than wood, the vast forests in the United States, especially in the South, furnished enough timber for most American companies' needs.

Still, it is difficult to understand this widespread aversion to coal, in view of the fact that the coal-burning locomotive had its advocates as early as the 1840's, and tens of thousands of dollars could have been saved in fuel if railroads had relinquished their dependence on wood. The forward-looking *American Railroad Journal* championed the change in an article in June, 1858, and argued that, if wood were replaced by coal in locomotives, the railroads would save approximately $10,000,000 a year, a sum which amounted to one percent of the entire cost of all of the nations railroads.[46] A year later, in 1859, the weekly journal carried a series of advertisements for the Boardman Locomotive Boiler Company, which stated that experiments in 1847 revealed that by using coal one railroad had reduced by 47% its expenses in fuel. Other figures cited by the Boardman Company showed that the fuel savings per mile for engines using wood was 20.1% to 10.6% with coal. Another company testified that changing to coal saved their shareholders $3,050 a year. Coal, they discovered, was not only less harmful to fireboxes and tubing in engines, but was also totally consumed.[47]

Similar testimony was offered from other sources as well. The Baltimore & Ohio Railroad reported that its line had realized an impressive 55% fuel savings by using engines burning coal.[48] A New Jersey railroad revealed that its engines fueled with coal cost one-third less to operate than those burning wood,[49] while the Columbia & Philadelphia Railroad reported that "measures have accordingly been adopted to prohibit the use of wood on this road, as fast as locomotives can be prepared for the use of coal."[50]

Passengers' objections to wood-burning locomotives also provided an incentive to switch to coal. The wood-burners ejected cinders from the engine, making travel by railroads dangerous and uncomfortable. Passengers frequently complained that the cinders, which entered the coaches, burned holes in their clothing and were hazardous to their eyes. The problem was as old as the railroads themselves, for even on the first trains of the Charleston & Hamburg Railroad passengers were harassed by sparks from the rich pinewood consumed by the *Best Friend*. During the 1830's, when many railroads were still operating open cars, those passengers brave enough to venture on a short journey were obviously at the mercy of the engine's fiery trail. Judging from the accounts of other passengers, however, the situation was hardly improved when carriages were enclosed.

One of those most annoyed by cinders and smoke was Harriet Martineau. During a six months' visit to the South from December, 1835 to July, 1836, Miss Martineau remarked there was an "incessant shower" of large sparks, annoying the passengers in her car and burning holes in the ladies' dresses. The only way one could be spared this fiery danger was to shut the coach windows, which was just as unbearable as the sparks on warmer days. While on the way to Charleston, she recalled that a near tragedy was barely averted when a lady in the car "had a shawl burned to destruction on her shoulders." Upon examining her own gown, Miss Martineau discovered that it had thirteen holes in it. Damage to her eyes was prevented only by covering her face with a veil, which had more holes burned into it than she could count.[51]

David Stevenson remarked in 1837 that not only were the sparks "vomited" from the engine a "source of constant annoyance to the passengers," but they frequently set fire to wooden bridges and houses along the line.[52] These hazards were also noted by James Buckingham. On his way to Richmond in 1839, Buckingham complained that sparks from the engine were a constant annoyance to everyone on the train, making "small holes in the garments of all."[53] Seven years later the same condition was so discomforting to Alexander Mackay that he viewed the wood-burning locomotives as equestrian monsters. The Englishman compared American and foreign engines thus:

> With us [the English] locomotives are fed on nothing but coke; in America they devour nothing but wood; and, like a

horse kept exclusively upon oats, the latter are difficult to
manage, from the nature of their diet. They are constantly
attended by a formidable train of obdurate sparks, and
sometimes amuse themselves on the way by setting fire to a
barn, a hay-rick, and the like, and, when they have nothing
else to do, burning down a fence.[54]

Resigning himself to the inconvenience, Charles Dickens
viewed the sparks from the engine as an interesting source
of entertainment. On night trains, while observing the effects of the wood fire, the usually critical author remarked,
"We were travelling in a whirlwind of bright sparks, which
showered about us like a storm of fiery snow."[55]

Attempts to reduce injuries and inconveniences resulting
from wood fuel were evident by 1847, when many railroads
installed spark arresters in the big balloon stack so commonly seen on antebellum locomotives. One model advertised by French, Baird & Campbell in Philadelphia was
recommended in *Hunt's Magazine* for use on every train and
especially for the cotton-hauling trains prevalent in the
South. The advertisement stated that the appendage was
"thoroughly tested, and found to surpass anything of the
kind, for that purpose, in use in this country."[56] William
Chambers, among those noting the device during his tour
of 1853, observed that many American engines had a
"capacious grating" placed over the stack to arrest ignited
sparks. Because of this grating Chambers did not find the
cinders as disagreeable as some other passengers, nor did
he "hear of any damage being done by them."[57]

The wood burned in these engines could usually be procured at a trifling cost in the South and could be seen by
travelers in stacks ready for use along the sides of the track.
But with the building of many new lines by the Civil War the
supply in some areas began to diminish. For instance, the
North American Review reported in 1829 that in building and
fueling engines of the Baltimore & Ohio the timber was

unavailable in the immediate area of the city.[58] By 1859 the Georgia Railroad had difficulty locating wood in the Athens area. The town was in the older and more settled part of the state where the woods had been cut back, requiring timber to be brought in from as far as twenty miles away.[59]

To cut and haul their wood some companies maintained slaves, a procedure considered necessary by the Charleston & Hamburg Railroad because of the "extreme difficulty and expensiveness of hiring suitable laborers."[60] Generally slaves were hired from local planters nearby. During a layover in March, 1859, a local citizen in Holly Springs, Mississippi, was known to have let his slaves work for the Cairo & New Orleans Railroad for $240 a year. An engineer for that railroad also told Richard Cobden that the company paid twenty dollars a month for slaves, and provided them all food but no clothes. That Negroes were used in positions commonly reserved for whites was also called to the attention of Cobden. The engineer added that some skilled Negro mechanics employed by his company were paid as much as $400 to $500 a year.[61]

Charles Lanman, while traveling in the South from Washington to Savannah, also remarked during the 1830's that he was surprised to learn that the railroad had been built exclusively by Negro labor, "and that an intelligent slave occupied the post of assistant superintendent."[62] As early as 1836, at a directors' meeting on September 20, the South Carolina Railroad entertained suggestions by its president to run freight trains with Negro engineers under the management and control of white conductors. The measure was approved and ordered to be adopted as soon as practicable but the plan never matured.[63] The evidence suggests, therefore, that at least some railroads did not rely on the persistent myths concerning Negro inferiority to maintain racial peace by keeping Negroes in positions of unskilled and untrained menial tasks.[64]

Several passengers commented on the labor of Negroes, including Philo Tower, Frederick Law Olmsted, and John

Abbott. Traveling in the South in the 1850's, Philo Tower reported seeing Negroes employed by railroads in every position except those of conductor and engineer.[65] Writing in December 1859, the Maine historian and educator John Abbott noted that he witnessed a gang of Virginia Negroes on their way to work on a road further South. Some of the other slaves remarked they were "through the considerate kindness of their owners and employers... returning home on a visit" for the Christmas holidays.[66] Frederick Law Olmsted commented that some Virginia Negroes were paid attractive wages by railroads for their labor. Olmsted had heard that Negroes there had commanded such high wages to work on some railroads and tobacco-factories, that farmers "were often driven to employ white men, and to give them very high wages by the day...."[67]

Whether fueled by slaves, passengers or crews, engines customarily took on wood at various stations along the route. However, the operation was sometimes subject to change, adding to the many schedule irregularities encountered by travelers. During a Southern tour in 1843 and 1844, Bishop Henry Whipple's train was delayed for twenty-five minutes in Forsyth, Georgia, so the crew could chop wood for the engine. This was strange to Whipple, who commented, "This is the first railroad I have ever seen where the cars were stopped to cut fuel."[68] Five years later Whipple's journey would have been hastened by one of the new horse-powered saws advertised in the *American Railroad Journal*. The blade was powered by a horse walking on an endless belt, and operated on the same principle as the Charleston & Hamburg's horse-car of the 1830's.[69]

As the American locomotive evolved from its basic form to more elaborate models, it began to resemble the steam machines of the twentieth century. The first engines did not even carry headlights, since most runs were short and accomplished during daylight hours. However, once railroads extended their tracks, the need for illumination was recognized. The problem was temporarily solved by

Horatio Allen, chief engineer for the Charleston & Hamburg Railroad.

Allen correctly reasoned that an effective light would have to be placed low on the front of the locomotive to avoid blinding the operator. To support such a light he built a small square car about five feet long to be pushed in front of the engine. A fire was built on the floor of the car with lighter wood resting on several inches of protective sand. This shielded the wooden frame of the car from the destructive yet illuminating flame. Although Allen's primitive invention was a poor arrangement at best, it did serve the needs of the Charleston & Hamburg Railroad temporarily. Although it was not generally adopted by other companies, at least the simple arrangement did demonstrate the practicality of illumination, so that by 1840 kerosene oil lamps with reflectors began to appear.[70]

Other innovations on locomotives often involved safety features which seem simply common sense today. A bell was added to warn pedestrians of oncoming engines and to announce the departure of trains. By the 1840's, engineers and firemen were sheltered with the addition of cabs.[71] Braking was improved by the installation of sandboxes. This accessory afforded better traction to the driving wheels, and was first installed on Pennsylvania engines because of a serious grasshopper plague in 1836.[72] The details of the emergency seem well known by travelers twenty years later, since John Abbott remarked: "I once heard of cars being stopped by grasshoppers. They lit in such numbers upon the rails, that, crushed by the locomotive, they so greased the track, that the ponderous engine could not move."[73]

Although machinists and designers in the United States profited from the knowledge and experiences of English engineers, locomotives produced in this country acquired other special characteristics that were distinctly "American." Some of these variations from European models were necessary because of geographical differences, whereas others were reflections of Yankee ingenuity or the efforts of an enterprising "locomotive-driver" to add a personal flair to his steaming machine. For example, locomotives were colorfully decorated before the Civil War and proudly maintained by their mechanics and crews. In a section prone to use imaginative nomenclature, Southern engines were usually named rather than numbered, adding a touch of romanticism to one's journey. The Central of Georgia entered the Civil War with a *New Hampshire* and a *United States,* but these emerged after Fort Sumter renamed *Beauregard* and *Joseph E. Johnston.* The Virginia & Tennessee Railroad had an engine in 1858 called the *St. Nazaire,* which the *American Railroad Journal* called "one of the most beautiful we have ever seen." Other engines belonging to the company were named *Chesapeake, El Paso,* and *San Francisco,* designations indicative of the future relations and connections of the road.[74] The *Southward Ho, Spring Hill* and *Dart* were names given to engines by other railroads, but the most imaginative of all seems to have been the *Flying Nelly* of the Western & Atlantic, especially when its assignment to switching duties is considered.[75]

That the American locomotive was an objective of curiosity to veteran foreign travelers and American neophytes alike is well established. Its shrill whistle and clanging bell announced the age of steam, and the addition of cabs and sandboxes were examples of American ingenuity. Perhaps the most fascinating feature to foreigners on American engines was the cowcatcher. This awesome apparatus was first installed on engines in the 1830's as a safety device to remove obstacles from the tracks and to prevent animals from being caught under the engine wheels. Its design was relatively simple, consisting of one or several forward-slanting bars of iron or wood appended to the front of the machine. The devices were mentioned in journals by the early 1830's and were praised for removing animals from the rails. One of the first recorded reports of a cowcatcher appeared in *Niles' Weekly Register* in 1833 when it was suggested that the Camden & Amboy Railroad in New Jersey follow the experiment of the Baltimore & Ohio by suspending in front of their engines a piece of timber forward of the machines leading wheels.[76] Two years later *Niles'* reported another train armed with a "lattice work platform constructed in front of the locomotive" engaged a herd of cattle on the track and that the "excellent contrivance" picked up and removed the animals without injury to the passengers or the cars.[77]

Foreigners visiting the United States could never fully comprehend why Americans did not follow the European practice of fencing in railroads. It was not uncommon to hear these travelers tell of their train traveling along at twenty miles an hour and suddenly smashing into a cow, a herd of sheep, or other obstacles that might be on the track. Léon Beauvallet, touring the United States in 1855 as a member of Rachel Felix's opera troupe, humorously wrote that the Americans should provide some kind of protective fencing for railroads, but, "Bah! How could Americans take time to think of such fooleries?"[78] Furthermore, the Frenchman added, all was well as long as American trains were pulled by horses but when steam was applied to trains, neither promenaders nor animals were safe from being ground under the wheels of the furious engines.

Other European travelers were fascinated by cowcatchers and described them in numerous ways. While visiting America in 1837, David Stevenson referred to a cowcatcher as a "guard," and noted the good effects of the device after his train had smashed into a large wagon loaded with firewood. Reflecting on the aftermath of the collision, Stevenson noted that the wagon and its contents were scattered on both sides of the engine, and the wagon was "literally shivered to atoms by the concussion."[79] Apparently well satisfied with the efficiency of the apparatus, he suggested that English railroads might utilize these bumpers in areas where accidents had occurred frequently because of obstructions on the track.

Another name for the cowcatcher was provided by William Chambers, who defined it as a "shelving-fender." To Charles Weld, however, the cowcatcher was an "iron barred vizor-like affair" which was not particular about what kind of animal became its next victim.[80] During the travels of Captain Frederick Marryat, an Englishman who had served with distinction in the British Navy, speculation was offered on how many animals had been "cut into atoms by the trains in America." To Marryat the cowcatcher was a "sort of shovel" that simply picked up a poor beast, "tossing her off right or left."[81]

A typical experience which involved a cowcatcher and a foreign visitor occurred between Baltimore and Washington during the travels of Alexander Mackay in 1846. For most of the trip the train whizzed along without difficulty. About ten miles from Washington, however, a violent jerk shuddered through the cars, indicating the engine had hit a formidable obstacle, but not one so large as to derail the cars. Once the locomotive came to a stop, the engineer climbed down and discovered that he had struck a cow which was lying on the tracks. Walking to the front of the engine, Mackay found that a mangled cow was caught in the "strong iron grating," which protruded a few inches above the tracks. The conversation that took place between the engineer and the foreigner revealed that to the former, the experience was not a novelty:

"Sure on't," said the driver, as soon as he had satisfied his curiosity. "You seem familiar with such accidents," I observed; "are they frequent?" "Now and then of a night," said he, "we do run agin somethin' of the kind, but they gin'rally manage to get the worst on't it." "But do they never throw you off the rail?" I inquired. "They seem to take a pleasure in doin' it, when they find us without the 'cow-ketcher,' " he replied.[82]

From some of the other passengers standing around the engine, Mackay learned that it was not uncommon to find a dead sheep or hog in the cowcatcher upon arrival at the depot. Yet he was told by the stoker that a horse or cow was too "formidable an obstacle" to run against without being detected at the time of impact. The stoker added that hitting a hog was not too serious, "but them 'ere cows are the devil to pay."

Once all the passengers were satisfied over the cause of the delay, Mackay thought it a shame to leave the carcass by the wayside and asked if it might not be taken on to Washington. One of the by-standers replied that this would be a good idea, but the engineer wanted to leave room for the next unfortunate animal. Formerly somewhat dubious as to whether he would reach the end of his journey safely, Mackay commented that such a remark enabled him to return to his seat "with a very comfortable feeling of security."[83]

By 1860 the great improvements made on American locomotives enabled passengers to travel about the country much faster than ever before. Nevertheless, railroad travel still left much to be desired in such areas as tracks, bridges, and general comfort of the railroad passenger coach.

4

The Railroad Passenger Car

In the three decades before the Civil War locomotives acquired only such moderately effective equipment as lights, brakes, and protective cabs, but passenger cars underwent more drastic changes, evolving from rudimentary carriages to coaches designed much like those in service today. In spite of certain similarities, however, between pre-Civil War and contemporary cars, the unsolved problem of assuring passenger comfort and safety definitely plagued the antebellum railroad. Numerous passenger complaints were registered at such discomforts as ventilation and heating systems, uncomfortable seats, inadequate lighting conditions, and the lack of efficient suspension and insulation equipment that would make traveling by train a relaxing and relatively noiseless experience.[1]

Since horses were extensively employed to pull trains before the lines acquired locomotives, coach designs naturally reflected their equestrian source of power. In spite of this common feature, the first passenger cars did not conform to any standard design or national plan. In 1831 in the *New England Magazine* it was recorded that carriages were constructed in many various forms and sizes, and evidence of such haphazard development is obvious in the case of the Baltimore & Ohio's first cars.[2] A warning to unsuspecting neophyte passengers was issued six years later by David Stevenson, who went so far as to remark that there were hardly two railways in the United States that were made exactly alike or constructed on the same uniform construction.[3] This fact was especially true in the 1830's and persisted until the Civil War.

That passengers would have to be content with pot luck when riding trains before the Civil War was one of the tacit challenges that travelers were forced to accept. It was not uncommon to discover that on some of the earliest lines the coaches were little more than tailor-made horseless carriages mounted on flimsy rails. In fact, some models operated by the Baltimore & Ohio Railroad were merely three-seated open coaches that exposed the occupants to the mercy of the weather and to clouds of cinders and dust. Consequently, before cars were enclosed and weather-proofed, extended rail journeys for individuals were very rare.

Both inexperienced and veteran travelers alike reacted to adverse conditions of traveling in horse-drawn cars in as many ways as there were vehicle designs. In 1831, Thomas Hamilton described a novel coach on the Baltimore & Ohio Railroad as resembling a wooden house or chamber like those used by itinerant showmen in England.[4] Even as late as 1853 William Chambers, speaking of a passenger carriage as "one of those houses on wheels which accompanies travelling shows and menageries," agreed that in reality it was "nothing more than a long wooden box, painted yellow, with a roundish shaped roof; a door at each end, and a row of windows at each side."[5] Other models of horse-cars, seen operating between Lexington and Frankfort, Kentucky, by James Buckingham in 1837 were described as being side-less, holding sixteen passengers on the floor level and eight on the roof. They were also remembered as the "least commodious and agreeable" vehicles that Buckingham had ever seen.[6]

Other specific models pulled by animals and machines and mentioned by passengers before the 1850's included coaches designed by Richard Imlay of Philadelphia,[7] and the "barrel car" patented by S. S. Hacker in 1841. The Imlay coach was distinguished by its stagecoach appearance and by the cabinet making skills of the artisan whose name the car was given. The "barrel" model was so-called because of its rotund shape. Utilized for both passenger and freight duties, Hacker's car was mounted on eight wheels, four forward and four in the rear, rather than the conventional four. Its barrel shape was the result of constructing staves around six iron hoops that measured two inches wide and one-half inch thick. The center diameter of the car was nine feet, tapering to eight feet at the cars' ends. Passenger models were identified by the twenty 15-by-30 inch glazed windows on each side, while freight cars were windowless and constructed to hold forty to forty-five bales of cotton, or 15,000 pounds of other goods. Overall the passenger and freight car was considered to be cheaper, safer, and more durable than the standard square design.[8]

Unlike most travelers of today, the antebellum passenger cannot be accused of having lacked an aesthetic appreciation for finely built cars, but the style and comfort of his vehicle were of secondary importance to the safety features of a machine. The record of accidents in horse-cars was alarming to the more timorous who were frequently reassured by leading magazines of precautions taken for their well-being. *Niles' Weekly Register* expressed confidence in the Baltimore & Ohio cars, reporting that they were hung on springs and built low to the ground, thus being difficult to overturn. Among other safety features, the *Register* noted one which allowed the motion of the cars to be arrested by the use of a powerful lever brought into contact with the wheels to check immediately the speed of an animal attempting to go faster than the driver desired.[9] Additional assurance was added seven months later in 1831 by the *New England Magazine*, which declared that the Maryland cars seemed safe, since the horses were attached to the vehicles in such a manner that they could not pull the cars from the tracks.[10] These and other accounts pointed out that the only certain dangers for most passengers were those accidents that resulted from their own extreme carelessness.

Even as early as the 1830's, when many companies were still utilizing horses, some railroads began operations with steam engines, causing additional safety and comfort problems in railroad cars. But the transition from horse-cars to steam locomotives did not occur all at once. As late as 1848, Ebenezer Davies traveled on a horse-drawn train to Baltimore, but in a coach that was modern for its time. The car was thirty to fifty feet long and featured a center aisle that separated the rows of double seats. Each of the seats was nicely cushioned and was of sufficient length to accommodate two persons. Of particular interest to the British abolitionist was the fact that the seats were constructed so the passenger could reverse them and face away from the animal and toward the end of the car if he so desired. This was undoubtedly a major advantage over stationary seats, and no one seemed to appreciate this luxury more than Davies, who remarked, "This part of the arrangement is indispensible, as these long carriages can never be turned. The hind part in coming is the fore part in going, and vice versa."[11]

Horse-cars were observed by some travelers as late as mid-century, but the great advances in railroad equipment which had occurred by the 1860's relegated these models to iimited duties. Seldom by the 1850's did coaches look like homes for itinerant showmen, having acquired dimensions and characteristics similar to passenger cars today. Henry A. Murray commented on the evolution of the passenger car in 1852, reporting that American coaches were approximately 42 feet long, 9½ feet wide, and 6 to 6½ feet high.[12] Charles Weld described the dimensions of his car, two years later, as being about 40 feet long, 8½ feet wide, and 6½ feet high.[13] The passenger capacity of antebellum American coaches was reported to be between thirty and eighty passengers, indication once again of the lack of a standard design. Charles Dickens, while visiting the United States in the 1840's, commented that American cars seating between 30 and 50 people, were "like shabby omnibuses, but larger."[14] Léon Beauvallet reported during a tour in 1855 and 1856 that American cars were immense and could "easily accommodate fifty people,"[15] whereas Dionysius Lardner stated coaches contained about fifteen to twenty seats, accommodating about sixty to eighty passengers.[16]

Such conflicting reports are partially explained by William Chambers, who recorded that a fully seated car held sixty passengers, thirty persons on each side, but that in allowing space for a stove, the number was generally reduced to fifty-six or fifty-eight.[17] A second explanation for accounts of cars holding more than sixty passengers is attributed to the belief of some companies that it was prestigious to build cars holding as many as seventy-two passengers. This idea, however, was not generally accepted by antebellum railroads, which mostly adopted the sixty-seated passenger car.[18]

The relinquishing of horses for locomotive power was responsible for numerous innovations on passenger cars, such as heavier four-wheel trucks and improved suspension systems. The change from the pioneer four-wheeled car to the eight-wheeled vehicle occurred about 1838, and resulted in a twofold advantage. Additional wheels not only provided passengers smoother rides, but also increased the road stability of trains. William Chambers was one of several foreign passengers impressed by the maneuverability of the double-truck eight-wheeled cars and marvelled at the adeptness with which coaches in the United States could "round a corner with the ease of a gentleman's carriage."[19] Likewise, Charles Weld remarked that American cars were ingeniously mounted on swivel axles, that enabled them to whisk around curves, "at the sight of which an English railway engineer would stand aghast."[20]

Along with their superior speeds, railroads issued another deciding challenge to stagecoach lines when improved springs were installed on eight-wheeled cars in the 1850's. Until this time most springs were inelastic carriage models and were as hard on the rolling stock as on the passengers in the cars. By the late 1850's these crude suspensions were replaced with India rubber in the form of blocks. However, despite the additional comfort afforded passengers by the new innovation, the processed rubber then available rapidly lost its resiliency and became rigid and hard. By 1865 the rubber-blocked spring was discontinued, but was installed on American coaches in later years.[21] George Foster Pierce seemed to appreciate these new advantages, proclaiming that railroads were very agreeable contrivances "for getting along" and should last forever. Pierce further added that he would "cheerfully resign all [his] interest as a traveller, in horses, buggies, and steamboats, to be assured on every route of a railroad." It was a grand invention to the Methodist Bishop, who saluted the railroad lines with a hearty "success to them all."[22]

By the very nature of their power, horse trains seldom exceeded twelve miles an hour and were relatively easily controlled. But once steam was applied to trains, major braking and coupling problems involving both safety and comfort confronted engineers. The first couplings on the tiny coaches of the 1830's were frequently nothing more than two to three foot chains that caused a severe jerking motion during the acceleration of the cars. The shock often disrupted passengers and scattered baggage, making rude couplings another drawback of early travel by rail. The confusion was repeated when the train decelerated, since the slack in the chains allowed the coaches to bump together. One novel attempt to reduce the shock involved placing padding at the points of contact of the two adjoining cars.[23] To reduce the jolts of stopping and starting on other models, chains were replaced by iron bars or even fence rails placed between the cars. The crude devices were frequently held fast by yarn packed between the rail connectors and the walls of the cars.[24] But these too were dangerously inadequate, frequently causing tragic accidents and fatiguing rides.

Another more acceptable plan incorporated before the Civil War was to couple cars with steel links and pins. Though this method eliminated much of the train's jerking motion, many careless crewmen lost fingers and hands while joining or disengaging the cars. Small wonder that as late as 1862, passengers referred to car couplings as "rude" and "simply hooked together."[25] Smooth rides were never fully assured until modern times, when coupling problems were finally solved by the automatic devices which not only held coaches firmly together and eliminated bumping, but were much safer than chains, rails, or links and pins.

Unreliable brakes contributed to excruciating and dangerous rides in cars along with the accidents resulting from hazardous couplings. Some braking systems were so primitive that several companies went so far as to employ laborers to race out to meet an incoming train and physically arrest the movement of the engine and cars.[26] Some models had mechanical brakes that consisted of nothing more than wooden blocks applied to the wheels of the engine and each car. Such an arrangement, similar to brakes used on stagecoaches, was but another of the many similarities between the two vehicles. If the passengers were lucky, the train would stop when a crewman applied pressure on a lever that placed a braking block against the wheels. But since each car had to be stopped individually, passengers experienced a journey of uneven stops and bucking motions throughout their ride. In later years wooden brakes were replaced by metal devices controlled by a central operator. But it was not until after the Civil War with the invention of the air brake by George Westinghouse that passengers could feel reasonably certain that speeding cars could be stopped within acceptably safe distances.

Europeans often commented on the strangeness of certain American passenger car features. One of the most frequently mentioned novelties of the car's interior design was the long center aisle, which came to distinguish the American from the European passenger train. Just why this change from the continental plan of individual compartments was made is not clear. But it does reflect Jacksonian egalitarianism, since it did place the American closer to his fellow countryman and provide him an opportunity to express publicly his many opinions, whether people were willing to listen or not.[27]

That the center aisle discouraged class distinctions and afforded everyone on American trains a high degree of freedom was verified by class conscious foreigners, who often protested against the democratic atmosphere they found in American cars. During the travels of Captain Marryat through the South he noted:

> The Americans are a restless, locomotive people: whether for business or pleasure, they are ever on the move in their own country, and they move in masses. . . . the millionaire, the well-educated woman of the highest rank, the senator, the member of Congress, the farmer, the emigrant, the swindler, and the pick-pocket, are all liable to meet together in the same vehicle of conveyance.[28]

Similar remarks were voiced by other foreigners. The American car with its center aisle was a nuisance to Fanny Kemble, who described it as a "long greenhouse on wheels" flanked by two rows of seats that ran the length of the car. The passageway was described by the English actress as a thoroughfare for the uneasy to "fidget up and down" in, and for "tobacco chewers to spit in." The lady also objected to the pandemonium that filled the cars at stations, when the aisleway was invaded by tribes "of little itinerant fruit and cake sellers . . . distributing their wares at every place where the train stops."[29]

The aisleway to Thomas Low Nichols seems to have been less annoying than to other passengers, since Nichols believed the arrangement had its practical aspects as well. Because of its public nature, not only were passengers capable of visitation from car to car, but the aisleway reduced the likelihood of train robberies.[30] Yet to most travelers the aisleway was but an easy avenue filled with stumbling tobacco chewers and full of constant noises from boisterous adults and children who were inconsiderate enough to go from car to car slamming the vehicles' doors.

Once railroad companies made the decision to build cars with a center aisle, a need was also realized for providing platforms at each end of the vehicle to permit conductors to cross freely from car to car. This facility was also utilized by passengers, but not without ever-present danger. The careless or inebriated traveler was liable to fall between two cars and be crushed under the wheels. Even with its dangers, however, passengers like William Chambers skeptically approved of the platform arrangement, cautiously adding "There is a placard within the cars cautioning persons from standing on the platforms."[31] Some companies conveyed this message more poignantly by painting gravestones on the window glass of each door. Other railroads in several instances tried the expedient of locking coach doors. This met with only limited success, and was abandoned after several wrecks occurred in which the passengers were imprisoned in burning coaches.[32]

The discomforts of rail travel resulting from abrupt braking and the noises caused by restless passengers walking through the cars were frequently accompanied by poor seating facilities in the cars. Modern comfortable accommodations were almost unknown to passengers traveling on the earliest trains, since most seats were usually little more than thinly padded two-seated wooden benches that were at best a minor improvement over stage coach seats. Abraham Hall, for example, failed to see anything favorable about the ill-conceived Lake Pontchartrain Railroad in Louisiana, which he called a "relic" and a "farce." During his travels on the line in the 1840's, he discovered the hard-backed chairs in this company's cars were so unbearable that he was "ricketed" over the Louisiana countryside. "Ricketed" was defined by Hall, who added, "If you have ever ridden Turkish fashion over the granite soil of New Hampshire in a farm wagon, you can understand, and only in this event," the meaning of the word.[33]

Léon Beauvallet also complained about seating during his tour of the South in 1855 and 1856. He found that sleep was almost impossible on most American coaches, since the backs of the chairs were of just such a height as to prevent passengers from comfortably resting their heads.[34] Peddlers and railroad attendants were aware too of these tiring discomforts and offered some degree of limited services to aid irate passengers. Head-rests could be procured from peddlers in some depots, and when attached to the back of a seat, these could be adjusted to a position that would accommodate the passenger's head.[35] (A similar pillow service is found on busses and railroads today.) Another feature that helped to alleviate the ennui of traveling was the provision of reversible seats, which allowed passengers on one seat to face those on the seat in front or behind, thereby rendering travel a potentially pleasant social affair.[36] By 1852 other car models included reclining chairs and lavishly furnished coaches with paintings and upholstery.[37] Other cars offered the comfort of "retiring rooms" for both sexes, and a safety cord which, when pulled, summoned the engineer to stop the train. But for the most part it was not until the 1870's that most American cars came equipped with comfortable seats and luxury accessories as a matter of course.[38]

That traveling was anything but pleasant on antebellum trains, despite the improvements that were made by 1860, is obvious when one considers that air conditioning, electric lights, and adequate heating were absent in passenger cars until well after the Civil War. But as in the development of so many other aspects of railroading, serious efforts were nevertheless made to improve the comfort of Americans on the move. Before the invention of air conditioning and modern ventilation systems, railroads were constantly searching for an efficient means to purify the air inside coaches. At first, since many of the first trains were open cars pulled by animals, passengers certainly could never complain of a lack of fresh air. But once railroads began using locomotive power to transport passengers over long distances in closed cars, the necessity and practicality of adequate ventilation was urgently realized.

Passengers traveling in stuffy, hot cars frequently found relief simply by opening a window and sticking their feet or heads out into space. Although such measures undoubtedly provided a refreshing breeze while the train was moving, they must have presented a strange sight to pedestrians who stood watching the train pass by. This relief, however, was only temporary, since when the train pulled into a depot, passengers became uncomfortable once more. To make matters even more unbearable, the opened windows allowed hot cinders and dust to fill the cars, as well as fumes from animal fats that were used for axle grease.

Accompanying the problems presented by dust and heat, coach interiors were made especially stale in the winter months when cars became stuffy from the fumes of cigar smoke and expectorated tobacco juice. Bold indeed was the traveler who sought relief by opening a window, however, since during the winter this permitted both cinders and cold air to fill the car. Traveling between Baltimore and Richmond in 1850, Lady Stuart-Wortley felt that her coach was in need of some invigorating ventilation and raised one of the windows to admit some fresh air. To her surprise, one man immediately shielded himself with a large umbrella, while another tried to escape the cold blast behind a carpetbag. Lady Wortley heard some of the other passengers complain, "We shall be frozen before we get to our journey's end." Others tried to protect themselves with raised collars and buttoned coats, while some tacitly protested by shrinking and shrugging, and slouching their hats. Nevertheless, the determined English lady kept the window open, reasoning that Americans must have a dislike for fresh air and a dread of catching cold. However, she did comment that the manners of the Americans in her car were admirable, since the passengers "were too courteous and obliging to remonstrate."[39]

Fanny Kemble, another traveler who felt uncomfortable in her poorly ventilated coach, complained of tobacco-chewers and of the anthracite stove which robbed the "atmosphere of all vitality." However, when she attempted to raise a window and free the "poison emitted at every respiration from so many pairs of human lungs," the other passengers gave her such a "universal scowl and shudder" that she decided to leave the window closed. Only after reaching her destination did the actress breathe comfortably again, for the stove, replenished with additional coals, had "almost suffocated the inhabitants in the crowded coach."[40]

Along with raising or closing windows, other attempts to render travel more comfortable amidst cinders and dust were often reflected in a passenger's mode of dress. At first persons traveling by train thought it fashionable to don their finest clothes. But because of the presence of the destructive particles that entered the car, some travelers had begun by the 1840's to wear dusters. These protective garments were simply long coats made of light materials that were worn over one's street clothes to protect them while traveling on the train. Although dusters remained fashionable into the twentieth century, such clothing was at best only a temporary solution for protecting passengers from dust and cinders, and obviously was of no value in clearing the air passengers had to breathe.

So irritating and serious had cinder and dust problems become by the 1850's that several companies registered a decline in passenger traffic and offered lucrative rewards to inventors who could solve the expensive and annoying problem.[41] The *American Railroad Journal* carried numerous articles discussing a possible remedy, and in May, 1859, stated that if some efficient dust-removing device could be perfected, passenger traffic would double.[42] Several unsuccessful solutions had been presented in earlier editions of the magazine, such as one in 1850 that proposed a series of vents on the tops of cars to trap air and force it through a series of cloth filters before it entered the cars. Yet, like so many other plans of this type, the device only collected dust and offered little ventilation for the passengers inside the coach.[43]

Numerous plans and machines were suggested in trade journals and travel accounts as to how railroads could improve air pollution problems within the cars. One plan that had previously been mentioned was the installment of spark-arresters which would be housed in the large cone-shaped smokestack so commonly associated with early American locomotives. But although these arresters were lauded by the *American Railroad Journal* and other promoters, they were never completely effective. Another interesting plan to purify the air was the Townsend horizontal smoke pipe. This apparatus consisted of a long tube attached to the engine smokestack and extending along the roofs of the cars to the end of the train. At this point the residue from the engine would fall behind the cars and not on the passengers.[44] Although the idea was never applied to a train, it did represent another of the many attempts to solve ventilation problems and make railroad travel safer and more comfortable.

Other solutions suggested included vented windows, series of baffles, ice trunks in sealed cars, and a device, filled with water, which cleaned dust from blasts of air entering the cars. Thomas Nichols, traveling between Memphis and Cleveland, Ohio, rode in a coach equipped with a water-cleaning device and praised it as a great advance in railroad technology. According to Nichols, the machine

> warmed in winter, cooled in summer, and thoroughly ventilated always. In the warmest days of an American summer, with the thermometer at a hundred and the train enveloped in clouds of dust, these cars were kept clean, airy, and cool. By ingenious machinery a constant current of air was cooled and washed clean from dust by being made to pass through showers of water. In winter they were warmed and ventilated with hot air.[45]

Attempts to reduce dusty conditions by other means entailed the installment of collapsible curtains, which covered the open platform space between the cars. This not only prevented great amounts of dust and cinders from entering the cars, but also deadened the sounds of the engine and kept passengers from falling under the wheels of the train as they roamed from car to car. Yet it was not until 1931, when the Baltimore & Ohio Railroad put on two completely air conditioned trains between New York and Washington, that railroad passengers could travel safely in cars free of dust and completely comfortable all months of the year.[46]

Passengers' notions of escaping uncomfortable journeys with a change of seasons were quickly dispelled on their first encounter with the primitive heating devices installed in the cars. The anthracite coal stoves that were usually located either in the center or at each end of a car naturally provided an uncomfortable distribution of heat, so that passengers farthest from the stove were usually cold, whereas those seated nearest it were overheated. Bishop Henry Whipple once had the misfortune of being placed next to a throbbing hot stove and complained that it almost changed him into bacon.[47]

Charles Dickens described coach stoves he saw in America as "red-hot" and "insufferably close."[48] Similar complaints were registered by Daniel Hundley, Henry Murray, and William Cullen Bryant. On the Orange & Alexandria Railroad in near zero weather between Richmond and Washington, Hundley complained the stove in his coach did not give out "the least bit of warmth."[49] Passenger Murray commented that he often burned on one side and froze on the other when he had to open the window of the car to free it of stinking odors of "Virginia juice."[50] A concurring opinion on the heating of American coaches was added by William Cullen Bryant, who criticized the inadequate stoves in the coaches on the Weldon to Wilmington line, describing them as "shabby" and "extremely uncomfortable" in cold weather.[51]

One's position in the car determined more than one's comfort, however, since a safety factor was also involved. In the event of a collision, passengers seated nearest the stove were liable to be fatally burned. Should the car derail or overturn, a stove could cause fires, so that seats nearest the doors offered precautionary safety advantages.

Most passengers, however, were more interested in the immediate issue of comfort than in the possibility of accidents. Two of these were Ebenezer Davies and Charles Lyell, who found the "pot-bellied" stove satisfactory in winter travel. During the winter of 1848, Davies was delighted to discover that a stove was provided in each coach on his train, which was "at that season a most important article of furniture."[52] Sir Charles Lyell, in 1845, was another passenger who welcomed the stove as a comfortable piece of furniture, and remarked that travelers frequently stood around it to keep warm. He himself took up the habit. On one occasion, while indulging in thought about the speed of the train, Lyell seemed to enjoy the warmth, his newspaper, and the safety and comfort of rail travel so much that a fellow passenger had to call his attention to the fact that his coat had caught fire from standing too close to the stove. Nevertheless, Lyell gamely congratulated American railroads for heating their cars so efficiently, even though his means of obtaining comfort had mesmerized his circumspection.[53] But stoves were perhaps praised universally only by ubiquitous tobacco-chewers, who found them tempting targets on which to test their aim. Chewing was nauseous to most other passengers, however, and some railroads posted signs in cars which read "GENTLEMEN ARE REQUESTED NOT TO SPIT ON THE STOVE."[54]

Railroad companies were well aware of the deficiencies of anthracite stoves and experimented with other systems. One plan included pipes which were designed to carry heat to the passengers from the locomotive firebox into the cars. Another heating idea was to install hot water pipes under the floor of the coach to keep passengers' feet warm.[55] Even with all these attempts, car heating remained in a primitive state until 1887, when "a durable and flexible joint for the steam line between the cars was invented."[56]

Lighting presented a challenge to the railroads' ingenuity as soon as short daylight runs of the early trains were augmented by the night runs made possible by longer lines. At first, lighting was provided by candles and oil lamps, but these methods had serious drawbacks. Common complaints were that candles failed to provide enough light and were easily extinguished by an open window or door. Oil lamps, which offered more light, were troublesome and dangerous. Gas lights were the most efficient source of illumination on railroads before the Civil War, and were cited by the *American Railroad Journal* in 1859 as brighter and safer.[57]

Lighting was seldom mentioned by passengers traveling in the South, probably because few of them used the services of night trains. When darkness descended they evidently broke their journey by spending the night in hotels or inns. However, Fanny Kemble noticed that a coach on the Weldon Railroad was furnished with lamps although other features on this North Carolina line were totally lacking.[58] Traveling in the early 1840's, Dionysius Lardner also reported his coach was furnished with good lamps, located in each end of the vehicle. Lardner reported that overall the conditions were agreeable, and "the vehicle is perfectly lighted and warmed."[59]

Of all the improvements made to insure passengers' comfort during the first thirty years of Southern railroad history, none was more welcome on long trips than the sleeping car. It was first introduced on a Pennsylvania line in 1836, when the Cumberland Valley Railroad provided this service between Harrisburg and Chambersburg.[60] But according to some passengers, railroads in the South were lacking these accommodations as late as the 1850's. In the early 1850's Frederick Law Olmsted, for instance, pondered while riding a train near Gaston, North Carolina:

> Why night-trains are not furnished with sleeping apartments, has long been a wonder to me. We have now smoking-rooms and water closets on our trains; why not sleeping, dressing, and refreshment rooms? With these additions, and good ventilation, we could go from New York to New Orleans, by rail, without stopping; as it is, a man of ordinary constitution cannot go a quarter that distance without suffering serious indisposition.[61]

Night traveling on trains without sleeping cars was at best a bad situation. To improve their lot, some passengers improvised some sort of bedding. Usually a traveler had to doze in an uncomfortable chair and share the miseries of the journey with his fellow passengers. For the more fortunate an entire seat was occasionally available, permitting one to lie down in something like a prenatal position. One of the most comfortable sleeping positions for men was achieved by propping their feet on the back of a seat. But for women, custom conflicted with comfort, since it was considered unlady-like to lift the "extremities" off the floor.

During the winter months, sleep was even more difficult to be won because "of the anthracite stove that glowed and throbbed in the middle of this locomotive den."[62] Chilled passengers were constantly attracted toward the heat to warm their feet on the stove fender. Besides this traffic to and from the stove, sleepy passengers were also bothered by the constant attention of the attendant replenishing the stove.

In 1853, while trying to sleep on a night train between Wilmington and Washington, Eyre Crowe protested that his slumber was interrupted by a Negro fireman who contaminated the air with cinders by raking them from the stove. The discomfort was only temporary, for the Negro returned later and doused the smouldering fire with a bucket of water. Once more the travelers settled down and dozed with their "stockinged toes" pointed towards the heat. The episode was ended, said Crowe, with "a fine democratic air of simplicity about the whole arrangement."[63]

Bothersome conditions that interfered with sleep also included the inadequate space in the cars for the passengers' baggage and other belongings. Over-crowding was an additional irritant. Charles Mackay protested that American cars were frequently filled with as many as sixty passengers of all ages and conditions. Crying children, drunks, and tobacco chewers were closely packed in an atmosphere "deprived of all its moisture and elasticity."[64]

Once the sleeping car had been introduced by the Cumberland Valley Railroad, however, these conditions were improved considerably. Other companies, such as the Baltimore & Ohio Railroad in 1838, were eager to include this service on their trains. Most of the first sleepers in the United States were merely day coaches that were crudely converted to sleeping cars at night. The only means of distinguishing between these first sleepers and ordinary cars were the words "Sleeping Car" painted alongside the coach by some companies. Other cars equipped with bunks that were built three high on one side of the coach did offer slight improvement. Limited privacy could be gained by hanging curtains in front of a bunk.

Only a hard mattress was available for travelers on the first sleepers; a passenger who wanted the comforts of a blanket and linen had to bring his own. Consequently, many persons simply slept in their clothes. In later years, most railroads did provide bedding which was usually stored in linen closets at one end of the coach. It was left up to a traveler's honesty to take whatever supplies he needed. This undoubtedly impressed foreigners with the simplicity and equalitarianism found on American trains. None of the berths on a sleeping car were reserved, and the charge for sleeping privileges was usually twenty-five cents. Since the sleeping cars reflected the dual hazards of dirty linen and lack of privacy, "women never ventured into them," but were allotted a separate sleeping section to which males were forbidden entry.[65] By 1838 some cars were equipped with collapsible seats that could be converted into beds at night, and two decades later sleepers even had separate compartments for passengers. Though George Pullman introduced some of his ideas for night travel as early as 1858, it was not until 1865 that his cars began to resemble the modern sleeping coach.[66]

Most antebellum travelers praised the sleeping car and lauded its innovation in their travel accounts. George Lewis, a Scotch Presbyterian minister, recalled in 1844 that he "slept rather comfortably in a sleeping apartment in one of the cars" between Augusta and Madison, Georgia.[67] Other testimonials were offered by Thomas Low Nichols and John Shaw. Nichols remarked that passengers traveling for two or three nights could rest on a sleeper, comfortable and undisturbed all night.[68] Shaw, on his way to Atlanta, in 1846, traveled on a train that had cars which contained beds "where the weary traveller might rest his limbs and sleep as soundly as if he were on a bed of down at his own home." Even with the shaking motion of the coach he "was enabled to pass a very good night," and when he awoke he was surprised to discover that the train had traveled 170 miles in twelve hours. Apparently well satisfied with these accommodations, Shaw remarked, "This is one of the many instances to be found in America, where something new and original will be constantly meeting the eye of the European traveller."[69]

Despite its many shortcomings, by 1860 the American passenger coach had far surpassed the description of Davy Crockett, who saw it as a group of "big stages hung on to one machine."[70] In fact, long before wealthy travelers sported over the country in lavish "Palace Cars," the presence of wealth was revealed by specially reserved private cars. This accommodation was accomplished by one of two methods. One way was simply to secure a carriage on a flat car, much the same as trucks were later to be shipped on railroads. The other arrangement involved an ordinary passenger car, which was reserved specifically for certain individuals or families. The fee charged for this exclusiveness was between five and twenty-five dollars in the 1830's, in addition to the regular fares charged for the persons transported.[71]

Additional evidence of sophistication was the inclusion of smoking cars and vehicles equipped with water closets, where passengers could take care of their morning ablutions.[72] Trains also included tenders and freight cars, as well as baggage, mail, and express cars. However, other conveniences, so common to travelers today, were not familiar to passengers until after the Civil War, coinciding with the changes brought by coal and electricity.

Undoubtedly, the introduction of sleeping cars and other improvements renewed the faith of travelers in railroads. Nevertheless, cars were often still poorly ventilated, inadequately heated, and miserably cold. Among other unsolved problems was that of road noises entering the cars as they clacked over rough and uneven rails. Carlton Rogers remarked in 1856 that he had "a great dislike to talking in the cars, when they are in motion, as the effort to raise my voice above the din and noise of the rattling train seriously affects my throat."[73] This problem, which involved the rails themselves as much as the passenger coach, was only one of several aspects that would have to be improved before the railroad truly came of age.

The characteristically American flavor of the early railroads reflected the country's spirit of primitive democracy in an age when rubbing shoulders with all classes was a uniquely American phenomenon. As American habits became more sophisticated, so did the railroads; but neither the populace nor the railroads ever lost entirely that peculiarly equalitarian character of early America.

Sail Car

Treadmill Car

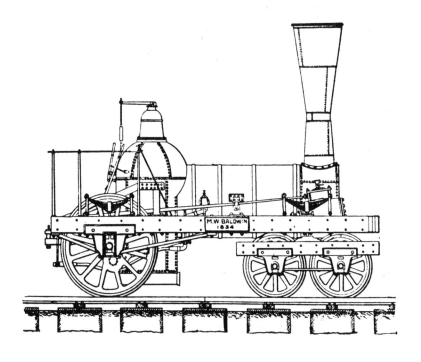

E. L. Miller Locomotive (1834)

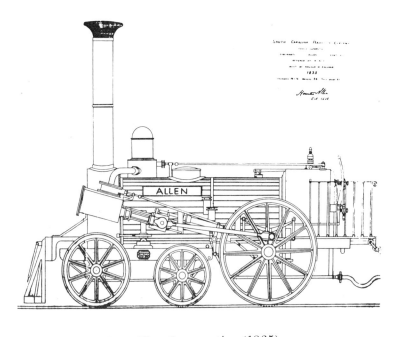

Last Allen Locomotive (1835)

SOUTH-CAROLINA RAIL-ROAD,

Between Charleston and Hamburg, S. C. opposite Augusta, (Geo.)

Distance 136 miles, performed in daylight, from 6 A. M. to 6 P. M. *President*, John Ravenel. *Directors*—Wm Aiken, A. Black, Wm. Bell, J. J. Bulow, Dr. S. H. Dickson, John Dixon, H. F. Faber, John Haslett, B. J. Howland, Dr. Joseph Johnson, T. Tupper. *Auditor*. Henry Ravenel. *Secretary*, J T Robertson, *Principal Engineer*, H. Allen.

RATES OF PASSAGE.

From Charleston to			Miles	$ Cts.	From Hamburg to			Miles	$ Cts.
Woodstock,	-	-	15	50	Aiken,	-	-	16	75
Summerville,	-	-	21	75	Blackville,	-	-	46	2 25
Inabnet's,	-	-	32½	1 62½	Midway,	-	-	64	3 25
Branchville,	-	-	62	3 00	Branchville,	-	-	74	3 75
Midway,	-	-	72	3 50	Inabnet's,	-	-	103½	5 12½
Blackville,	-	-	90	4 50	Summerville,	-	-	115	6 00
Aiken,	-	-	120	6 00	Woodstock,	-	-	121	6 25
Hamburg,	-	-	136	6 75	Charleston,	-	-	136	6 75

And from one intermediate Station to *another*, Five Cents per Mile. *Children under 12 years and Coloured Persons, half-price.*

Regulations for the Passenger Carriage.

1st. All baggage at owner's risk—75 lbs. allowed. 2d. servants the not admitted, unless having the care of children, without the consent of all the Passengers. 3d. Passengers not allowed to stand on the outside platform. 4th. moking prohibited, 5th. No Gun or Fowling Piece shall be permitted to enter the Car unless examined by the Conductor. 6th. The feet not to be put on the Cushions, nor the Cars soiled, defaced or injured in any way. 7th. Dogs not admitted into the Passenger Cars. 8th. At the ringing of the Bell, Passengers will be allowed one minute to take their places. 9th. Seats must be engaged and paid for fifteen minutes previous to the hour of departure. As a general direction, the conductors of the Carriages are instructed not to permit any conduct that is inconsistent with good order, or the comfort and safety of the Passengers: for which especial end these Rules have been established, and are required to be enforced with civility but strictly.

HOURS OF DEPARTURE AND ARRIVAL.

UPWARD PASSAGE.

Leave Charleston, at 6 A. M.

To Woodstock, running time and stoppages 1h. 5m. *Not to arrive before 5m. past 7 A. M.*—Breakfast 20 minutes.

Time Table

Simple "sleeper" construction used on the surface and in excavation, where the ground was firm.

Reinforced "sleeper" construction, with the track supported on foundation timbers running parallel to rails, was used where soil was too soft.

Piling construction supported track above surface. As needed, the pilings were steadied by single timbers, X-shaped cross braces or outside bracing.

Trestles or "truss work" came into use where soil conditions were particularly bad and the road was more than 12 feet above the ground surface.

Track Supports

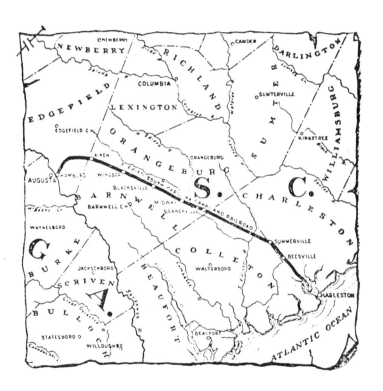

Map of the Line

5

The Hazardous Roadway

Railroad passengers were primarily interested in such immediate factors as their own comfort and safety, but railroad companies were also forced to struggle with constructing and correcting the technical difficulties of early rail transportation. Since many backers invested in companies only to realize profits, the natural tendency of many was often to neglect such tedious details as roadbeds, bridges, and tracks until a line could be pronounced a financial success. This reluctance to commit the necessarily large amounts of funds to building safer roads resulted in hasty, unsafe construction, which revealed itself all too clearly to the nervous passenger in the form of flimsy tracks, hazardous curves, unstable bridges, and dangerous inclines.

As in so many other areas during the first decades of American railroads, construction costs varied greatly not only in the different regions, but also within the Southern states. *Appleton's Railroad and Steamboat Companion,* cited in 1849 that the cost of track per mile in Massachusetts was $36,000, compared to $24,000 in the South.[1] Two years later other sources asserted that the average cost for a mile of Southern track was approximately $20,000.[2] In 1828, one mile of single track on the infant Baltimore & Ohio Railroad was built at an estimated cost of $15,000,[3] while further South, in South Carolina, the 136-mile Charleston & Hamburg Railroad was built at a total cost of $700,000.[4]

Higher expenses for constructing such lines as the Baltimore & Ohio Railroad were due to the fact that much of the track bed had to be cut over and through hills of rock. Yet in other parts of the South construction costs were accelerated by dense swamplands, swarms of insects, alligators, and snakes. In fact, so difficult were conditions encountered by the New Orleans & Jackson Railroad, that an entire year was required for surveyors to chart a distance of only eighty-eight miles.[5] Despite the high costs and obstructions presented in building these roads, however, the excitement and ease of opening railroads in the United States soon made the new mode of transportation a common affair.

The simplicity with which a railroad could be organized, and the lack of regulations governing their operation, made roadways as widely varied as their costs. In many areas where companies tried to realize greater profits at the expense of safety, the upkeep on certain bridges and tracks was completely neglected. One extreme case in point was the St. Marks Railroad in Florida, which ran trains that were frequently derailed, leaving the passengers no alternative but to detrain and assist the Negroes in righting the cars on the track again. Conditions were so disgraceful on the line that, according to a passenger of the 1830's, practically nothing had been invested in the road, and the roadbed was completely incapable of supporting steam engines, even being unsafe for horsecars. Constructed of metal-capped timbers connected with one bolt, rails on the line were laid crudely on the bare sand without benefit of any ties at all. Small wonder that this company's tracks were said to be as "undulating as the sea."[6]

Minimal expenditures were also made by those lines fortunate enough to take advantage of already existing animal or carriage trails.[7] Conversely, new roads built in rocky areas, were initially expensive, but offered lasting permanence, by using available fill and stone for roadbeds, sills, and blocks. In most cases, however, cheaper wood proved best for cross ties since its shock absorbent qualities provided greater passenger comfort and reduced operating costs by diminishing the damage to rolling stock.[8] These rails of the 1830's were mostly wooden, plated with a strap of iron ⅝ inch thick. They measured approximately 15 feet long, and 2½ inches wide, and were supported on ties that were sometimes spaced up to four feet apart. Whenever horses were used, the ties were hewn cut in the center to provide room for the horse path. The better beds were filled with crushed stone, although ties were on the most rudimentary lines of the 30's occasionally laid on bare ground.[9]

Since passengers' records show that most railroads seldom invested excessive time and money in carefully laid tracks, accidents on antebellum trains were caused as often by rail problems as by exploding boilers and unsafe cars. One major deficiency that caused untold misfortunes was the use of poor quality timber causing the rapid decay of ties. To preserve the wood numerous schemes were suggested such as the use of a compost of tar and sand,[10] solutions of salt, boiling ties in common gas tar,[11] or even immersing timbers in liquor for long periods of time.

Sometimes tracks would tear loose and come crashing through the bottom of a car. Several passengers reported such incidents, including Dionsyius Lardner and Bishop Henry Whipple. Lardner remarked he had often heard of the thin bars piercing the under carriage,[12] whereas Bishop Whipple reported that passengers using a Georgia line out of Macon commonly experienced rails piercing the car floors, derailments, and other "amusements of the kind calculated to make one's hair stand on end."[13]

In the event a train was delayed by a loose rail, the repair procedure was pragmatic and rudimentary. Included among a train's accoutrements were sledgehammers that the crew used to beat rails back in place. Some wags reported that Negroes were detailed to walk in front of some trains to search for "snakeheads," or bent rails, and that when they found one, the locomotive was positioned to hold one end of the track down while the Negro scout secured the other.[14] "Snakeheads" remained a problem to many railroads as late as the 1850's. However, during the late 30's and 40's most lines began to replace wooden rails with a piece of iron fastened to the surface with the new and improved U-rail.[15] But most efficient was the T-rail designed by Robert L. Stevens about 1830. The rail was in general service by 1860, and it was so practical and advanced for its time that its basic design is retained even today.[16]

Besides "snakeheads" and wood decay, another road problem both costly to companies and irritating to passengers, was the absence of a standard national gauge. Since most engines in the United States were at first imported from England, that country's gauge of 4 feet, 8½ inches was adopted by American lines. But once Americans began constructing locomotives for their own needs, any plan of standardization rapidly disappeared. New England and the Middle West generally retained the English standard, while the South usually preferred the 5-foot gauge. Pennsylvania and Ohio used other variations, ranging between 4 feet 8½ inches and 4 feet 10 inches, while other companies argued for the larger 6-foot gauge.[17]

The dilemma was moved toward a settlement only when President Lincoln issued an order in 1862 to establish a standard gauge for the proposed trans-continental railroad to California. But even the President's influence could not settle such a knotty problem of vested interests. Missouri argued for 5½ feet, Chicago and New York suggested 4 feet, 8½ inches, and California clamored for a 5-foot gauge.

Finally, the dispute was taken to Congress, where after eight long months of debate, a law was passed in March, 1863, establishing a national gauge of 4 feet, 8½ inches.[18] The standardization was completed when railroads in the former Confederate states converted their tracks on May 30, 1886.[19]

The railroads' notoriety because of unsafe tracks was a fact of much concern to Americans and foreigners, and the latter were especially fearful of the poor roads and disastrous collisions that occurred before the Civil War. The foreign traveler could never understand how Americans could tolerate the large numbers of accidents occurring in the United States, and pointed out that one major cause for so much carnage was that the Americans insisted on unduly hurrying the completion of their lines by building only roads with but one track. Michel Chevalier warned the wary of single tracks in the 1830's, recording that on isolated and scarcely used railroads up North, and on all those in the South, there was usually but a single track.[20] Another who seemed to take sardonic delight in criticizing the absence of double tracks was Léon Beauvallet. In 1855, he critically observed:

> Another folly in this country is to have only one track; which is charming, because when two trains rush upon each other, one of them is sure of being finished; but they are in such a hurry—these sons of the New World!

The Frenchman added that double tracks might have saved several thousand lives in America, but "Fudge! what is the life of a man worth in this country?" Americans to Beauvallet, could not think of taking twice the time to build double railroads, for "they care for one thing only, to do quickly what they do at all."[21]

Ebenezer Davies wholeheartedly concurred. This observer, after traveling between Cumberland and Baltimore, Maryland, complained that Americans were quick to boast of the "hundreds of thousands of miles of railway they have constructed" but forget "to tell us that they are nearly all single."[22] Davies and William Chambers both mentioned that occasionally they found double sets of rails to enable trains to pass safely,[23] but that passengers were often delayed for as long as an hour at these sidings awaiting an approaching engine from the opposite direction.[24]

Whenever sidings were found they were often of little use in preventing collisions because of reckless engineers, who had to rely on faulty time systems to avoid approaching trains. Nevertheless, the neglect of life and property was always difficult for some foreigners to understand, since the country had adequate natural resources to build additional tracks and other safety features as well. Especially in the South, some noted that virgin forests of pine and oak afforded an "inexhaustible supply of timber . . . free to whoever wishes to use it." This timber could have been used, according to Chevalier, not only for double tracks, but for guard rails on bridges and station houses too.[25]

David Stevenson joined the protest in 1837 and queried since American railroads were less elaborate and cheaper to build than European roads, why, especially in view of the availability of wood, more safety features had not been built in.[26] Fanny Kemble also remarked that some companies were so irresponsible that they retarded their own progress "by hurrying unduly the completion" of their lines.[27] Still, extra construction time and a desire for increased profits all too frequently outweighed the concern for safety on lines that were "merely laid out with the design to make money."[28]

Railroad bridges were another hazard feared by passengers. Although some bridges, such as the Baltimore & Ohio's granite structure spanning the Patapsco (from Baltimore to Washington) was listed as "among the noblest bridges ever built,"[29] this double tracked, 700-feet-long, 60-foot-high $120,000 bridge was an exception to the norm.[30] Most bridges were simply constructed of timber, which despite their rapid decay were preferred to such bridges as the Patapsco bridge. It appears the wood was not so liable to damage as stone in cold weather, and of course wooden bridges were cheaper to build.[31] According to the *Atlantic Monthly* in 1858, Americans seemed to prefer the wooden structures so much to those of stone that "stone bridges so rarely occur upon the roads of America, that they hardly need remark." Thus, because of the availability and preference for wood, and despite the fact they were often built in a rude though substantial manner at little cost, the *Atlantic* proudly boasted that "nowhere in the world has the design and building of wooden bridges been carried to such perfection and such extent as in the United States."[32]

Based on travel accounts, one of the most discussed series of bridges built in the 1830's and "calculated to terrify travellers," were those belonging to the Charleston & Hamburg Railroad between Charleston and Aiken, South Carolina. Michel Chevalier described the construction of these bridges and their tracks as "peculiar," since much of the line was built over the water, on pilings 15 to 25 feet high. Supported by stilts, and leaving "something to be desired in regard to the safety of travelers,"[33] Harriet Martineau (who visited South Carolina about the same time as Chevalier), called the line which spanned pools, creeks and gullies, "the most interesting railroad we had ever been on."[34]

James Davidson also used the Carolina road, as did David Stevenson. In 1836 Davidson also found that a large part of the road passed over swamps, and was raised on wooden stilts 25 feet high, that reminded him of supports holding up "race troughs which convey water to Mill wheels in Virginia."[35] Stevenson, dubious of the passengers' safety when using the line, referred to the elevated road as a series of "structures on wooden truss-work[s] that were by no means stable enough to bear the weight of a locomotive," and "as may naturally be expected, very serious accidents have occasionally occurred on them." Furthermore, he remarked that on the highest parts of the road the company had failed to provide ledges for pedestrians, "who, if overtaken by the engine," had no means of safety except "only by making a leap to the ground."[36]

The Charleston & Hamburg Railroad was by no means the only line that used stilts, since passengers reported others in Georgia, Virginia, Mississippi and Louisiana. In April, 1844, George Lewis traveled by train on a Georgia railroad described as "the worst I have yet seen in the States." From Augusta to Madison, Lewis "slept rather comfortably," but was roused from his sleeping apartment at four in the morning to board a mail stage for the next segment of the journey. It seems that the stage route had been recommended as being safer than the railroad, since the tracks on the next section were elevated over marshes, and were so poorly constructed that "the whole concern was in danger of collapsing into the swamp."[37]

Two other accounts that reveal the concern of passengers when crossing bridges were those of Amelia Murray and William Chambers. Miss Murray became so giddy and frightened while crossing a bridge that she could not bear to look out of the coach window. The terrifying span was built on stilts that were 180 feet high. Despite the presence of the engineer who had built the bridge, and who assured her the structure was safe, the comforting words were of little solace to the English lady who found it "difficult to feel at ease during the transit."[38] Conversely, William Chambers stated that American bridges were sometimes built so close to the water that the cars seemed to be running on the water. He added that he seldom saw any ledges or railings on the structures, and "nothing could have saved the trains had they slipped from the track."[39] The stupendous wooden bridge over the James River prompted a similar comment from Alexander Mackay, who noted that because of a lack of railings, the "least freak of the engine might in a moment precipitate the whole train" into the foaming water below.[40]

Rainstorms, wash-outs and landslides also added to the hazards, discomforts and delays experienced by passengers. One intrepid traveler recording the danger of wash-outs was Bishop George Foster Pierce, of the Methodist Episcopal Church, South. Journeying in 1855–1856 from Georgia to Texas and back, on the return trip, between Montgomery, Alabama and Columbus, Georgia, he recorded that prolonged rains had disarranged all the roads as far as Macon, "and made travelling comparatively slow."[41] Even average speeds were dangerous, and rumors filled the cars of landslides, broken engines, and overturned cars along the road. Soon the clergyman had concrete evidence of these statements, since an engine had broken down and capsized east of Opelika, Alabama. Crossing into Georgia, nearly a mile from the Chattahoochee River, another engine was bogged down in mud and dirt from washouts caused by the torrential rains. The misfortune halted Pierce's train and forced the passengers to abandon their journey and return to Opelika. Not to be denied, Pierce and several others decided to press on by foot, using a second nearby bridge. Below them the water was "swollen, rushing and foaming," while a gale whipped about the intrepid travelers. A little wiser in retrospect, Pierce later warned that walking on cross ties over long, high bridges was ill-advised, and that it was safer to wait for another train.[42]

Apprehensions over poor bridges and washouts were also reported during the travels of John Abbott and Léon Beauvallet. Abbott, on a trip to Augusta on a very dark and rainy night, feared that before morning his train and its passengers would encounter some serious disaster, because of floods, yet "all night long, through the rain and darkness, we went careening on in perfect safety."[43] Beauvallet's observation of American bridges was that many of them were improperly constructed of inferior timbers, were improperly graded, and thrown together in haste. He bitterly criticized the railroads for using second rate wood for ties and supports, maintaining that the timber would bend under the weight of the cars and seemed likely to break at any minute. In anticipation of such a disaster, the Frenchman warned that cars were liable to be criminally flung "into the midst of interminable marshes, immense rivers, torrents which thunder at your feet, and immeasurable precipices." Succinctly, he concluded that railroad bridges were but another of the "thousand and one opportunities to break your neck" in America.[44]

A controversial engineering problem to be solved by the earliest companies was how to traverse mountains and the steeper grades. At first numerous skeptics maintained that locomotives would never come into general use except where the terrain was uniform and level.[45] Another school of thought held that undulating railroads were the answer. The locomotive in a roller-coaster fashion would gain speed on the downward slope so that it could ascend the upward slope to the crest of a hill.[46] But, in an age of limited power, the position that was finally accepted as most plausible was that of the inclined plane.

By 1860 the adoption of the inclined plane was a common affair in the mountain states, both North and South. Considered uniquely American, and largely responsible for many companies' success, it nevertheless was not without a multitude of hazards.[47] The operation involving these planes would separately attach the engine and cars to large hawsers, sometimes measuring up to nine inches in circumference. A stationary engine of perhaps sixty or more horse power then pulled the vehicles to the summit. To lower the cars down the reverse slope the plane engine arrested the descent of the vehicles. Sometimes horses were added to the operation, and in order to conserve the animals' strength, and to prevent their being run down by the cars, some engineers suggested provisions for the horses to board flat cars during the downward trip. This eliminated a waste of power, but it also required some fancy footwork, the career of a less than agile beast usually terminating under the wheels of a rolling car.[48]

Although most planes in the slave-holding states were not as large as those in Pennsylvania and other free states, those planes of the Baltimore & Ohio and Charleston & Hamburg railroads were impressive and an engineering feat for their day. *Niles' Weekly Register* described in 1831 the Baltimore & Ohio's three and one half miles of incline over Parr's Ridge, between the Patapsco and Potomac Rivers as among "the most interesting and imposing features presented on any part of the road." To overcome approximately 550 feet, one section of the incline was 2,150 feet long, while a second section added 3,000 feet more. Between the two sections was a level stretch of 3,674 feet. For the descent, the sections were 3,200 feet, then a level stretch of 3,678 feet, and a final downward grade of 1,900 feet.[49] Less spectacular was the Charleston & Hamburg's incline at Aiken, South Carolina. Although described as being "perfectly successful," the incline was shortened in 1835, and later completely replaced by discarding stationary engines for powerful mobile locomotives in 1841.[50]

Railroad inclines were immediately recognized as being as dangerous as they were impressive in mountainous areas where the angles were acute. Most companies, therefore, first used them only to negotiate freight cars. But with the pressure for better service in later years, passenger cars were included at the risk of "breaking the necks of travelers."[51] Thus, another aspect of antebellum travel was the contemplation of possible power failures and cable breaks, which could send a coach plummeting down an incline to be smashed to bits.

Several measures were taken to minimize this tragic possibility, one of which was to reduce a car's downward motion by thrusting wooden poles under the wheels after the manner of a wagoner going downhill. Eyre Crowe witnessed this precautionary action on a steep grade between Fredericksburg and Richmond, Virginia, and remarked that the passengers were given "quite pleasing jerks in the process."[52] Another device was the "safety car." This vehicle served as a brake by following or preceding the regular cars on the incline, and prevented their rapid descent in case of a failure in the power machinery.[53] But despite safety cars and such, dangerous conditions on steep inclines were not finally obviated until the mountains were penetrated by tunnels, or planes were ascended by more powerful locomotives with efficient brakes.

For irresponsible lines that failed to incorporate then-available safety features, results of neglect were often tragic and fatal. One of the most macabre accidents concerning inclines occurred on the Blue Mountain Railroad in Virginia. During one of the first passenger runs over the entire line in 1854, the locomotive *F. Harris* pulled a handsome passenger car with about twenty-five or thirty occupants, including engineer, fireman and brakeman. Also in the car was the chief construction engineer and his assistants. Before the descent of one of the steeper grades on the road, the engine and car were disengaged so that they could negotiate the grade separately. On the way down the latter's brakes, which were "somehow fastened with chains" failed to function. The brakeman, seeing he had no way to stop the vehicle, "leaped from the car and left it to its fate," while ahead, an occupant in the engine, Mr. George Clemens, jumped from the machine onto the tracks. The passenger car rolled over him, "cutting off both his legs, one below and the other above the knee, and one of his arms, from the effects of which he died in a few hours."[54]

The story concerning the unfortunate Mr. Clemens was but one of the many that travelers heard and read about while touring the country. Other mishaps involved greater amounts of machinery and personal injuries and were even more gruesome. But most intrepid travelers thought the risks involved were better than having no railroad at all.[55] Regardless of the hazards involved, the Age of Steam had captivated the minds of Americans and stimulated their appetite for increased rapid transportation.

First Headlight

6

The Perils
of the Road

Normally impatient Americans were remarkably willing to accept the delays and frustrations that accompanied rail travel before the Civil War, and in view of the omnipresent possibility of serious accidents, a touch of reckless abandon was as necessary to the early traveler as his infinite patience.

Because of their newness and haphazard expansion, one would conclude that the first railroads were the most dangerous of all. Yet, the accident rate from 1829 to 1841 was amazingly low.[1] Several factors help to explain this comparative safety enjoyed by railroads up until the carnage of the 1850's. First, accidents in the 1830's were fewer since trains ran slower, and ran on roadbeds, poor as they were, specifically designed for the lighter engines of the earliest lines. Second, accidents were restricted by the fact that trains were not permitted to run on Sunday, and that night trains were seldom used, unless they were preceded by pilot engines that searched for obstacles on darkened roadways. Third, the accident rate increased as more companies were founded, so that by the 1850's traffic was so heavy that railroads were faced with a veritable accident explosion.

As the railroad mania spread to the corners of the country, the hazards of travel were also increased by the employment of uninformed and inexperienced engineers and officials, who were incapable of even working with the antiquated systems of the 1830's. Thus, with faster trains, attaining normal speeds of twenty-five and thirty miles an hour, recklessness and neglect were also in large part responsible for the numerous rail disasters of the 1850's. Add to the above, collisions, derailment by misplaced switches and obstacles on the tracks, engine explosions, poor brakes, and wrecks caused by poorly constructed bridges and track beds, together with accidents resulting from carelessness of the passengers, and one is not surprised to discover that American railroads on the eve of the Civil War were regarded as among the most dangerous in the world. Yet, despite the alarming accident rate, the railroad mania by 1860 had become so infectious that the American desire for track mileage surpassed technological and managerial improvements necessary to protect the traveling public.[2]

The many perils encountered by the average railroad passenger of the antebellum years are in some ways reminiscent of today's calamities on our highways. In fact, in the first sixty years of the last century, one's chances of being killed or maimed in America led Léon Beauvallet to charge that, if one managed to avoid an accident in this country, it could be concluded that fate had greatly favored him.[3] Although Beauvallet was usually inclined to exaggerate conditions on American railroads, the Frenchman was correct in this instance. Typical reports submitted by the *American Railroad Journal* and *Hunt's Merchants Magazine* reveal that in no year of the 1850's were there less than 116 persons killed, or less than 417 injured. It is also significant to note that these figures do not include those run over, persons killed and maimed by jumping from moving trains, or passengers attempting to enter and leave while the trains were in motion.[4]

Although many Americans stated that American railroads were as safe as those of other nations, the records indicate otherwise.[5] The total number of deaths on English railroads, in 1857, in accidents directly involving railroads, amounted to only twenty-five. This figure, reduced to more impressive terms, meant that only one Englishman was killed for every 5,200,000 passengers transported.[6] Yet, another survey of the mid-1850's revealed that on American railroads one person out of every 188,000 revenue passengers was killed, as compared to one in every 1,703,123 in France, and one in every 6,680,324 in Great Britain.[7]

The railroad companies were constantly criticized for these alarming statistics, but they at least had the satisfaction of knowing that trains of the antebellum years were safer than steamboats, and that most accident-conscious travelers preferred to take their chances on land.[8] Several decades before the rail disasters of the 1850's, magazines were reporting that "the destruction of life and property, have become so frequent upon the Western rivers, that we look as regularly, when we open a newspaper, for a steamboat disaster, as for the foreign news."[9] Typical of other disasters were such notices as:

> *Amulet*—Sunk in Arkansas river; boat and cargo a total loss.

> *Concordia*—Boilers exploded opposite Plaquemine, Mississippi river, September 17th. Thirty persons scalded and missing.

> *Westwood*—Burst her boilers twelve miles below New Orleans. Twelve to fifteen lives lost, and several persons severely injured.[10]

> Vessel *Moselle* burst her boilers on a trip for Louisville and St. Louis (going South). Heads, limbs, bodies and blood was seen flying through the air in every direction, attended by the most horrible shrieks and groans from the wounded and dying.[11]

If horrifying accounts such as those carried by the newspapers did not persuade travelers to forsake the pleasures of the steamboat for the safer locomotive, other comparisons of boat and rail disasters did.[12] For instance, the editors of *William's Traveller's Guide Through the United States and Canada* applauded the construction of the Mobile & Ohio Railroad to provide safer transportation than the Mississippi steamers that were destroyed by snags and other navigational obstructions "such as are hourly met with on the 'Father of Waters.'" The railroad also afforded

> less liability to the fearful and heart-rending scenes which may happen again and again, until nearly every family in our country have to record the loss of "one loved one," at least, by either fire, explosion, "snags," or utter recklessness of human life on the part of those whose business and care it should be, to regard the lives and property of those entrusted to their care with the greatest sacredness.

The *Guide* added that, besides the railroad's speed, the Mobile & Ohio line also permitted persons to travel "without those feelings of danger which are so frequently experienced on going on board" one of the up-river steamers.[13]

Other examples showing that steamers were more dangerous to travel on than railroads are found in *Hunt's Merchants Magazine* and the *American Railroad Journal*. Typical is a report in *Hunt's* that noted in 1853 that there were thirty-one river accidents which killed 319 passengers, and wounded 158. In 1854, out of forty-eight accidents, there were 587 killed and 225 wounded. Such carnage on the nation's rivers led the publication to add, "The idea of five hundred and eighty-seven human beings being sent prematurely to their long home, in one year, by collision and explosion, on our inland waters, is too heart-rending to contemplate."[14]

The *American Railroad Journal* conceded that traveling by river steamers afforded passengers greater freedom of movement and a more pleasant ride concerning safety, adding, however, that these comforts were not obtainable without a price, for "the ratio of hazard to life and limb is vastly greater on board the steamboat than on the car." For instance, it would take only one steamboat disaster to exceed "the entire loss of life" on all the railroads in the United States during a year, since "on a ship the carelessness on part of *one* passenger can be gross." But on railroads a passenger's safety was for the most part secure if his arms and head were confined within the protection of the coach, and if he refrained from moving about while the train was in motion. The safety of railroads over river travel was also supported in the *Journal* because trains were seldom subjected to the dangers of storms, and were not likely to be completely destroyed by explosions and fires.[15]

Two of the numerous travelers who preferred rails instead of rivers were William Kingsford and George Rogers. Kingsford's fear of steamers was based on his personal observations during a voyage in 1858, when he noticed that the showers of sparks belched from the engines made the vessel liable to catch fire and explode. Such possibilities, he concluded, led "serious men to see on going to bed if their life-preserver is at hand."[16] The likelihood of fires and explosions frightened the Reverend Rogers into commenting that "one can repose on board of one of these floating volcanoes with about as comfortable a sense of security, as if he were to take lodgings in the crater of Vesuvius or of Cotopaxi."[17]

That railroads were preferred by cautious passengers with an eye for longevity, does not negate the fact that they also viewed passenger trains as being lethal too. Travelers seemed always to try and include some grisly accident in their accounts, with these accidents usually falling into three major categories. They were boiler explosions, collisions, and derailments. The latter included accidents caused by reckless railroad employees, poor roadbeds, sabotage, and mechanical malfunctions of the machinery.

Of these three areas of accidents, judging from remarks made by passengers it appears that the fear of boiler explosions was most prevalent in the 1830's, although explosions were not so numerous as collisions and derailments. Many of these explosions were excused as part of learning to control the power of steam. But those mishaps attributed to careless crewmen and negligent safety regulations were criminal. The most famous explosion of one of the earliest engines was that of the Charleston & Hamburg's *Best Friend.* The celebrated and needless accident occurred on June 17, 1831, when a Negro fireman, failing to relish the music of the steam blowing through the engine's safety valve, attempted to stop the hissing noise by closing the valve. His ignorance nearly proved tragic. The machine exploded, and the force of the blast hurled the engine twenty-five feet. Injured were Nicholas Darrell, the engineer, and two Negroes, one of whom suffered a broken thigh.[18]

Although the *Best Friend* was rebuilt and toiled on the road for many years as the *Phoenix,* the incident prompted the Charleston company to undertake additional precautions to safeguard travelers from future accidents. One new plan was to relocate the steam valve so that it could not be accidentally closed. Passengers were given additional insurance against shrapnel from boiler explosions when a flat car "on which was built a pyramid made of cotton bales" was placed behind the engine and the tender. Later the company added another vehicle behind the "barrier car" to give even better chances for survival. This car carried a Negro brass band that functioned as a back-up to the "barrier car." Theoretically, if an engine exploded, the engine, tender, "barrier car," and band would go first, before the passenger cars.[19] This arrangement undoubtedly eased the minds of the passengers, but the music produced by a band expecting to be blown to eternity at any moment may have been less than melodic.

Explosions could be frequently attributed to an unfamiliarity with new steam locomotives, but railroads were still confronted with boilers exploding as late as 1860. Most mishaps were caused by failures on the part of engineers to understand boiler limits so as to realize the necessity of maintaining sufficient amounts of water in the locomotive boiler. The *American Railroad Journal* suggested the number of explosions could be reduced if the companies hired more educated men, who should be kept constantly informed on new mechanical innovations by reading the latest publications concerning their business.[20] This magazine also offered advice concerning the neglect of railroads in the use of boiler safety plugs. These were plugs inserted into holes in the boiler, that would pop out when the steam pressure became dangerously high. However, a certain amount of water leakage occurred with plugs, and prompted companies to seat them permanently in the boiler, thus eliminating the safety valve.[21]

When railroads and crewmen ignored safety precautions like boiler escape valves, the results were sometimes disastrous. Typically, three men were injured due to an explosion of the Georgia Railroad's engine *Altonna* in 1849.[22] Four years later the company experienced another explosion that destroyed an engine and killed three persons near Marietta, Georgia.[23] The likelihood of explosions on steamboats and railroads caused Reverend Enoch M. Pingree several sleepless nights during his travels. The Louisville preacher was so frightened by transportation facilities in America by 1848, that he identified himself as a "timid" traveler, and never felt safe on any means of public conveyance. Being a man of the cloth, he remarked that his friends had often ridiculed his fear of being scalded or burned to death, or being blown up or sunk. When asked why he would be afraid to die, "seeing that I fear no evil beyond death," the Reverend replied that "besides the violation of the instinctive love of life, and anxiety for those dependent upon me for protection and subsistence, *I don't want to go to heaven in that way.*"[24]

To allay the fears of passengers such as the Reverend Pingree, railroad journals sometimes carried safety tips advising passengers of the safest sections on a train. Hence, to reduce the annoyance and hazards caused by dust, the car nearest the engine was recommended by one guide. In the event of more serious accidents, the rear cars were the safest. Specifically, the safest car in a train was the next to the last one, unless rammed from the rear, or in the event the train ran over an object on the tracks. In the latter event, the forward cars were safer since they were not affected by the whipping motion of the cars as the wheels passed over the obstacle. Of course passengers were aware they could not predict the type of accident they might be involved in, but they nevertheless considered that, overall, the safest position in a train was a center seat in the next to the last car.[25]

When puffs of black smoke and steam whistles announced to farmers by the 1830's that their open range lands were being invaded by locomotives, another serious safety problem was added to those already present. Soon locomotives began colliding with roaming cattle, much to the consternation of their passengers. Strangely, the solution adopted to protect trains from the animals was developed in New Jersey, rather than in the rangeland areas of the South or West. Commonly called the cowcatcher, the apparatus was the brain child of the Camden & Amboy Railroad's, Issac Dripps, who had previously gained fame by assembling for that line the engine *John Bull* in 1831. Dripps was apparently a prodigious jack-of-all trades when it came to railroads, in actual fact never having seen a locomotive at the time he assembled the *John Bull*. His inventiveness was further demonstrated when he also built a tender for the engine which included an empty whisky cask for the water tank.[26] His career had hardly begun however, when he invented "the deadly parent of all cow-catchers, which *speared* the rambunctious bulls and tamed them somewhat."[27]

Dripp's first cowcatcher consisted of one or more pointed wrought-iron bars that extended parallel with the track and about four or five inches above it.[28] Precisely, the first model was little more than a spear attached to the front of the engine. So confident of the success of his invention was Dripps that he is reported to have said just before the weapon was tested that "it ought to impale any animal that may be struck and prevent it from falling under the engine wheels." Dripps was not a prophet, but was obviously an excellent engineer. For when the first bull fell before a Camden & Amboy locomotive armed with a cowcatcher, it struck the animal so severely that a block and tackle was required to remove the impaled carcass from the front of the machine.[29]

The success of the cowcatcher, though perhaps a sad occasion for roving animals, was a happy one for railroad passengers throughout the nation. However, despite the fact that it made trains safer, Dripp's cowcatcher had one major drawback: it worked too well. Consequently, the spear model was later discarded in favor of some bumper types that extended at right angles across the rails. Another type used by antebellum railroads was composed of a series of iron bars that resembled a "V." London businessman, Joseph Briggs, spoke of the V model in 1837, calling it "a sort of large shovel in front, which removes obstacles on the rails." Attesting to the efficiency of the device, Briggs reported that one night he saw a cow standing in front of a speeding train near Washington and "expected a terrible concussion." Much to his surprise, however, the "shovel" scooped the animal off the rails and carried it a few yards where it fell by the roadside. The engine survived the incident "scathless."[30]

The V model became common on most antebellum locomotives, and though it was modified in later years, other types were retained on American engines until recent times. But with the construction of heavier locomotives and the abandonment of open ranges the device began to be discarded by railroads, and is now little more than a wide metal fan that is a part of a diesel's design. In its evolution from the "steam-propelled lance" of the 1830's, however, to models used in the twentieth century, the American cowcatcher has set apart locomotives of this nation from those of most other countries.

For foreigners visiting the United States, the fascination for cowcatchers was matched by the bewilderment over why American railroads were not enclosed as they were in Europe. One can well speculate what the reaction of an Englishman may have been had he been in an encounter between a bull and an engine, as reported by *Niles' Weekly Register* in 1835:

A bull-fight with steam—A few days since, as the locomotive steam engine was passing along the Columbia rail road, the engineer espied a noble bull driving across the field, apparently to give battle to the machine. He was coming at the top of his speed, his tail stuck right into the air, and his head down, as if for immediate attack. As the bull errant rushed onward, the director checked the car, and received the blow upon the front wheel. The animal recoiled several steps —the puffing of the steam pipe seemed to challenge him to a second onset, and on he came, bellowing and tearing up the earth, while his eyes seemed to shoot forth baleful fire. The engineer thought that his safety consisted in moving; he therefore put on the whole head of the accumulated steam, and the car started like the wind. The enraged beast struck short of his aim, he missed his footing, and rolled down a high embankment, to the infinite gratification of those who had watched his behaviour, and to the glory of the engineer.[31]

Amelia Murray was one foreign visitor who gave such circumstances considerable attention during her travels in 1854 and 1855, and reasoned that Americans neglected to fence their lines because many railroads did not pass through sections having enough cattle to warrant fencing the tracks. Traveling by train near Charlottesville, Virginia, the British authoress noted that cows and sheep were frequently killed by trains, but usually "when not more than fifty beasts can be seen in as many miles."[32] She also added that enclosures were not as evident in the United States as in Europe, because horses and their riders had become so accustomed to trains that they usually stayed out of their path. Likewise, Henry A. Murray expressed the opinion that many Americans seemed so unconcerned about their children playing near the tracks because he believed the children had developed an instinct for avoiding on-rushing locomotives, which was a sixth sense.[33] Yet both of these travelers, who were unrelated, failed to understand the short-sightedness and lack of economy in killing cows and damaging engines by not erecting *some* fences, in a country where fencing materials were so easily obtained.[34]

Collisions with cows were not necessarily fatal to passengers, but they did cause concern over frustrating delays. During his travels in North Carolina in 1845, Charles Lyell was upset when his train was delayed on the way to Wilmington by ice on the rails and an encounter with a cow.[35] In April, 1855, Amelia Murray was distressed by a Louisiana railroad's poor schedules, caused by locomotives continually running over cattle. While at one station awaiting her train she heard it had been involved in a collision and was knocked off the tracks and into a bog. Later she learned that when the engine left the tracks, its coupling had snapped and left the cars on the roadway. Fortunately, Mrs. Murray missed being stranded in the middle of a swamp and sitting in the cars all night until the train was rescued the following day.[36]

Even more dramatic illustrations of the dangers caused by animals on the tracks turn up in reports of serious wrecks like the one recorded by an anonymous seaman of an accident that killed several persons on the Lake Pontchartrain Railroad in Louisiana. It was the first time the sailor had ever traveled by rail, and on a train that went so fast "you could scarcely see anything near by." On the engine was a "piece of wood fastened in front to throw things off the track" such as hogs and cows. Unfortunately, the device was not always effective. On one occasion the sailor recalled he once saw a train run over a slow moving cow that could not get out of the way of a train fast enough to avoid a collision. The engine was heavy enough to remain on the track and did not topple over. But several passengers were killed in cars as they overturned one by one.[37]

Another mishap which nearly ended in tragedy occurred during the travels of Joseph Ingraham in the early 1830's. His train had completed about two-thirds of its trip when the passengers were alarmed by "sudden and tremendous shouting from the forward cars." As the alarm spread throughout the train, the New England teacher heard "such yellings and whoopings" as "were never heard before on this side [of] Hades," for, resting less than a quarter of a mile in front of the speeding locomotive, a cow was lying quietly and calmly directly in front of the speeding train. Apparently the screams of the passengers petrified the animal, for she held her position "with the most complacent nonchalance." Although the engineer feverishly attempted to stop the locomotive, it was all in vain. The momentum of the train carried the engine and cars over the poor animal that was frozen to the tracks. With a "jump—jump—and a grinding crash," the shock of the impact was so violent that it nearly threw the cars off the track. Fortunately, the train was not derailed. But by the time the last cars passed over the carrion, the animal had been so completely severed that Ingraham noticed no perceptible shock.[38]

An incident of an even more serious nature occurred in 1847 on the Baltimore & Ohio Railroad near Cumberland, Maryland. While waiting at one of the stations along this line, Munch Raeder, a member of a prominent Norwegian family, engaged a number of passengers at the depot who had recently survived a collision. It seems their train had jumped the track and hit a covered bridge twenty or thirty miles away, when the engineer had jammed on the brakes to avoid hitting several cows napping on the rails at dusk. The animals were cut to pieces, and the ensuing collision with the bridge converted three of the cars into splinters. Later, after talking with some of the passengers on the ill-fated train, Raeder was told that not a single person was hurt, even though several had jumped from the windows of the speeding train. One uninjured passenger narrowly escaped drowning by hanging over the water, suspended by a beam that had been part of the demolished bridge. Although the engine had gouged large gaps in the bridge and along the roadway, Raeder seemed relieved to report that the ladies on the train, though thoroughly frightened, had not even fainted from the ordeal. The next morning at breakfast, the Norwegian spoke with one of them who "was eating heartily to make up for any possible loss of strength." The crash apparently had affected neither her appetite nor her disposition, for "she seemed to be in the best of humor."

That evening Raeder saw the wreck himself. Little had been done during the day to clear the demolished train from the bridge, so large numbers of people had gathered around the piles of wreckage. Indicative of the violence of the crash, Raeder found the bars on the cowcatcher were bent out of place, and the forward parts of the elegant cars were "utterly demolished." The side walls of the vehicles were "flung hither and thither." Amidst the debris Raeder saw two pools of blood which marked the place where the cows had met their fate. The track was useless, and the only way he and the other passengers could continue their journey was to walk across the damaged bridge, and board another train on the other side, that had been sent to pick them up.[39]

Wandering cows, sheep, and swine remained a serious problem for railroads throughout the antebellum years. Potentially more dangerous, however, were collisions involving two or more trains. Two such accidents that occurred on the Charleston & Hamburg Railroad in 1837, and on the Georgia Railroad in 1839 are typical. Returning from a winter vacation in St. Augustine, Florida, Henry Summer, between Aiken, South Carolina, and Charleston, marveled at the advantages of railroads, commenting, "What a triumph of art is that mode of travelling." But his appreciation for steam locomotive was dampened somewhat when a train of freight cars, pulled by the locomotive *Georgia,* rammed into Summer's engine, the *Marion.* The lawyer recalled that the shock was severe, and that the *Marion* was disabled. The only casualties from the incident, however, were two injured horses, and a gentlemen who hurt his shoulder when he jumped from the car after the alarm was sounded.[40]

The accident on the Georgia Railroad in 1839 involved three trains. According to an article in the Augusta *Chronicle and Sentinel,* two trains dispatched to haul cotton forty-five miles from the city were traveling on the same track. During their journey they encountered a third train coming from the opposite direction. The engineer of the leading train apparently panicked, stopped his machine, and began backing up to gain the protection of a siding. He then collided with the other train that was following behind. No passengers or crewmen were injured, but the engine of the following train, and five freight cars of the retreating train were seriously damaged.[41]

Other strange accidents involving collisions include one that occurred in 1858 on a line between New Orleans and Canton. In this instance, a parked train with a broken axle was momentarily abandoned by the engineer. During his absence the train, still under steam, lurched forward and threw the passengers standing on the platform of the rear car to the ground. The runaway engine then collided with a second train in a head-on collision. The engineer, a Mr. Odell, made his escape to the woods as a hunted fugitive from justice, and obviously as an ex-engineer.[42]

Sharp curves and carelessly built roadways, navigated by reckless engineers, also added to the alarming number of wrecks occurring in the United States by the 1860's. Sir Charles Weld was one passenger who indicated concern over the number of sharp curves on American roads, and stated that locomotives in America rounded curves with "rocket-like impetuosity," which no English engine could manage. Sometimes, however, a zealous engineer taking these curves at excessive speeds brought on disastrous results.

Because of one foolish engineer, the high speed of a train on which Weld was traveling loosened the car's accessories which began falling on the passengers. A lamp-glass fell on Weld's head, and another in the lap of a lady. The Englishman "felt certain we were on the eve of a smash," and anxiously approached the conductor in an unsuccessful attempt to have the engineer reduce his speed. All endeavors to protect the passengers having been in vain, the car's occupants feared the worst, and one passenger in the car began giving instructions to the others on what to do in case of a wreck. The Englishman's fears were justified, for the train soon left the tracks, and Weld, climbing from the debris half stunned, recalled that he was "highly delighted when I found my limbs sound." The only equipment that escaped severe damage was the engine and about half of the middle car. The coach wheels had been flung great distances, and the rails were wrenched from the sleepers and "converted into snakeheads." Along with the damage to the equipment, Weld also reported a group of slaves on the train were considerably bruised, and the baggage car presented a curious mixture of bags, boxes, and ice. Overall, "the spectacle was extraordinary."

Weld and the other passengers placed the blame for this accident on the conductor for not requiring the engineer to reduce his speed. However, one passenger who had extricated himself from the wreckage and was sitting under a sumac tree smoking a cigar seemed unconcerned at the spectacle. Weld could not understand the aplomb displayed by the man and asked him how he could remain so calm. The traveler, an Englishman who had lived in Wisconsin for some years, philosophically replied that he was used to accidents on steamboats and railroads, adding that they were so numerous and so little thought of in America that it was useless to remonstrate. Somewhat dismayed, Weld took it upon himself to investigate the tracks which he described as only a "mere ribbon." The wonder was how the train had stayed on the rails as long as it did.[43]

Another accident resulting from poor conditions of roadways was witnessed by Henry A. Murray on his travels between Petersburg, Virginia and Wilmington, North Carolina. The first indication that something was wrong was the curious motion of the carriages and their "slantingdicular position." Among the confused and anxious passengers who anticipated a wreck was a Spanish colonel. Hugging a "beloved fiddle," he leaped out of one of the windows in Murray's coach in a manner "far beyond his years." The passengers' fears of an impending crash were soon confirmed, and amidst the sounds of bending metal and the screams of the ladies, the cars left the rails. The English naval captain reported, "Thank God! no lives were lost or limbs were broken." After the passengers "unkenneled" from the cars, it was discovered that if they had derailed a few yards further, the train would have plunged down a thirty foot bank. Later investigations revealed the train had derailed because of worn switching. The faulty equipment was reported by Captain Murray to the engineer, who said he had previously reported the weakened section of track to the superintendent, but was merely told "it would do very well for some time yet." Disgusted with the negative attitude of the railroad official, the Englishman hoped that in the future the superintendent "might break every bone in his body" at "the first favourable opportunity."[44]

Amelia Murray and Ebenezer Davies reported two other typical accidents concerning derailments. In Mississippi, in the mid-1850's, Miss Murray's engine took a wrong turn and plunged into a quagmire. Although the machine was later retrieved undamaged, a young boy who had been oiling the cowcatcher had jumped from the grill when the engine derailed. The boy's move was imprudent, for he was injured so seriously that he died.[45] Less serious were the woes of Davies. Because of an accident involving a "luggage-train," fourteen miles from Baltimore, the British minister's train was slowed to about nine miles per hour. He later discovered that the cause of the delay was another engine which had left the tracks further up the road, tearing "up ground in a frightful manner."[46]

Much of the labor done on railroads was performed by inexperienced men: other road hazards that caused accidents included unsafe bridges and faulty maintenance of equipment. George Foster Pierce experienced several moments of anxiety and typified the general apprehension of many passengers concerning bridges during his travels in the 1850's. The minister exclaimed that bridges, curves, and gorges along the route between Chattanooga and Nashville were frightful to weak nerves, and "even the strong man feels safer when he is over them." Yet despite the hazards of railroads, he found them a boon to the man who "has been long from home," for they swiftly bore the homesick traveler on his way.[47]

American railroads, which mixed Senators and rednecks in the same cars, also did not discriminate as to who was

included in the cars in serious accidents. Faulty equipment
was responsible for a wreck that included ex-President
John Quincy Adams in 1833, and President-elect Franklin
Pierce in 1853. On the Camden & Amboy Railroad from
Philadelphia to New York, on Friday November 8, 1833, an
axle of one of the lead cars broke on a train in which Mr.
Adams was riding. No one was hurt in the Adams car, but in
another car with twenty-four passengers, the vehicle overturned "with great violence" and injured many. Because of
injuries received in the wreck one Mr. J. C. Stedman, Esq.,
of Raleigh, North Carolina was horribly mangled and later
died, having been dragged for a considerable distance in
the car that overturned. Another passenger, a Dr. Rex of
Pennsylvania, was also badly mangled and died, while a Mr.
Wells, of Lebanon, Pennsylvania had both legs and arms
broken and was not expected to live. The cause of the
accident in which President Adams was involved was attributed to a broken axle that was not detected by the agent in
charge of constantly surveying the train. It seems the agent
was putting out a burning cotton bale at the time the axle
broke.[48]

The accident in which President-elect Pierce was involved took the life of his only surviving child Benjamin,
who was twelve years old. The tragedy, which many believed strongly affected President Pierce emotionally during his entire administration and after, occurred one mile
north of Andover, Massachusetts, on the Boston & Maine
Railroad. It seems the Pierce family was just returning from
visiting with friends in Andover when the only passenger
coach in the train overturned and "fell among the rocks,
down a precipice twenty feet and was turned so as to change
ends." The other coach of the train, a baggage car, and the
engine remained upright, but the passenger car was
broken in two. The Pierce family had been sitting four or
five seats from the front of the car, and when it overturned
the child was struck by a piece of framework that crushed

his head and dashed out his brains. President and Mrs. Pierce were not injured, although several others in the car were. The cause of the accident was attributed to a broken axle that may have snapped in the zero temperature.[49]

Illustrating the dangers of faulty equipment were accidents occurring on the Lexington, Kentucky Railroad in 1835, and those witnessed by George Combe and Tyrone Power. On the Lexington line the company had introduced "an elegant locomotive engine" which stirred the curiosity of the local people who came to view the wondrous machine. Two "burden cars" were attached to the engine, and these were minus safety rails around the sides of the open cars. On the return trip of an excursion for the populace, the wheels of the leading car came off and the occupants tried to abandon the disabled car. Several of the passengers fell under the wheels of the second car from the initial shock, while others met the same fate as they jumped from the car. Many of the passengers suffered broken limbs, and one required part of the car to be disassembled to free him of imprisonment under the wheels. The railroad was criticized for negligence, since it was believed that had the persons been transported in regular passenger cars or on flat cars with rails they would have been adequately protected in the wreck.[50]

In the late 1830's, near Washington, D.C., George Combe, regarded as "the world's outstanding phrenologist," was involved in an incident that resulted from a broken axle on the train's baggage car. Fortunately, none of the passengers were injured, even though trunks and packages in the car were thrown about and dashed to the ground.[51] A broken axle caused more serious consequences on the train used by Power in 1836. Near Baltimore, the first indication that something had gone wrong occurred when "our attention was quickly arrested by loud cries to 'stop the engine.' " Once this had been accomplished the "carriages were deserted in a moment," because the broken axle had overturned the rear car, resulting in only one out of the twenty-four passengers escaping unhurt. Included among the casualties was one man dead, another dying, and five suffering fractures, some serious. Several women who had been in the car were also hurt, and the children of one of them, two little girls, had suffered broken limbs. The Irish comedian noted that it was three hours before the injured passengers were removed from the sandy bank on which they had been stretched, and the scene of bloody, disfigured bodies exposed to the glare of the hot sun was an afflicting sight to behold.[52]

By the 1850's the public had been so aroused over horrible railroad accidents that companies were encountering strong pressures for improved safety precautions from all quarters. In New York, for instance, a code of 1856 stated that the passenger's safety was to be the major concern of a company, and that in matters of construction and interpretation all operations and policies would be governed by the primary rule of safety to passengers in the cars. Railroad conventions such as The National Convention of Railroad Engineers, convening at Baltimore on November 6, 1855, also demanded greater safety measures for the public, and suggested, among other things, that railroads establish higher standards in employing engineers. To meet the requirements of competent and responsible engineers the delegates stated that a good engineer should be able to supervise and repair locomotives, and should be a sober man, in good standing with the society. With the exception of men who were already employed, the delegates also suggested they should be able to read and write fairly well.[53]

The companies themselves were fully aware of the public clamor and need for additional rules to govern their respective lines, and in many instances had turned their attention to the problem as early as 1831. Shortly after the explosion of the *Best Friend,* The Charleston & Hamburg Railroad established regulations concerning the speed of the cars.

On trains consisting of a single car, the engines were restricted to fifteen miles an hour. When two and three cars were included in a train, maximum speeds were limited to twelve and ten miles an hour. Later, additional regulations stated that engines were never to exceed twenty miles an hour, "unless greatly behind time, then not to exceed twenty-five miles per hour."[54]

Similar rules regulated other aspects of railroading. To prevent losing a car during the train's movement, in 1853, Rule Number Three on the South Carolina Railroad stated that "no passenger train will run without a cord connecting the rearmost car with the whistle or bell of the engine." Other rules required an inspection of the locomotive and its train before engineers were permitted to leave a station. To avoid collisions with approaching locomotives, trains were never allowed to depart from stations ahead of schedule.[55] The engineer of a returning train was cautioned to imagine "that at any station he may find a train out of place."[56] Regulations also required that a warning be given a mile in advance of a station or crossing, when extinguishing coals, or in the event cattle were seen on the track.

On one Virginia railroad, watchmen were stationed at every road crossing to prevent collisions with other vehicles. A similar system, involving sentries stationed at four to eight mile intervals, was adopted by other companies. Besides serving as a safety precaution, the watchman and his Negro crew were also responsible for keeping the track in good condition and having wood and water available for the engine at all times.[57] Other schemes included ways to keep trains from hitting objects on the rails at night. Charles Lanman reported that in South Carolina he witnessed a "number of negroes bearing bright torches" who were sent in advance of the train. This practice had an eerie appearance to Lanman who said the Negroes "sometimes seemed like evil spirits gathering angrily around the locomotive monster which had dared to penetrate their forest home."[58]

Other attempts to promote safety included the use of flags as markers and signals to announce opened drawbridges, or to notify officials that trains bearing standards were ones with special purpose. Express trains, for example, were marked by red flags, while a white flag could mean that two trains were following one another on the same track. Flags were also used by conductors (lanterns being substituted at night) to signal engineers, and in the event of a breakdown some companies required that a watchman with flags be posted no less than three miles from a disabled train.[59]

Trainmen and engineers faced a communication problem on the earliest railroads which improved very little with the expansion of the antebellum railroads, and added to the hazards of the road. The first signals were often bizarre and inefficient; if the conductor needed to communicate with the "engine-driver" he would simply climb to the top of one of the cars and shout or wave. To capture the attention of a preoccupied engineer, he used the simple expedient of throwing a rock at the engine or pounding on the cars. Later, flags and hand signals came into general use, accompanied by other personalized systems such as lifting the steam valve or ringing the bell to relay instructions.[60] If the train was without a bell, a piece of wood was sometimes substituted which, when pulled, would thud against the engineer's platform.[61] One device mentioned in the columns of the *American Railroad Journal* in 1858 involved a whistle that was secured on the end of a long stick. When thrust outside a speeding car it gave a shrill sound, the faster the train moved, the louder the sound. The *Journal* stated it had been used efficiently on Chinese railroads and could be heard by either the engineer or the conductor.[62]

To reduce the number of collisions at road crossings and to lower the number of collisions due to poor signals, were other challenges that railroads had to accept and solve if they were to make trains the safest way to travel. William

Chambers, among others, criticized American railroads for their general indifference to regularity or safety and commented that in the United States the only protection afforded citizens was a sign which read, "LOOK OUT FOR THE LOCOMOTIVE WHEN THE BELL RINGS."[63] As newspapers of today sadly attest, many crossings in this country are still as poorly guarded as those a century ago.

Also associated with single tracks and signals was the problem of a safe procedure for engineers in the event that two trains met on a single track. This problem was so serious as late as 1855 that *Hunt's Merchants Magazine* editorialized as follows:

> No road between important points should be permitted to convey passengers *without a double track;* and upon every single track, the most definite and precise provisions should be exacted to prevent collisions. The time-table should be specific, and a violation of its directions should be made, in every case, a criminal offense. Until public sentiment compels our legislators thus to provide for the public safety, we shall be compelled day after day to chronicle these wholesale slaughters upon our railroad lines.[64]

During the days of horse-trains the safety of passengers and guards against public clamor were hopefully prevented by the use of center-posts erected mid-way between two sidings. The train first reaching the pole was supposed to have the right-of-way, the other engine being forced to back up and take refuge in the nearest siding. Unfortunately, this system was sometimes more productive of disputes than safety, as engineers engaged in slugfests over who had reached the marker first. In the most daring encounters, both trains would race to gain access to the pole, often with disastrous results.[65]

Although many accidents were caused by poorly built roads and faulty equipment, other disasters undoubtedly resulted from human error. Two such problems discussed by the *American Railroad Journal* involved faulty time-pieces and the health of the engineers. In 1853 the magazine stated that railroad accidents could often be traced to the fallibility of unsound watches. Even with reliable timepieces there was still the problem of synchronization and the possible malfunction of each official's personal watch. Only with efficient signals could these human and mechanical errors be solved, and it was the *Journal's* opinion that watches were the "most treacherous means of protection relied upon."[66]

In a time before medical science had come of age, the *Journal* also pondered the possibility of wrecks being caused by the effects of gasses from the locomotive on the engineer's nervous system. To illustrate this point of view, the magazine carried a statement made by the French Academy of Medicine in Paris, which suggested that an engineer's nervous system was often upset because the driver breathed oxide gas and carbonic acid that escaped from the fire hole of the engine, thus impairing alertness and efficiency.[67]

Another way suggested by leading magazines to lessen the tragedy wrought by serious railroad accidents was that of railroad insurance. *Hunt's* pondered the question that railroads were held responsible for cargo in their cars, and likewise should offer passengers the same protection with railroad insurance. Although railroad insurance was not offered by a company for each individual passenger, it was possible for some insurance to be obtained as early as the 1830's. With the increase of accidents in the 1850's the number of available policies increased, one of which offered $1,000 worth of insurance to a passenger for the sum of $1.00. On longer trips a $1,000 policy was offered by certain companies at 24 cents per $1,000.[68]

Newspapers of the antebellum years graphically illustrated the horrible accidents that had occurred on railroads by using "accident broadsides" and other lurid accounts. For some unknown reason, however, the attack on the railroads changed abruptly just before the Civil War. This change in policy possibly can be explained by the tenacity of some travelers in insisting that railroads were safe and not the brutal killers they were often painted. Two such defenders were Charles A. Goodrich and Dionysius Lardner. Goodrich, as early as the 1830's approved of continual expansion of railroads that were "coming fast into use in this country," advocating their construction "throughout the length and breadth of the land." The Congregational clergyman, a popular author, reported that actually only a few accidents had occurred on railroads, as must be expected.[69] Later, Dionysius Lardner, a self-proclaimed experienced traveler, stated that during his travels in the United States in the early 1840's, he had "never encountered an accident of any kind, or heard of a fatal or injurious one." Apparently unaware of the numerous accidents that did occur, the Irishman attributed the security of American trains to the absence of heavy traffic on the rails.[70]

The change in attitude of the press concerning railroad accidents in the late 1850's may also be the result of pressures exerted on the papers by the railroads themselves. In addition, the number of accidents did diminish shortly after the Civil War when modern accessories were being added to trains.[71] Yet whatever the reasons, passengers riding the rails after 1865 could feel safer and more comfortable than the passengers who used trains before the Civil War.

The years before the Civil War were filled with strange railroad mishaps frequently as comic as they were tragic. The humorous and critical reporting of many British visitors can be at least partially attributed to troublesome Anglo-American relations in a period when the expanding democracy was more concerned with growth than refinement. Yet under the witticisms and ridicule directed at American railroads, a hint of appreciation can be de-

tected for the raw, untapped power than expressed itself by
confidently continuing to build hundreds of miles of track,
heedless of all obstacles. By 1860 Americans had a vision,
and it was not to be derailed by caustic pens, unstable
roadbeds, or even the Civil War.

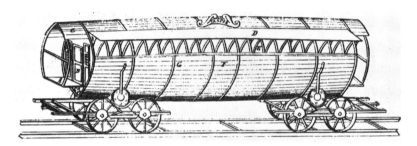

Barrel Car

First Sleeping Car (1837)

7

The Railroad
Station

In the furious pace of pre-Civil War railroad developments
the railroad station itself was at times all but entirely over-
looked. In their enthusiasm to accumulate miles, companies often ignored meeting places for passengers until
the 1880's. And before the Civil War the structures were
usually crudely designed and roughly erected. Most of the
first depots were constructed of wood, were as varied as the
lines they served, and were square and stark in appearance,
virtually without accessories for the passengers. The picture was somewhat more attractive in larger cities since
architecturally some railroads built their depots of stone
and brick, and experimented with the "L," "T," and Greek
Temple designs.[1] But regardless of whether the depot was
an urban or rural one, throughout the era the American
railroad station continued to reflect the egalitarian elements which set the railroads in the United States apart
from their Continental counterparts.[2]

To the European traveler American depots in some cities
and in thriving smaller towns were usually the best that
could be found. Few stations indeed could boast of having

gaslit smoking rooms equipped with inside shutters, of offering barber shops, telegraph offices, or newsstands, lavatories, bootblacks and check rooms.[3] Yet, representative of the improvements being made by the 1850's was the new depot in Washington, D. C. Built in 1852, the terminal measured 106 feet across and 68 feet deep. Overall it presented a striking facade, since the building, constructed of Connecticut brownstone, was crowned by a tower displaying a clock. During the day the station was partially lit by skylights, for which gas was substituted at night. Ticket and freight offices distinguished the main entrance as well as ladies' and gentlemen's saloons. The latter, furnished elegantly with dressing rooms, were equipped with mirrors, sofas, and numerous other comforts seldom, if ever found elsewhere.[4]

The same year the Washington station was completed, the Carrollton Railroad renovated its 1835 depot which was enthusiastically hailed by the Louisiana town as a sure sign of progress. The building was described by the Carrollton *Star* of April 24, 1852 as "extremely beautiful," spacious, and of a neat and plain color. The architectural style, "light and graceful" according to the *Star,* was well adapted for its intended purpose. Like the Washington depot, it was equipped with a clock, gratefully accepted by the community as a private donation from the railroad to the town. Carrollton was especially proud that the conspicuous position of the city's new acquisition made it the first thing to meet the eye of a traveler approaching the city.[5]

Two other stations which included modern conveniences were constructed in Macon, Georgia and Louisville, Kentucky, in the 1850's. The Macon depot was a two-story affair built on Fourth Street. Its spacious dimensions measured 370 feet long and 100 feet wide. Comfort and welfare of the passengers were assured by providing "a ladies' and gentlemen's waiting room," washrooms, baggage rooms and storage facilities. Besides rooms for porters, the station was equipped with ticket offices, a large dining saloon, a kitchen and a bar. The terminal was lighted by gas and qualified as one of the better stations in the Deep South.[6] The Louisville & Nashville Railroad constructed a modern $34,000 depot in Louisville, Kentucky which was opened for service with a gala celebration in 1858 that included speeches and inspections. The yard of the depot contained three platforms and six tracks, that served the twenty-three acres and the depot building which measured 400 by 153 feet.[7]

The Washington, Carrollton, Macon, and Louisville depots represented the better ones, but they were by no means the kind that most travelers touring the South normally encountered. The greater number of depots were poorly built low wooden structures that trapped the wood-burning engine's cinders and smoke. Engines fueled with coal were even worse. Besides being fire traps, stations also at times took on the appearance of cow barns, because of the various wagons and bales standing nearby. One writer has commented that except "for the presence of trains instead of hay wagons, a train-barn was indistinguishable from a substantial farm barn."[8] Generally, terminals lacked the canopies needed to protect passengers when leaving and entering the trains during inclement weather. The depots also neglected loading ramps, and were short of spacious waiting rooms that were comfortable and warm enough. Most stations were also short of necessary officials, and were sometimes even barren of restroom and eating facilities. In the most isolated areas conditions could even be worse. According to Charles Lanman, in 1846, the crudely built rough pine depot in Weldon, North Carolina was described as a discredit to the state. Lanman could never comprehend how "so glorious a State as North Carolina" could contain "such wretched accommodation for the traveller, and such vindictive swarms of the insect race." Continuing south, the Englishman called his journey into South Carolina a "kind of exploration expedition into an unknown land" where he still failed to discover "cheerful station-houses."[9]

Other travelers complaining about American depots commented that they were usually cheaply constructed, were sometimes not walled-in at all, and were without the services to be found in European stations.[10] However, most exasperating to the traveler, was to detrain and find no station *at all.* William Edward Baxter, an experienced traveler who claimed he had journeyed over ten thousand miles of railroads in the United States, was dumbfounded when he detrained in the middle of a Georgia cornfield with "no edifice of any sort being in sight." After inquiring the whereabouts of the depot, the British merchant and politician was informed that the *field* was the site for boarding and leaving trains. Undoubtedly dismayed, the Englishman remarked that Georgians, for all their enthusiasm in building railroads, had apparently forgotten to build stations as well.[11]

William Chambers was involved in a similar incident in Virginia. Near Richmond he was set down in a public street, seeing "no trace of a station-house, further than a small office where tickets were obtained."[12] Charles Dickens and Fanny Kemble expressed concern over out-of-way stations. In the 1840's Dickens could not understand why Americans built stations so far removed, "where the wild impossibility of anybody having the smallest reason to get out is only to be equalled by the apparently desperate hopelessness of there being anybody to get in."[13] Fanny Kemble concurred in the author's judgment. In North Carolina, the depot and small junction town of Weldon was described by her as a "small knot of houses . . . pretending to be a place . . . where a place was intended to be."[14]

Explanation for the lack of quality stations in the South did not necessarily stem from an aversion to refinements, nor because the citizenry accepted the new mode of travel reluctantly. Instead, it seems that most Southern companies were more concerned with profits and moving commodities such as cotton rather than passengers. Travelers visiting the cotton states were impressed by the great numbers of bales they saw stacked in depots awaiting further disposition. During several trips, covering a six-year period, Lillian Foster spoke highly of a cotton and freight depot in Augusta, Georgia. According to Miss Foster the 280 x 80 foot building was most conveniently arranged for efficient freight operations. The roof projected eleven feet beyond the walls on each side. Cars received their goods under the over-hanging eaves on one side, while "loaded drays drive into all parts of the building through the doors of the opposite side." This allowed constant protection from the weather as well as continual loading. In Chattanooga Miss Foster referred to the buildings of another "freight-house" as "fine."[15] Charles Parsons of Maine in 1852 was fascinated by the great amounts of cotton stacked in the Central Railroad depot in Savannah, Georgia. Amidst "acres" of cotton bales piled "mountain high," twenty to thirty cars were waiting to be dispatched. Passenger traffic was slow on the line, according to this Maine abolitionist and temperance leader, who observed that on six trips from Savannah to Macon never more than one passenger car was included with the freight cars or "burden cars" in the train.[16]

For those making long distance trips before the Civil War, a pleasant vacation to visit a loved one usually developed into an ordeal of fatigue. All too frequently, anticipated services expected by passengers were nonexistent, and brought numerous complaints concerning this aspect of railroad travel. To Charles Mackay and Henry Murray the lack of station officials was particularly annoying. Mackay protested this deficiency in South Carolina, where his train stopped at a station and he found neither clerks, check-takers, porters, "nor officials of any kind."[17] Henry Murray disappointedly remarked that much remained to be accomplished "in the way of organizing the corps of officials" that one did find.[18] Other discomforts in depots included a lack of heating in the winter months. Passing through a Washington station in the late 1850's, Alexander Mackay described it as miserable, cold, and poorly lighted,[19] and Henry Murray complained that station attendants sometimes neglected to provide sufficient supplies of wood for the station stove, leaving passengers unprotected from the weather.[20] Comfort, however, is a matter of individual taste, and in Alabama, Daniel Hundley complained bitterly that he was "nearly cooked by the red-hot stove and almost stifled by that horrible stench which always is emitted from burning iron."[21]

Such inconveniences were, to say the least, puzzling to aristocratic foreigners who did not understand the reluctance of less comfort-minded Americans to build adequately furnished attractive stations. Sir Charles Lyell commented in May, 1846, that he saw "more prudence and economy" displayed in the United States than he had anticipated. Critical of all aspects of American railroads, he also noted that railroads avoided digging tunnels or building double tracks, and were content with speeds of fourteen or sixteen miles per hour.[22] William Chambers believed American economizing was most marked in rural areas, with the better accommodations being made available in stations in principal cities, which were furnished with offices and waiting rooms. Yet, after comparing the impressive English depots with those in the United States, Chambers described American depots in most instances as "exceedingly cheap," and "shabby affairs."[23] Other travelers protested that not the "least notice is taken as to convenience and accommodations for passengers," a disregard which was apparent in the lack of adequate station-houses, watchmen, and various safety features.[24]

Besides the annoyances found inside the station, passengers were subjected to other abuses outside. According to the *American Railroad Journal* the railroads often irritated many travelers by pressuring them to use certain lines by employing "runners." This competition, was in fact, carried to such extremes by some lines, that fares were in some instances reduced far below the remunerative point.[25] These "runners" were described as being "entirely destitute of character," and were the result of the "intense rivalry" existing between the railroads. Although the *Journal* questioned their effectiveness, the purpose of "runners" was to convince passengers "that their particular line is the shortest, fastest, and cheapest, and most comfortable."[26]

Passengers were also frequently annoyed by representatives of opposing business interests who engaged in the practice of soliciting customers for the various taverns, hotels and inns. En route to Charleston, in December, 1836, James Davidson witnessed such a spectacle in Aiken, South Carolina. No sooner had the train entered the yard than several "landlords" approached the passengers, "bowing and inviting" them to walk to Major Marche's. The procedure was apparently novel to Davidson who said it was "the first time I had ever seen strangers invited to a tavern in that manner."[27] In Washington, Edward Waylen noted during a stopover that, as soon as the passengers from his train alighted from the cars, a crowd of blacks approached them, "each offering to carry the luggage, and clamourously urging the superiority of the respective hotels to which they were attached." The Episcopal clergyman stated that most of the Negroes were slaves, "yet who would suppose it from their comfortable sleek appearance, and the look of contented glee that marks every face?"[28] Charles Richard Weld also reported being met by large groups of Negroes at stations that clamoured in favor of the hotels which they represented.[29]

More irritating than "runners" and zealous "landlords" were the large numbers of cabmen competing for the right to transport passengers to hotels. Greeting passengers with "take your baggage, massa," "want a cab," and "a nice conveyance I've got for your honor," the cabmen in New Orleans were described by one traveler as being ethnically composed of "Irish, American & niggers," an unethical lot that cared little for earning an honest dollar.[30] Fares charged by drivers were usually determined by the law of supply and demand. The amounts varied from day to day and it was not uncommon for a driver to raise the price of his services, even though the rates were published and clearly stated in numerous railroad guides and other publications as well. For instance, *Williams' Traveller's Guide* stated in 1855 that a passenger visiting Baltimore should pay no more than fifty cents for transportation from the depot to a hotel or private residence within the city limits. For each additional passenger thirty-seven cents should be charged, and for each trunk, box or bag "of sufficient size to be strapped on," the cost was normally twelve cents. The *Guide* warned that parcels small enough to be carried inside the carriage should be taken without a fee.[31] *Disturnell's Guide* posted similar rates, but added that porters' fees were usually twenty-five cents. For information pertaining to other stations, the *Guide* advised passengers to refer to "the laws relating to Hackney Coaches, & Co., which can be found in carriages, as required by law." When drivers failed to adhere to the established prices, the *Guide* suggested that passengers not employ them at the rates they asked.[32] Regulations and warnings posted in books did little to curtail the activities of these men, who unscrupulously continued extorting excessive fares from passengers. Numerous travelers registered complaints, including Charles Mackay and Archibald Maxwell. In New Orleans, the former was infuriated when charged one dollar by a driver for transportation from the St. Charles Hotel to the Lake Pontchartrain depot less than a mile away.[33] Such practices would never be tolerated in London, Mackay added, since English drivers were not permitted by law or the police to "extort as much as they please from the fear, the ignorance, or the indolence of the public." Mackay advised London drivers who wished to amass a fortune that they could do so in Louisiana or "any other state in the wide dominion of Uncle Sam."[34] Lieutenant Colonel Archibald Maxwell expressed his contempt for hack drivers during seven weeks' leave from the disputed frontier of the Aroostook War. To the Colonel the drivers were a "race of extortioners," who had no idea of a sum "under a half of a dollar."[35] Perhaps the attitude toward stations and hack-drivers was best summed up by Thomas Cather. Critical of American democracy and the trend toward egalitarianism he witnessed in the United States, Cather reported that Americans viewed "everything with reference to how many dollars and cents they can make out of it." The Americans, said Cather, are continually on the move, have deplorable table manners, and the public conveyances were always crowded and the hotels always full. "You, here, see nothing of the quiet decorum of an English inn."[36]

If one were fortunate enough to survive the discomforts of the station and the extortions of the cabmen, another obstacle related to depots involved overnight accommodations. More fortunate passengers on lines that failed to provide night trains, took lodging in one of the railroad inns or local hotels near the depot. The accommodations were without uniformity, and standards were as varied as the railroads themselves. However, between 1830 and 1860, the hotels, like the railroads, improved with time. Take, for instance, the description of discomforts found in an early inn by one of the first passengers using the Charleston & Hamburg Railroad in 1833. The train stopped at nightfall in the town of Blackville, South Carolina, a town which consisted only of "two or three log houses, and one half built 'tavern.' " The name of the town seemed appropriate to the chronicler since the surrounding area was "a half burnt forest of pitch pine." However, such circumstances were the facts of travel and were stoically accepted. The building to which the passengers were directed was a "square roughboarded" structure along the roadside. Normally intended as a storehouse, it was furnished only "with a few old chairs and a table." Spirits were further dampened by the miserable food served, which some of the more critical believe was prepared by slaves. Privacy in the inn was nearly impossible since the five rooms were shared by twenty-five to thirty passengers. The rooms resembled a "row of stalls in a stable" and "anything said at one end could be heard at the other." One of the stalls, which was open above, was assigned to the ladies.[37] The arrangements were at best poor, but this did not prevent the passengers having a sound night's sleep. Early in the morning all were awakened by a bell and continued the trip.[38]

At other stations poor conditions led passengers to suspect collusion between hotel and railroad officials. George Rogers and several other occupants in a train were quite indignant over an unnecessary delay in 1856 in Chattanooga, Tennessee. It was "intimated that the railroad company had a pecuniary interest in the badly-kept hotel at the station," and that delays were intentional to promote business at the inn. The sleeping conditions were so poor here, said Rogers, that he "would rather have spent the night on a *rail* than in a seven-by-nine room, on a bed of straw, between sheets *not* as immaculate as the driven snow."[39]

If the accommodations in Chattanooga and Blackville were cited as some of the worst, the St. Charles Hotel in New Orleans, and Barnum's Hotel in Baltimore were listed among the best. Even meticulous foreigners praised the efficient Mr. Barnum who provided for one's every need:

> If there is an hotel-keeper in the United States who merits the commendations of a traveller, the veteran Mr. Barnum may claim to be that person. His neat private parlours and

bed-rooms, his quiet house, his excellent table, and the ready and obliging attendance found there, leave the traveller little to desire.[40]

To help alleviate the irritations of railroad travel, some assistance in overcoming obstacles were afforded by judicious consultation with a railroad guidebook. Besides warning passengers of unfair cab rates, guidebooks also informed travelers of the most comfortable clothes to wear, the etiquette of travel, prohibitions of the line and information concerning its operations. Additional information, which included advertisements, historical sketches, maps, telegraph prices and other items to assist the traveler, seemed at times almost to obscure the pamphlets' main purpose, that of listing fares and schedules.[41] Yet, nevertheless this helpful little pamphlet was of incomparable value in preparing passengers for the many discomforts they might experience.

Words of caution to the passenger about to begin a trip often included the advice that he purchase his tickets at the depot before boarding the train. Some stations issued the tickets at attractive counters which occasionally reserved special sections "exclusively for ladies." In other instances, however, tickets were obtained at ordinary counters or from officials in post offices or general stores. William Chambers expressed an intense interest in the American system in one of the larger depots in 1853. Besides having booths where one could procure tickets, he observed that other stalls were staffed with "competitive agents," the various railroads represented being identified by "flaming placards" hung on the office doors. One method used by agents to attract passengers involved distributing handbills. Like the "runners" these naturally recommended the advertised railroad as the fastest and cheapest line to travel on. It seems these bills were also circulated in hotels. On the premises of Chamber's hotel the ground was literally "sown" with yellow and pink advertisements "thrown about by boys" hired by agents. Papers were also seen lying on the hotel chairs and tables "to be picked up and read according to pleasure."

Once the traveler had survived the task of purchasing his ticket, he discovered that the stubs used for fare were printed in various shapes and colors according to the tastes of the railroad. Those used by Chambers were described as about three inches long. On one side was listed the essential information regarding the trip, and on the other side distances between stations. This information proved most useful to passengers, since officials were sometimes difficult to locate in the stations. Chambers also reported that his tickets were minus dates, with the exception of the year they were issued. This arrangement facilitated the use of tickets issued by several companies patronized during one's journey.[42]

The prices of railroad tickets varied from state to state, and line to line, and was usually higher on the earliest lines than on those in operation on the eve of the Civil War. That transportation became cheaper is revealed by the fares charged by the early trains on the Charleston & Hamburg Railroad. To travel the entire distance of 136 miles the sum was $6.75. Clergymen on official duties rode the train free, while children under twelve and servants with their owners were allowed transit at one half-fare. Free persons of color paid the full fare. Between 1844 and 1857 the passenger fare on the Carolina Railroad fluctuated from five to three cents per mile.[43] Although according to *DeBow's Review* the National rate in 1852 was two cents per mile.[44] By 1855, other railroads listed in *Williams' Traveller's Guide* listed the fare from Savannah to Atlanta as $9.50, from Savannah to Memphis the price was $30.00, and from Savannah to Holly Springs, Mississippi, $28.00.[45] To travel between New York and Charleston, according to *Disturnell's Guide*, required sixty-three hours at an expense of $20.00.[46]

As noted, children under twelve received special consideration on most railroads. According to *Appleton's Railway*

Guide in 1849 a child's age was determined by the conductor. If the official accepted the word of a young lad, he was charged only half price. For children under five accompanied by their parents the ride was free. Arrangements concerning fares and rates were new to many Southerners who never quite understood the logic of the system. For instance, a passenger on the New Orleans & Cairo Railroad remarked,

Men are perfectly willing to pay five dollars for riding a hundred miles in a stage coach; but give them a nicely warmed, ventilated, cushioned, and furnished car, and carry them four to five times faster, with double the comfort, and they expect to pay only half-price,—as a friend of the writer once remarked, "Why, of course we ought not to pay so much when we a'n't half so long going,—" as if, when they paid their fare, they not only bargained for transport from one place to another, but bargained for the luxury of sitting in a crowded coach a certain number of hours.[47]

Delinquent passengers who failed to purchase tickets at the depot paid a surcharge for the infraction when the ticket was obtained from the conductor in the cars. Charles Mackay spoke of this policy during his travels in the 1850's and reported that one was fined a ten per cent penalty if the ticket was purchased in the cars.[48] The policy of other companies, such as the Southern Railroad in Mississippi, was to charge late passengers ten cents extra for the first station, and five cents extra for every station thereafter.[49] Sometimes, however, the assessment was paid because of unavoidable delays. This nearly happened to Joseph Holt Ingraham at the Lake Pontchartrain depot in New Orleans. After hurriedly reaching the depot he barely had time to hasten to the ticket-office to deposit "six-bits" for two tickets.[50] William Cullen Bryant was not so fortunate. On a trip between Baltimore and Charleston, in 1843, the famous writer had to pay a penalty which boosted his fare considerably, from $22.00 to $29.00.[51]

Purchasing tickets was a simple affair compared to planning schedules, which not only involved transfers to one or more railroads but to stage lines and boats as well. Six years later, traveling from Baltimore to New Orleans in 1845 by the most expeditious route required an expenditure in transportation charges of $62.50. While en route the traveler had to use five railroads, two steamboats, and two stagecoaches. His average rate of speed would be eight and three-quarter miles per hour.[52] Traveling from New Orleans to Washington in 1851, also required the services of three modes of travel. Beginning in New Orleans, one took a steamboat to Mobile, where a change was made to a coach for transit to Montgomery. The next segment, to West Point, Georgia, was a railroad, followed by coach to Covington, Georgia. Travel from Covington to Charleston, South Carolina was accomplished by rail. To travel further north the passenger boarded a steamer for Wilmington, North Carolina, where he changed to the passenger cars for Fredericksburg, Virginia. The last part of the trip to Washington was completed by steamer. In total the journey involved eight changes by three conveyances to travel 1,377 miles.[53]

Scheduling was one of the most confusing aspects of railroad transportation to the inexperienced traveler. Some passengers were ignorant of the importance of schedules and failed to understand why locomotive "captains" could not delay a departure long enough for passengers to visit local taverns.[54] The absence of a standard time system added to the confusion, since before the nation adopted four standard zones, conductors' watches were regulated from many different sources, including depot and courthouse clocks, or by the engineers themselves. For example, rule number one of the South Carolina Railroad stated in 1853 that each conductor set his watch by the timepiece in the Charleston depot. The regulations further stated that "no excuse will be received for any accident caused by his time being wrong."[55] When one considers that trains were also poorly scheduled because of weather, uncompleted tracks, mechanical break-downs, and illnesses of the crew, it is not surprising that antebellum travelers considered it prudent to arrive at the station at least one hour in advance of boarding the train.[56]

Another aspect of traveling associated with the depot was the handling of baggage. Foreigners as well as Americans often complained of the general equipment and services on railroads, but travel accounts of the times indicate an approval of the method of checking baggage. Essentially the system was the same one in practice today. With the purchase of a ticket the passenger was given a stub, used to claim his belongings. Bags other than those carried in the car were transported in a specially reserved coach usually placed between the engine and the cars. The vehicle was simply referred to as the "luggage van" or the "baggage car."

William Chambers explained the American system in detail during his tour in 1853. The Scotch author reported that every train had a "luggage-van" or "crate," which was under the supervision of a "baggage-master." This official was responsible for the passengers' baggage at no additional charge. Shortly before coming to the stations along the road the "baggage-master" patrolled the cars to be alerted by passengers wanting to detrain and claim their bags. Possession of an article was proven by presenting a numbered brass plate.[57] The number shown on the plate was also registered in a log book by the name of the traveler's hotel. If all went well, "in half an hour or less after arrival, there lies your luggage on the floor of your bedroom." This added special service, used mostly in cities, was provided by paying a small fee that was attached to the hotel bill. Although these arrangements were highly praised by

Chambers, he advised passengers who might want certain articles during transit to carry a "hand-valise, or carpet-bag" which could be taken in the cars.[58]

Ebenezer Davies and Thomas Low Nichols were also satisfied with the system. Davies was "struck with the simplicity and suitableness" of the arrangement on the way to Baltimore in 1848. According to him, bags were labeled by a piece of tin marked by a certain number. The duplicate was presented to the passenger to claim his gear.[59] Nichols reported similar experience, and was amazed that luggage was handled so efficiently "through five or six sovereign states" by several railroad lines.[60]

Should one's luggage be lost in transit, it appears that by 1860 the courts were usually solidly behind the passenger in contested cases and not the railroad lines. For instance in 1839 the *Commercial & Statistical Register* reported that the New York Supreme Court upheld two cases in 1838 that railroad, steamboat, and stage lines were responsible for the belongings of their passengers.[61] Nine years later *Hunt's* noted in its pages that the state of New York also attempted to protect the passenger by requiring, under penalty of the law, that railroads be certain that passengers receive duplicate baggage stubs for the passenger's identification of his bags.[62] In 1849, the magazine added that on several New England Railroads, if baggage was checked with the baggage-master, and damaged due to any neglect by the companies, the railroads would be held responsible.[63] Likewise, *Hunt's* in 1852 reported that the loss of a baggage check by the passenger did not relieve the railroad from liability.[64]

Of all the discomforts that travelers encountered concerning stations, perhaps the most serious was the lack of suitable eating accommodations. Few accounts were recorded that equalled the description of a backwoods feast afforded Charles Lyell near Chehaw, Alabama. Here, at a small log house in the woods, poor looking from the outside, "we saw on the table a wild turkey roasted, venison steaks, and a partridge-pie, all the product of the neighboring forest, besides a large jug of delicious milk, a luxury not commonly met with so far south."[65]

Many passengers were lucky if they could find eating places at all, and for those who did, the establishments were frequently poorly stocked, or insufficient time was allowed by the conductor to consume the food that had been found. For instance, the *American Railroad Journal* reported that it was not at all uncommon for passengers to swallow a "hasty plate of soup" for fear of being left behind. The solution, the magazine suggested, was the development of a locomotive dining car which would allow passengers to eat whenever and wherever they wanted to. It was added that such an improvement would be a boon to gentlemen and ladies, especially when the women were traveling with children.[66]

The plight of travelers regarding eating accommodations was perhaps best appraised by Thomas Hamilton, who commented that for "a traveller, to get on comfortably," he must accept things "as he finds them, assume nothing, and get rid as soon as possible of all superfluous refinement." Traveling on one of the Baltimore & Ohio trains of the 1830's, Hamilton complained after being served a "wretched breakfast" in the hamlet of Ellicott's Mills.[67] Other passengers of the period had similar reasons to complain. Traveling to Savannah, Fredrika Bremer grumbled that the food during her tour was so terrible that she had to rely on a basket full of bananas she had fortunately carried into the car. Later apparently satiated, her appreciation for the fruit was revealed when she proclaimed: "Long live the Banana!"[68] William Chambers also joined the criticism and blamed the poor quality of food on the fact that the railroad's policy was to purposely serve meals at stations where trains were always late. This along with other inconveniences, reasoned Chambers, was apparently the reason why American passengers were so patient concerning delays in their traveling habits.[69]

While some passengers were treated to delightful meals served at leading hotels and quaint backwoods homes, others were not so fortunate. For instance, William Thomson remarked that as the train approached the station in Aiken, South Carolina, passengers' meals were prepared after a "signal is made to the clever and indefatigable Mrs. Schwats, who, *it is said,* can kill and cook a dozen chickens in ten minutes."[70] Fanny Kemble, having dined on chicken in Weldon, North Carolina commented that the birds were "swimming in black grease," and were so tough that "I should think they must have been alive when we came into the house, and certainly died very hard."[71] Conditions were hardly better for John Shaw during a dull journey from Charleston, South Carolina to Augusta, Georgia. At eating stations along this route, dinner was always served late. This discomfort had been compounded by the jolting and shaking of the coach which so "thoroughly agitated the digestive tube that it contained nothing but empty space." Succinctly, Shaw protested that the shaken and hungry passengers had been treated worse than the "poor man's pig."[72]

To alleviate the hunger of passengers on some lines, vendors boarded the trains when they stopped at stations. Those seen by Henry A. Murray were mostly juveniles selling lollipops and peanuts, who roamed about the cars "crying out their respective goods."[73] Charles Lyell also reported the presence of young boys walking up and down the cars selling apples and biscuits. At Fredericksburg, Virginia, William Cullen Bryant recorded that Negroes visited the cars selling cakes, fruit, and additional refreshments.[74] Other travelers spoke of vendors selling oranges, hymnals and books.

According to Captain Marryat, the lack of proper eating facilities was responsible for passengers' behaving like starved animals. During his travels, whenever trains stopped at refreshment stands at fifteen-mile intervals, the passengers rushed out of the cars "like boys out of school." This exodus was quickly followed by a mad rush to the tables, where hungry passengers purchased "pies, patties, cakes, hard-boiled eggs, ham, custards, and a variety of railroad luxuries, too numerous to mention." When the bell was sounded for the departure of the train, all the passengers hurried on board again, clutching the food that aided them in relieving the monotony of the trip "by masticating without being hungry." At the next stop the scene was re-enacted.[75]

The railroad station and its attendant devices had to endure the same growing pains as the rest of the railroad industry. As scheduling and ticket selling became familiar processes, they also became more streamlined and less frustrating. From modest and uncomfortable beginnings, the station itself was to develop into a haven for the harried traveler. Like the other aspects of American railroading, however, it never lost its peculiarly egalitarian character. Private entrances and special clubs were not a part of the antebellum railroad. The prevalent spirit of *laissez-faire* may have freed companies from some responsibility, but it also acted to produce a system where all mingled freely, from the time of purchasing a ticket to the time of arrival.

8

Society
in the Cars

The early railroad car was a conspicuous example of the American concept of an egalitarian society. Unlike his European counterpart, the American traveler was almost totally lacking in the type of class consciousness which would have resulted in different cars for each social class. With the exception of most Negroes, some immigrants, and those cars reserved for ladies, all passengers mingled together and shared equally the uncertainties of the road.[1]

Foreigners, often totally unprepared for this democratic spirit of give-and-take, frequently found the lack of first and second class accommodations distasteful, and believed the incongruous mixing of persons to be absurd and detrimental to those lines aspiring to attain the efficient standards existing in Europe.[2] Thomas Low Nichols, was one traveller who complained that the most repulsive thing an Englishman meets with in America is the want of any distinction of classes. "On the railroad there is but one class and one price."[3] Richard Cobden and Dionysius Lardner likewise failed to discover first or second class cars in

America and concluded that all coaches are of the same class.[4] Such degrading conditions were harmful to the manners of the polished traveler, said William Chambers, who contended that "it will not be difficult to understand how certain obnoxious practices should obtrude themselves" on persons who are required to live and travel in American conveyances and inns.[5] But perhaps the best evaluation of the democratic way Americans preferred to travel was very simply stated by Ebenezer Davies, who contended that to have class accommodations in the United States would be "too aristocratic."[6]

Since American railroads failed to afford passengers the opportunity to select traveling companions, aristocrats and those of the upper-class frequently found themselves placed among a mixture of persons who, they felt, left much to be desired. Thomas Cather was one of the many who discovered that in the United States there was "a desire among the mass to produce a perfect equality by reducing those above them to their own standard." In the passenger car there could be found:

> the slaveholder from the South, the abolitionist from the North, the merchant, the Congress man, the lawyer, the artizan, [sic.] and labourer, all huddled together in glorious equality, smelling of anti-fogmatics, and in the most independent manner, spitting and smoking almost in each other's faces.

An Englishman in America, said Cather, would be "shocked at the abominations he witnesses around him," since the gentleman class in the United States is minute and seldom seen. "One man thinks himself as much entitled as another to dub himself gentleman. If they could assume the character along with the name, it would add immeasurably to the comfort of those who travel among them." Overall, the American to Cather was a money-making person engaged in a headlong race after wealth. "Their altar is their counter, their Bible is their ledger, their God is their gold." In no country was "Mammon pursued with greater keenness" than in the United States.[7]

Other sensitive passengers were startled by the company found in the cars, which included immigrants, species of "crackers," eccentrics, "rednecks," and tobacco-chewers.[8] George Featherstonhaugh, for one, was surprised after leaving Barnum's Hotel in Baltimore to find himself most unceremoniously emptied into a car with a group of "unshaven, unpromising looking fellows as ever I was shut up with." In Alabama Featherstonhaugh complained of white, yellow, and black passengers being "indiscriminately packed together in a long sort of omnibus." To make matters worse, the coach included several country boys who cursed and swore every time they opened their mouths. Having no desire to engage in the conversation, Featherstonhaugh remarked that he had been ignored during the journey by the other travelers because his questions were not introduced "with an execration suited to the taste of those I was addressing." Understandably, this erudite traveler was infuriated, remarking that he received no more response to his questions than "if I had spoken Polish or Italian." Thoroughly disgusted by the filthy talk of the men, Featherstonhaugh later remarked that the English language was in a strange way in the slave-holding states and altogether unfitting for educated men whose lot is cast there.[9]

Other travelers who objected to the absence of classes and the indiscriminate mixture of passengers also found it strange that even Senators and Representatives were mixed among the common people, and voiced the opinion that these everyday, "dirty" people should not be allowed in the cars.[10] Nevertheless, most Americans were apparently eager to communicate with the more lordly passengers, whether invited to or not. Lady Stuart Wortley observed this during her tour, adding that Americans were the most

philosophic and patient travelers in the world.[11] Likewise,
John Shaw discovered the Southerner was a much more
communicative and agreeable traveling companion than
the men of the Northern States.[12] Other characteristics
were noted by Thomas Low Nichols. This New Hamp-
shire-born editor observed that American passengers preferred a spacious car having a capacity of fifty or sixty
persons. They also enjoyed walking through the cars and
were not the least bit reluctant to intrude upon a conversation with passengers throughout the train. The American
was usually gregarious and social, and always ready to dis-
cuss trade or politics without paying attention to rank.[13]
However, Charles Dickens warned that during election
years feelings toward presidential elections run high and
should not be mentioned. Otherwise, the author added that
a great number of newspapers were seen in the cars but
were seldom read. Instead, "everybody talks to you, or to
anybody else who hits his fancy."[14]

Sometimes the monotony of the road was broken by odd
and eccentric persons along the line who entered the cars.
In Georgia, Bishop Whipple commented in the 1840's that
"we had nothing to interest us except watching the crackers
at the stations and hearing their comments on the railroads
etc."[15] In his car, Henry Murray was fascinated to note that
all the men had "cigars in their mouths," and that in
America to put one's coat on was a luxury.[16] Amelia Murray, however, lamented with good cause that her trip from
Acquia Creek to Richmond, Virginia would have been
more enjoyable had she been with "pleasanter neighbors in
the car." Miss Murray noted that in front of her was a man
"who called himself the American dwarf." She described
him as "about two feet high, with fin-like hands, and a head
nearly as large as his contorted body." Sitting to her right in
the car was a Negro woman attired in a fancy straw bonnet,
trimmed with white and artificial roses. Unfortunately, the
stale interior of the car caused the Negro to become ill, and

soon she was leaning across Miss Murray in order to use an opened window.[17] In Charles Lanman's car the only passenger worthy of note was a blind missionary. However, Lanman talked with an eccentric traveling to Savannah whose only possessions were a violin, a gold watch, a huge cane and cloak. The anonymous Arkansan proclaimed himself a citizen of the world traveling in search of a wife. Once in South Carolina the passengers were ferried across the Pedee River "to the music of this man's fiddle."[18]

Although lack of classes in the cars and traveling eccentrics brought numerous complaints, the most disgusting passenger was the tobacco chewer. According to Charles Mackay the vice was so common in America that a spittoon was provided in every car. In fact, Mackay found the habit so widespread, that on one occasion he considered it would be appropriate if the American eagle were armed with spittoons rather than thunderbolts in its claws.[19] Judging from the numerous complaints of passengers, Mackay's suggestion to change the national emblem might have received wide support. One who would have favored such legislation was George Combe. When visiting the United States in the late 1830's, he became annoyed at the "constant showers of tobacco saliva squirted on the floor at our feet."[20] A similar protest was issued by Henry Murray who witnessed whittling in the coaches and "Virginia juice on the floors."[21] Likewise, James Buckingham saw chewing in steamboats, on railroad cars, "and other places of great public resort," even though "it is very common" to see notices prohibiting the offensive and nasty habit.[22]

Throughout America the mark of a tobacco-chewer was easily seen, since the practice necessitated a constant spitting operation regardless of time or place. The discarded quid was evident on steamers, in the streets, and on stoves and grates. In railroad cars and barrooms it was not uncommon to see the floor covered with the "filthy scum." Although the offensive cigar in "everybody's mouth" caused smarting of the eyes within the coaches, the tobacco-chewer was believed to have had no manners at all. Joseph Biggs reported that even at dining tables, persons "sitting between two ladies turn round deliberately to spit on the floor, or will even spit across the table into the fire."[23] If there were smoking on trains, Thomas Nichols asked, why not have chewing cars as well? Nichols reported that judges chew on the bench, lawyers at the bar, doctors when calling on patients, and preachers in church. At the theatre, in the pauses of an impassioned oration, he had "heard a pattering shower" of tobacco fall upon the floor from gaping mouths of an excited audience. Even in Washington the "senator removes his quid to make a speech to Congress, and pauses in the midst of his most eloquent period to look for the spittoon." And in some instances, the carpets in courts of law were protected by an inch of sawdust, "and so converted into one big universal spittoon."[24]

Alexander Mackay, a journalist who recorded many sides of American life in an accurate, yet often humorous style, presented a detailed picture of the tobacco-chewer. Mackay came to know the species in 1847, while traveling to Baltimore on assignment for the London *Morning Chronicle*. North of Wilmington he was placed beside a man carrying what appeared to be a large carefully wrapped picture frame covered in canvas. Because of its size, the package not only covered its owner's knees but most of Mackay's as well. The journalist had scarcely taken his chair when he observed the American "cram his mouth full of tobacco." A few minutes later the Englishman was asked, "Stranger, will you let me spit?" Mackay replied that he had no objection to it as long "as he did not spit on me:"

> "That's just," said he, "what I didn't ambition to do; but you see, with this 'ere thing I'm a carrying,' unless you spread out your feet a bit, I have no place to do it in." "If that's all," I replied, "I'll exceed your wishes by giving you the whole place to yourself;" whereupon I left him, and sought the

platform, preferring the cold, but fresh air, to the deleteri-
ous fumes within the car, and to having my neighbour cooly
deposit his filthy expectorations between my knees.[25]

Mackay observed when taking his exit that the floor of the
car was incrusted with tobacco. The "pestiferous concoc-
tion" had also stained the seats and windows, and the interior walls of the car as well. Some of the stains were the
work of a drunk, who took delight in using a quid to trace
his initials on a part of the car. The journalist regarded such
displays as one "of the many stupid things that men 'a little
sprung' would sometimes do."[26]

Equally humorous was the Englishman's experience
on the Charleston & Hamburg line. In South Carolina
Mackay was approached by a man who asked the traveler if
he chewed or used snuff. A negative motion being the
writer's only reply, he was then asked if he smoked. "Occasionally," Mackay replied, to which the rustic returned, "I
don't—it's a dirty habit." He had no sooner finished the
sentence when he ejected "a quantity of poisoned saliva"
from his mouth, part of which fell on the guardrail on the
end of the coach. The fluid was removed by a brush of the
hand. "Following this, he bent his head forward, opened
his mouth wide, and the reeking quid fell at my feet. I turned aside in disgust."[27]

It seems that refuge from chewers was attainable only in
drawing rooms or in the presence of ladies, and not in
depots or passenger cars. However, little did the ladies
realize the agony to which their admirers were subjected by
this gallant bit of self-denial. Mackay recalled that on one
occasion he overheard a man in the presence of ladies
moan, "Oh! for a chew." The cry was uttered in tones
indicative "of the deepest distress." The Englishman advised him that if he were in any pain to step into the next
room, and indulge in one. But the man shook his head
despondingly, saying that the ladies would smell the to-

bacco on his breath. About an hour later the two men departed from the room together. The man's first exclamation on gaining the street was, "Thank God! I can now use my box."[28]

In rural America, where chewing was especially popular, it was almost impossible to abolish the habit in stations, on river steamers, and in railroad cars. But once more the most effective deterrent was the presence of a lady. Other and more official warnings were provided, however, by posting signs in the cars and the addition of smoking coaches on some of the lines.[29] It was not until the twentieth century was well underway that chewing was greatly curtailed as an undesirable and dirty habit.[30]

A large number of travelers made the trip South to see the institution of slavery first hand. Some came with predetermined ideas and saw exactly what they had hoped to see before they boarded their trains. However, others came to support their aristocratic interests and to buttress the philosophies of such pro-slavery writers as George Fitzhugh and Edmund Ruffin. On the other hand, some actually attempted to record an accurate account of their findings.

Two of slavery's bitterest critics were John Abbott and Charles Parsons, both Maine abolitionists. In 1859, Abbott toured the South, using railroads and visited such cities as New Orleans, Mobile, Atlanta, and Wilmington, North Carolina.[31] Throughout his tour he wrote exaggerated accounts of slavery that are considered some of the best propaganda the abolitionist could invent. Parsons came South in 1852–1853, and established his headquarters in Savannah, Georgia. His accounts, like those of Abbott, depicted lustful overseers and the crack of the whip. During part of his tour the preacher described vivid accounts of slaves being forcibly marched to the "nigger car," after they had been torn away from their "wives and husbands at the sound of the whip."[32]

Conversely, the pro-slavery travelers revealed an equal amount of prejudice and propaganda in their accounts. The well known Virginia historian and biographer Edward Alfred Pollard toured the South in 1858 to correct "the false views of northern spies" infiltrating the South. Typical of Pollard's writings was an account written after a return from Europe:

> The first unadulterated negro I had seen for a number of years (having been absent for the most of that time on a foreign soil), was on the railroad cars in Virginia. He looked like *home*. I could have embraced the old uncle, but was afraid the passengers, from such a demonstration, might mistake me for an abolitionist.[33]

Among the moderates attacking slavery were Frederick Law Olmsted and Alexander Mackay. Traveling out of Richmond in the 1850's, Olmsted noted that his train included two passenger and two freight cars. The latter were filled with about forty Negroes belonging to a slave trader, who was sending them south to be auctioned on the block.[34] A similar incident was reported by Charles Dickens. He saw two newly purchased slaves placed in a car set aside for Negroes on their way south. They were a mother and child who had been separated from the father. The author stated that throughout the journey the child cried, and the mother was "misery's picture." Dickens reported that "the champion of Life, Liberty, and the Pursuit of Happiness, who had bought them, rode in the same train" and at every stop checked the car to see that they were safe.[35]

Alexander Mackay in 1845 witnessed a commonly seen incident. During one of his sojourns by railroad a dark looking man was expelled from the coach because of his color. The incident to Mackay was repugnant:

> These bold defenders of "life, liberty, and the pursuit of happiness," these chivalrous assertors of the Declaration of Independence, looked with utter indifference on this practical violation of the "rights of man."

Greatly concerned, the Scottish-born journalist asked the conductor where he had been sent. "Put him?—in the nigger crib, to be sure, where he should be," was the reply. The remaining passengers in the car approved. In fact, one young man remarked that it "sarved the d—d nigger right." Others in the car added, "He'll know his place better the next time, the b—y mongrel!" The passengers laughed again. Mackay's curiosity by this time could not be contained. He asked the conductor if he might not see the "crib" to which the Negro had been directed. He was shown to a luggage van that contained about a dozen other Negroes. Some were silent in the "crib," but others laughed. It seems that some of them thought their latest associate had believed himself too good to ride with them.[36]

That segregation of free and bonded Negroes had long existed in the Southern states is a recognized historical fact. However, that racial discrimination in the North was often just as severe was somewhat surprising to travelers visiting that region before 1861.[37] Charles Dickens noticed, for instance, that Negroes were hardly seen traveling with Northern whites since the colored passengers were placed in a "Negro car." One of the vehicles was described by the English author as "a great, blundering, clumsy chest, such as Gulliver put to sea in from the kingdom of Brobdingnag."[38]

While visiting the United States in 1833–1835, Michel Chevalier found that Negroes were allotted a distinct place away from whites in all sections of America. Whether rich or poor, ignorant or educated, the Negro was avoided "as if he were infected with the plague."[39] Racial barriers throughout the country were noted by Thomas Low Nichols as well. According to this traveler the resentment against Negroes was not determined by the darkness of the skin, since the prejudice was shown to mulattoes as well as the darker blacks. According to Nichols, if "it be known that there is even one drop of the blood of Central Africa in the veins of an American," it would be "better for him that he had never been born."[40]

The observations of David W. Mitchell, who lived mostly in Richmond, Virginia, during his stay in America, reinforce the view that the Negro faced equal discrimination in the North and the South. In the North the Englishman noted that the Negro was frowned upon as an outcast, an obstacle and a nuisance. In the opinion of Northern whites, said Mitchell, the Negro was viewed as the "Western pioneer looks on trees, and wolves, and Indians." The Irish-Americans hated them "worse than they do the British." Mitchell added that while people in the North were reluctant to sit with Negroes in coaches, in the South "it was a common thing to see master or mistress and slave sitting in the same stage, without any nose being turned up at Pomp or Dinah." The author said, "There can be no mistake about it," the Northern Negro was "regarded as an alien, an outcast, a pariah."[41]

During his travels Eyre Crowe witnessed an incident in which a Negro wearing a "chimney-pot hat" was ejected from the car on the way between Philadelphia and Baltimore. The Negro was ordered to go to "the first car" after being admonished for "sitting here among white people, indeed!" The man obeyed the official and entered a poorly lighted coach just behind the engine.[42] Maine abolitionist Charles Parsons reported that ironically the colored race in the North was excluded from social positions, churches, school, hotels, steamboats and railroad cars. For instance, on a trip from Georgia to Pennsylvania, Parsons noted that little was said about a Negro woman in his coach until the train reached Philadelphia. Further north a great stir was made when a Negro man took a seat among the passengers.[43] A similar opinion was offered by Joseph Biggs in the 1830's. He commented that even though Pennsylvania was not a slave state there existed "the same strong animus against the dark-coloured race as in the Slave

States." Whereas the Negro is treated with great care in the South, according to the Englishman, "in New York, Philadelphia, and indeed all over the Free States, the negroes are treated with great contumely and insolence."[44]

Although the "nigger car" varied from line to line, the baggage car was customarily designated for colored passengers. Some passengers, however, referred to the segregated car as the "first car." Charles Weld's observations reveal that American railroads were without class distinction with the exception of immigrants and Negroes. Traveling near Washington, Weld's train was composed of three coaches and a baggage car. The first car was set aside for colored passengers, the second for gentlemen and the third for ladies.[45] Dionysius Lardner noted the lack of distinction in the cars concerning class but did mention as an exception the coach set aside for Negroes. According to Lardner, colored passengers, free or slave, traveled in the baggage car or in "the carriage in which the guard or conductor travels."[46]

Considering the agitation of the abolitionist and the debates in Congress over slavery, it is surprising that so few travelers reported non-segregated coaches in the northern states. And even those who did had reservations. For instance James Stirling, who toured the nation in 1856–1857, stated that he had traveled with colored people on steamers and in railway cars, but had never witnessed their being ordered out of their seats or "ignominiously treated." However, the Scotsman also admitted that he had heard of their being put off trains in Pennsylvania, and that the "antinigger" prejudice was strongest not in the South, but in the states adjoining the slave states.[47] That slavery and the concern over the free Negroes in the South made Southerners racially prejudiced cannot be denied. However, there is also evidence to show that "physical repulsion" to the Negro certainly was no stronger in the South than in most parts of the North.[48]

Although segregated cars for Negroes may clearly be classified as an opprobrious form of discrimination, separate cars for women represented quite the reverse. In an age when women in some places were relatively few in number and difficult to replace, the ladies' car was both a tribute to their value and a concession to their sensitivity. If the antebellum American railroad was too democratic to allow special reserved cars for the lordly and affluent, it was at the same time sufficiently refined to provide special facilities for the protection and comfort of the American woman.

Foreign travelers in America were as impressed by the special treatment afforded ladies as they were by the absence of class distinctions in the cars. This was especially true in the hospitable and chivalric South. While touring the country in 1837 Joseph Biggs was one of the numerous passengers who was struck by the great attention given women in the United States. The London businessman noted that American ladies were never referred to as "women" since this was a classification reserved only for "a negress or mulatto." In public places, said Biggs, no self respecting "lady" could be seen holding the arm of a "gentleman" unless she was "affianced or related to him," since in America such actions are "considered a mark of great familiarity." The mere presence of a lady on public conveyances caused men to bolt from their seats, and offer their chairs. In such places as dining tables on steamboats, unsophisticated hungry males were given a lesson in *savoir-faire* by posted notices reading "Gentlemen are requested not to sit down at dinner until the LADIES are seated." The sanctuary of a ladies' cabin on the vessel was announced by the warning, "Gentlemen not to go into the Ladies' Cabin without permission."[49]

On railroads the female passenger was always given "the first accommodation, and until she has it no man will think of himself."[50] For instance, a lady was never concerned over

the availability of a seat in the coach, for if she took a fancy
to one already occupied by a gentleman, her escort had to
do nothing more than indicate this to the male occupant
who immediately evacuated the chair with great po-
liteness.[51] Women, seated in the best cars, occupied the
better seats. Men often found dinner delayed until "some
young miss has fixed her last curl, and taken her seat near
the head of the table." Whether she be old or young, pretty
or ugly, the American woman could travel from one end of
the country to the other encountering "kindness, civility,
and every assistance she needs from every man she
meets."[52]

Men were forbidden to enter reserved sections of cars
specifically designated for women unless invited by the
ladies or given permission from an official of the railroad.[53]
Charles Weld reported that he was given permission from a
station manager to sit in the coveted car, "which, being the
last carriage of the train, gave me an opportunity of seeing
everything very well from the end windows and exterior
platform."[54] Traveling to Baltimore in 1840, George
Combe mentioned there was a car on each train provided
for ladies and the men accompanying them. Combe reported one car he saw had a place for retirement which "is a
great accommodation, particularly when children are in the
party."[55] Other passengers who mentioned the strict regulations applying to the ladies' car included Dionysius Lardner and Munch Raeder. Lardner noted that the ladies'
section in his car was appropriately furnished and that men
were forbidden entry.[56] Munch Raeder learned of the strict
regulations pertaining to the ladies' car after his car had
been taken from the train because of a wreck. With no place
to sit, he unknowingly entered the ladies' car from which he
was quickly ejected. Later, in a "filthy, open baggage car,"
while sharing a seat with a wounded sergeant on his way to
Washington to see about a pension, Raeder grumbled that
women in America possessed "an almost despotic power in

all public places, and with the slightest nod drive even the oldest and portliest men away from their places, just as one blows a feather away from a glass."[57]

Criticism of railroads and the attention given all women in American coaches also antagonized Charles F. Adams. Traveling in 1835 Adams was emptied into a hot, smelly coach that was soon overflowing with the addition of twelve working girls. "Make room for the ladies," cried the conductor who found space for the dozen new passengers who began sucking lemons and eating green apples. Obviously irritated, Adams unleashed his wrath on the privileges given the female sex in the following account:

> talk of ladies on board a steamboat or in a railroad car. There are none. I never feel like a gentleman there, and I cannot perceive a semblance of gentility in any one who makes part of the travelling mob. When I see women whom, in their drawing-rooms or elsewhere, I have been accustomed to respect and treat with every suitable deference, —when I see them, I say, elbowing their way through a crowd of dirty emigrants or lowbred homespun fellows in petticoats or breeches in our country, in order to reach a table spread for a hundred or more, I lose sight of their pretentions to gentility and view them as belonging to the plebeian herd. To restore herself to her caste, let a lady move in select company at five miles an hour, and take her meals in comfort at a good inn, where she may dine decently. . . . After all, the old-fashioned way of five or six miles with liberty to dine decently in a decent inn and be master of one's movements, with the delight of seeing the country and getting along rationally, is the mode to which I cling, and which will be adopted again by the generations of after times.[58]

The man responsible for the comfort and safety of ladies and gentlemen alike was the conductor. Although the engineer and brakeman played the most significant role in keeping the engine running, the conductor's jurisdiction

included the proper maintenance of schedules, the obser-
vance of safety rules, and the command of the entire train.
He was also responsible for announcing arrivals and depar-
tures as well as collecting tickets from the occupants in the
cars. Passengers pictured him in various ways. Some saw
him stepping into the prestigious shoes of the steamboat
captain, while the more caustic viewed him as irresponsible
and shiftless. To others, however, he was a well respected
and gallant gentleman assisting passengers in times of
need. But regardless of his prestige, in the minds of travelers his familiar cry of "All o'board" was an integral part of
railroading, as the engine was itself.[59]

The only uniformity in dress among conductors on the
earliest lines was the badge designating their position. The
appearance of these men varied from line to line, with
ordinary clothes often being their usual attire. However, by
the 1850's some railroads began a movement to regulate the
appearance of officials by requiring conductors to be uni-
formed in distinctive clothes. Surprisingly, the *American
Railroad Journal* opposed the plan. It seems the magazine
believed that Americans were unfavorable to the idea of
dressing conductors like the "liveried lackeys of European
noblemen," and that little would be accomplished by the
plan other than decorating the interior of cars. Furthermore, the magazine asked why police-type uniforms were
necessary, when conductors could be plainly identified with
only a hat, arm band, or badge.[60]

Apparently common sense was the only preliminary re-
quirement for a conductor in the antebellum years. A large
frame and strong muscles were desirable features to enable
him to cope with the problems of his position. Conductors'
duties ranged from the disposition of drunks and rowdies
to assisting frail ladies with their bags. Appreciative travelers were always quick to applaud a tactful and adept official
during a trip. William Chambers, for example, seemed
delighted observing these officials during the fall of 1853.

The conductors encountered by this traveler were usually respectable, well dressed men, of good standing in the community. Some even held the rank of colonel in the militia. Traveling in the best of company, they were frequently seen in the better hotels accompanied by a "fashionable wife." Besides their other virtues, conductors were men of integrity. Their reputation and honor, according to Chambers, were supported by the company they kept and the "infinitesimally small" supervision of their duties. Yet most amazing to this writer was the manner in which conductors performed their duties.[61]

Viewed as "half clerk, half guard, with a dash of gentleman," the most interesting aspect of all to Chambers was to watch the conductor collecting tickets and maintaining order in the cars. Demanding tickets in a "dry, callous tone" that sounded as though "it would cost something to be cheerful," he noticed that hardly anyone escaped his attention. To facilitate collections at night he carried a lantern. Equipped with a strong reflector, the instrument allowed the official to "scrutinize the equivocal bank-notes that may be tendered in payment." The lantern apparently resembled models of today, since they were held by a giant ring through which the conductor could thrust his arm, "so as to leave both hands disengaged." Besides his lantern and badge, another characteristic marking the conductor was the small change box carried under his arm.

The conductor was known for his alert mind. Whether a passenger was engaged in a local trip or one involving several days, persons were seldom asked to show their tickets over two or three times. Once tickets were checked and the passengers were settled in their seats, Chambers then observed that the conductor escaped to the baggage car. Here "he [had] a kind of den for counting his money, and cogitating over his affairs." Satisfied that all was well, the official later returned to the cars to keep a watchful eye on the passengers until the train arrived at the station. At the depot the conductor mysteriously disappeared like a phantom in the night. Chambers' explanation for this sorcery was that once the station was gained, the official removed the badge from his hat and became an "ordinary human being." At the sound of the bell the mysterious man resumed his duties again "like a wandering spirit."[62]

The attentiveness and courtesy shown to travelers by conductors was lauded by many passengers. For instance, Misses Mendell and Hosmer, traveling as book peddlers about 1853, applauded the policy of conductors caring for ladies traveling alone and seeing them safely to their hotels.[63] Likewise, Lillian Foster gratefully praised a conductor in Savannah, Georgia who located her misplaced baggage. According to Miss Foster, ladies could always count on every polite attention and protection afforded travelers, if "put under the care of a handsome and gentlemanly conductor."[64] Additional praise was heaped on these men by Solon Robinson. To this "Connecticut Yankee" they were "the most gentlemanly, well-bred, kind and accommodating officers of my acquaintance."[65] The courtesy and helpfulness of these officials was cited by other sources as being responsible for making railroads such a comfortable method of travel.

Although some travelers praised conductors for their assistance, others criticized them for their deficiencies. Charles Dickens found their informal appearance and lack of uniforms distasteful. Fraternizing with the passengers was another sore spot with Dickens. The author remarked that strangers, or passengers having a questionable appearance to the official were watched with a suspicious eye. At other times the "check-taker" wore on the nerves of the author by placing his hands in his pockets and leaning against the coach door.[66]

Charles Weld identified the conductor by his badge and hearty "All o'board" to the "engine-driver" to start the train. However, such impressive appearances did little to

improve the official's performance in the eyes of this critical
Englishman. Weld's first complaint was that conductors
were often unavailable and negligent in their duties. One
sought their services in vain. The lack of concern for safety
was demonstrated on a mountain railroad when Weld witnessed a conductor attempting to make up for lost time.
This conductor was a reckless and determined man who
attached little value to his own life or the lives of the occupants of his train.[67] Charles Mackay criticized the railroads
for failing to supervise properly the duties of conductors.
Concerning his liberty to collect ticket money from the
passengers, Mackay considered that should one be dishon-
est, what would prevent him from putting the money into
his own pocket without anyone knowing the difference.[68]

Besides taking tickets and announcing stations along the
line, conductors were often forced to assume the duties of
policemen and guards. During the travels of Charles Lyell
there was witnessed an incident in one of the remote areas
of the South in the 1840's. The affair involved the conductor and a boisterous drunk who was annoying the passengers. The fracas began when the drunk placed his feet on
one of the seats and began to sing. The conductor was
summoned to end the noise and politely asked the man to
remove his feet and he reluctantly obliged. No sooner,
however, had the official left the car than he began his
revelry once more. By this time the conductor was
thoroughly irritated by the persistent annoyance and per-
sonally removed the man's feet from the chair. But even
this stern warning was to no avail. The conductor now
realized that more drastic means would have to be employed. The cars were stopped, and the obnoxious offen-
der was ordered to detrain. Lyell described the inebriate as
a "strong-built laborer" who would have been more than a
match for the smaller conductor if there were to be a fight.
However, Lyell, the conductor and the remaining passengers had witnessed enough of the drunk's conduct and
made it known that this was their fight too. The laborer was

apparently sober enough to realize he would be overpow-
ered and reluctantly left the car. He was left "many miles
from any habitation," with no prospect of another train
passing for many a long hour.[69]
   Traveling west in 1855–1856 to study Choctaw Indians,
George Pierce witnessed a frontier brawl between a passenger and conductor that smacked of the violence of the
Old West. The first sign of trouble, in this case, occurred
when the conductor entered Pierce's coach to collect the
tickets. One of the passengers did not have his stub, believ-
ing his money would be more valuable at a station further
up the line. The conductor explained to him that regulations forbade such speculation, and that he would have to
buy a ticket now or leave the train. The frugal passenger
was not to be denied, however, and refused to pay his fare.
After being ordered to leave his seat, the passenger refused
and sneered that he knew how to defend himself. Pierce
sensed a fight was about to begin that might involve a little
"blood-letting." The train was stopped and the scuffle
began. The man was reluctant to offer any aggressive resis-
tance, but tenaciously held on to his seat. However, the
dutiful official was no match for the rugged passenger. It
was only with the assistance of a gang of infuriated passengers that the man was dragged from his moorings and
unceremoniously hurled down an embankment. As the
train began to move it seemed the encounter had ended.
But the enraged speculator charged the platform on which
the conductor was standing. The latter resorted to kicking
his antagonist about the head and shoulders and stamping
on his fingers in an attempt to disengage him from the car.
The motion of the train rendered the effort successful; the
late passenger lost his hold and fell by an embankment over
which the train passed. The affair ended when the man
dropped from sight.[70]
   In 1846, a less violent incident occurred during the journey of John Shaw. It ended in nothing more than a crushed
hat. While Shaw was sleeping in an "admirably constructed

shelf-bed" in one of the cars, two laborers entered his compartment without permission and occupied the vacant berths. Before retiring, Shaw had placed his hat on one of the empty beds where he thought it would be safe. However, one of the "weighty gentlemen laid himself down in such a manner" that it was flattened like a pancake. The men were finally removed after the conductor was summoned, and commanded them to refresh themselves "with a little walking exercise."[71]

Frederick Law Olmsted made an amusing observation concerning a conductor during his travels in the South during the 1850's. At one of the stations "smoke was to be seen" coming from one of the wheel trucks of one of the cars. The conductor had his attention called to the malfunction and approached it nonchalantly. Standing back from the smoking car he "nodded his head sagely, took a morsel of tobacco, put his hands in his pockets," and "looked at the truck as if he would mesmerize it." Apparently puzzled by the problem he "spat upon it" and ordered the engineer to proceed to the next station. At this point the smoking was furious. Again the official returned to the car and examined the situation in an attempt to decide what to do:

> he suddenly relinquished the attempt, and deserting Mesmer for Preisnitz, shouted, "Ho! boy! bring me some water here." A Negro soon brought a quart of water in a tin vessel. "Hain't got no oil, Columbus?" "No Sir." "Hmmm —go ask Mr. Smith for some, this yer's a screaking so, I durstn't go on. You Scott! get me some more water. D'ye hear?"

Salt, oil, and water were crowded into the smoking box until the train reached Petersburg. The cause of the trouble was probably a "neglect of sufficient or timely oiling." While Olmsted was waiting in a carriage for a porter to bring his baggage, he noted another Negro oiling the trucks without going to the trouble of elevating the outlet of his oiler. The result of sloppy maintenance led to additional problems and deterioration of the equipment as well.[72]

American traveling habits were often criticized by visitors; however, another school of adventurers upheld the American in varying degrees. For instance, their inquisitiveness and disregard of rank was to David W. Mitchell a characteristic "much to the stranger's advantage, since it allows him to question in turn, and to learn much which he could arrive at in no other way."[73] John Robert Godley, after having seen "the mixture of ranks which one so often meets within this country," cautioned during his tour in 1842 that Americans were frequently misrepresented by the English. Too quickly do foreign visitors label the Americans as "impertinent, prejudiced, conceited, and ignorant of the common refinements and courtesies of civilized life," forgetting that in their own country certain eccentric acts one sees in America would hardly stir any interest at all. Not even Godley thought he was immune from exaggeration and reported that he had often been tempted to stretch the truth himself.[74]

Even tobacco-chewers were given some protection from the wrath of those travelers who most frequently noted their filthy habit. William Chambers stated that his observations generally led him to believe that passengers "exaggerate the chewing and spitting of the Americans." Actually, said Chambers, the nauseous practice was "as disagreeable" to Americans as to any "well-bred European." However, many foreigners visiting the United States remembered only the unfavorable habits of Americans, while at the same time they were "either ignorant or neglectful of the manners of their own country," a view shared by Hugh Tremenheere, Munch Raeder, and Charles Lyell.[75]

Richard Cobden was another traveler who questioned the numerous criticisms leveled against Americans after he saw the country in 1859. Although his travels were confined mainly to the North and the area around Memphis, Cobden

recalled that Americans were quite orderly while traveling
in the cars and that he had never been confronted with a
"rude or boisterous remark." The American's independence and honor were praised by Cobden, for he never
expected a porter to carry his bags or call a cab, and should
someone mistakenly occupy a claimed seat in the car he was
always quick to vacate it and take another chair.[76]

For legitimate and personal reasons most travelers were
usually more favorable to the North than the South. Especially discussed was the institution of slavery and its many
ramifications, the debilitating Southern climate, and the
inferior railroads that traversed the Southern states. However, the states south of the Mason and Dixon Line did have
their defenders. Just before Harriet Martineau was about
to make her visit to Dixie in December, 1834, the eminent
humanitarian was warned in Baltimore of the perils awaiting her in the South, but she decided to see the truth for
herself. By December, 1835, this indomitable lady had visited Richmond, Charleston, Columbia, Augusta, Montgomery, and New Orleans, where she began the final phase
of her journey up the Mississippi River. The threats the
Englishwoman had heard "proved idle, as I suspected they
would." In almost every instance, she reported:

> Throughout the South I met with very candid and kind
> treatment—I mention these warnings partly because they
> are a fact connected with the state of the country; and partly
> because it will afterward appear that the stranger's real
> danger lies in the north and west, over which the south had,
> in my case, greatly the advantage in liberality.[77]

In 1836, James Davidson was even more effusive. He was
pleased with the energy and enterprise of the Southerner,
as well as his frank manners and generous customs. "I have
scarcely seen a Bowie knife," Davidson said, and nowhere
did the traveler hear a quarrel or one man insult another
throughout the entire journey.[78] But perhaps best of all

compliments paid to American travelers was that of Thomas Hamilton in 1831. It was not denied by Hamilton that passengers must often associate with persons "whose companionship he cannot but feel carries with it something of degradation," yet it will be found in America that "a person of true breeding will rarely be treated with disrespect." "Even in this democratic country," one received "tribute without exacting it" and "[might] safely leave it to 'men's' opinion, to tell the world he is a gentleman."[79]

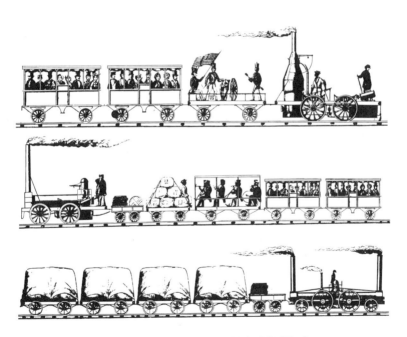

Three Early Southern (1830–31) Trains

9

Traveling
Through the South

Once the practicality of steam locomotion for passenger service was accepted, Americans began taking to trains in increasing numbers as additional miles of tracks made travel more readily available to the masses. By 1860 some foreigners noted that rail travel was so popular that many Americans took long and frequent journeys of a hundred miles or more.[1] The enthusiasm for travel resulted not only from a successful adaptation of the railroad to spacious lands and prevalent democratic attitudes. Each new line brought greater service and increased competition as well. Even as early as the 1830's, Michel Chevalier observed that competition among companies was so keen that "the line that has the advantage of half an hour over its rivals will be sure to crush them."[2] This was an "era of traveling" which ignored the odds. To promote transport by steam, masses of granite and acres of swampland were spanned to afford avenues of rails for both passengers and freight.

The reasons for traveling South were as varied as the menagerie of roads encountered. During the 1830's and 1840's the section was crossed to reach the troubled lands of

Texas and the Old Southwest. The issue of slavery drew humanitarians and reformers; others made the trip for health. Some travelers visited Florida and wrote of the Indian Wars. New Orleans was a favorite target for ministers, and aristocrats took delight in Charleston. Other visitors represented foreign governments, whereas many simply traveled for pleasure. But regardless of the motive, hundreds of travelers left numerous records which have contributed to a better understanding of the South before 1861.

Of all the various routes that led to the South, the most popular originated in Washington and Baltimore. The first half of the American "Grand Tour," completed at New Orleans, was accomplished by combination of stage, steamer and railway car. This point was often reached via Richmond, Weldon, North Carolina and Columbia, South Carolina. Layovers in Georgia included Augusta, Macon and Columbus. During the 1830's the trip through Alabama included a jaunt through the Indian country before reaching Montgomery and Mobile. Leaving New Orleans, the passenger undertook the second half of the tour by steamer. Ports of call on the northward trek included Baton Rouge, Louisiana; Natchez and Vicksburg, Mississippi; and Memphis, Tennessee. Another preferred route of travel entailed visits to Charleston, South Carolina; Savannah, Georgia; and St. Augustine, Florida. Points of special interest in the South included visits to historical sites and outstanding natural features such as Mammoth Cave.[3] Most tours of the South terminated at the Ohio River.

Because of the speed and hazards of the railway, passengers were not afforded the time or leisure to record their observations as extensively as from the deck of a steamer or the back of a horse. Most passengers nevertheless found time to jot down their impressions of the major points of interest. Once the train crossed the Potomac River and entered Virginia, foreigners and abolitionists were usually impressed that they had entered the land of the slave. In Richmond, Virginia, Eyre Crowe recalled that he saw a gang of slaves, carrying "scanty bundles of clothing," being herded to the railroad station by their masters to leave for their new homes in the Deep South.[4] Other groups of Negroes were seen in 1838 by Fanny Kemble at the depot in Suffolk, Virginia. Fascinated by the locomotive and cars, they gathered around the equipment with an intense curiosity that bordered on the ridiculous.[5] In 1852, Frederick Law Olmsted showed an interest in the "close cohabitation and association of black and white" Southerners seen from his car. He remarked that their faces "are constantly thrust together out of doors, to see the train go by."[6]

Many travelers reported by 1850 that North Carolina railroads were among the worst in the South. The Weldon to Wilmington line received special criticism. Europeans considered the railroad "too slovenly an example of railway construction to call forth the admiration of the foreigner."[7] Olmsted described the equipment on a railroad serving Gaston as very old and dirty, the cars being furnished with "dilapidated and moth-eaten furniture." The company's poor business, however, afforded Olmsted a comfort seldom enjoyed, since he had an entire seat to himself on which to stretch out and sleep.[8] Whereas the presence of gangs of slaves were an indication the train had reached Virginia, arrival in North Carolina was indicated by the sight of increasing swamplands and forests of pine. Fanny Kemble recalled that when she traveled through the state in the late 1830's she could see cypress and juniper trees growing in the swamps, and noted snakes among the region's animal life. The actress declared, "So forlorn a region it never entered my imagination to conceive."[9]

Throughout the coastal states, passengers spoke of the numerous pine forests which obstructed their view for miles and miles.[10] Fredrika Bremer seemed displeased that the railroad passed through "one continued stretch of pinewood" while traveling to Richmond. The only relief from the tedious ride was provided at breaks in the woods, where she saw cotton and corn. From the sap extracted from the pines, the nineteenth century reformer said, North Carolina derived its popular name of the "Old Tar and Turpentine" state.[11]

Charles Mackay noted while traveling through South Carolina in 1858, that one could travel for hundreds of miles and see no other vegetation for days but monotonous forests of Southern pines. Only here and there could be seen a village or town to break the spell. Between Charleston and Savannah Mackay was so moved by the interminable forests that he set his thoughts to rhyme:

> Where, northward as you go,
> The pines forever grow;
> Where, southward if you bend,
> Are pine-trees without end;
> Where, if you travel west,
> Earth loves the pine-tree best;
> Where, eastward if you gaze,
> Through long, unvaried ways,
> Behind you and before,
> Are pine-trees evermore.[12]

James Stirling, visiting America in 1856 and 1857, described the route from Charleston to Columbia as desolate, and lacking any towns of consequence. The Negro slaves seen on the way were "absolutely in rags" with dwellings "in fit keeping with their clothing."[13] In 1844, George Lewis commented on the numerous pine forests of South Carolina and suggested the state get rid of the view-obstructing trees. However, this Scotsman was informed by a contractor for the line that the country would become uninhabitable without the trees, since the heat reflected from the sandy soil would convert the state into "a furnace alternated with pestilential mud swamps."[14]

Besides Richmond, New Orleans and Savannah, Charleston was lauded for its European influence and the manners and hospitality of its citizens. Touring the United States in 1827 and 1828, Captain Basil Hall and his family undertook the "Grand Tour" with servants and a rented carriage at the time the first railroads were being built. During their stay in the Carolina city Mrs. Hall found "the people [to be] very hospitable, which is indeed the character of all the Southern States."[15] A similar impression was made on Captain Hall, who recorded that "we proceeded to the plantation of one of our obliging Charleston friends, who, in the style of hospitality universal in the South, had begged us to make it a resting place."[16] Aristocractic in mind and occasionally piqued by the dining customs of Americans, Mrs. Hall criticized the Charlestonians for their poor use of silverware. However, she seems to have forgiven her hosts for their breach of etiquette, finding Charlestonians "remarkable, not only in inviting strangers into their houses, but lending the carriages, which is a much less common piece of hospitality."[17]

Achille Murat was also pleased with the manners he found in the Carolina city and remarked there is "nothing wanting either as regards finish, or elegance of manners."[18] Murat, though extremely critical of Georgians, believed that in Charleston American manners were at their best. Touring the South in 1856, Carlton H. Rogers commented that the polished manners and hospitable attention of the people in Charleston were hereditary:

> They are proud and imperious in their bearings, yet courteous and graceful in their hospitalities, retaining in an eminent degree many of the peculiarities of the French Huguenots, from whom they are descended.[19]

Among other interesting experiences of passengers in South Carolina was that of Fredrika Bremer who detrained in the state's woods to visit a revival during her tour in

America from 1849 to 1851. In another instance, at a depot, she reported seeing a hundred soldiers on their way to visit the Georgia militia in Macon. The well-known Swedish reformer described the men as "handsome, pleasant, merry young fellows" who left the train at each station to refresh themselves.[20] At a station between Charleston and Branchville, James Buckingham reported seeing alligators along the route.[21]

As for the efficiency of the South Carolina lines, most travelers were pleased with the railroads in the state. Lillian Foster, in 1855, reported they were as good as those in the North "and as well, if not better, managed."[22] Politically, John Abbott in December, 1859 remarked that while in South Carolina, as well as four other Southern states, during his entire trip *"I did not meet one single individual who advocated disunion!"*[23] However, in contrast to John Abbott's observations, Joseph Stirling, several years earlier, complained of the speech restrictions in the South. Traveling between Macon and Montgomery in 1856 and 1857, this traveler "experienced another instance of that espionage" which one found "so disagreeable in the South." Stirling mentioned his observations to a lady and her daughter in his car who "agreed one could not be too cautious" as to what he said on the train. Just recently, they said, "some persons who had expressed themselves too freely" in Macon "had been escorted to the station by a party of inhabitants, and forced to take their departure."[24]

According to the accounts of travelers, by 1860 it appears that Georgia was one of the most progressive states in the South. James Stirling expressed this opinion while enroute from Richmond to New Orleans on the "Grand Tour." According to this Scotsman, Georgia was the "most go-ahead state of the South," and deserved to be called the "Southern Yankeeland." He was especially pleased with the Georgia Central Railroad which was "a most creditable concern." Stirling reported the railroad was far better than the average lines in the South, since it was well managed, adequately constructed, and maintained better schedules than any railroad he knew of in the states.[25] Similar praise was lavished on railroads in Georgia by Olmsted. Traveling from Savannah to Macon in the 1850's, Olmsted noted that Georgia trains were punctual "to a second." The speed of some of them, however, was "not great, but regular," since less time was spent at way-stations than one would expect. Olmsted claimed that he had traveled over five hundred miles on Georgia roads and was pleased to find "that all of them seem to be exceedingly well managed." The equipment of some companies compared favorably with any of the lines on the continent.[26]

Although the equipment on the railroad between Savannah and Macon rated enthusiastic praise, the countryside was apparently monotonously dull. In 1856, Carlton H. Rogers, of Palmyra, New York toured the South from Richmond to Savannah. On his way to Macon he described the region as "level and monotonous," the scenery being in most part "tame and uninteresting." Throughout the trip the train passed through immense pine forests and innumerable swamps, dotted with tall and melancholy cypress trees adorned with "garments of moss." Rogers described the view as the very "impersonation of gloom." The soil was mostly sand and red clay. The farmlands, said Rogers, were planted in corn, cotton and tobacco, and sometimes, "whenever the land could be over-flowed," in rice. Along the line numerous gangs of slaves were seen working in fields or walking between plantations with their tools in their hands. As the train whizzed by they would sometimes lay down their implements and watch the cars pass out of sight.[27]

Lillian Foster and Solon Robinson were also impressed by the Georgia roads. In 1855, Miss Foster spoke highly of the "Waynesborough and Georgia Railroad" whose cars she boarded in Augusta.[28] Robinson was impressed with the route from Barnesville to Atlanta, citing it as "one of the excellent railroads which abound in Georgia."[29]

Other visitors to the state were less enchanted. In the early 1840's Bishop Henry Whipple referred to the railroad between Macon and Barnesville as one of the slowest he had ever used. It seems that the traveler's ire was aroused when the train covered only forty miles in seven and one-half hours. Whipple found the pace ludicrous and proclaimed that "stage coaches can well laugh at such railroads."[30] The visitor from up-state New York was critical not only of the railroads, but of the countryside as well. The counties through which he passed "certainly gave us a miserable idea of Georgia." In fact, Whipple said, "An owl would hardly live here were it not for the mildness of a southern climate."[31]

Atlanta, however, provided a distinct contrast. Because of its strategic location, the town was experiencing by 1860 a new-found prosperity brought in part by railroads. In 1846, John Shaw had described the community as a backwoods place which consisted of only a few houses.[32] Several years later, however, Charles Lanman was impressed with the city's growth, reporting that what had been only a "wilderness . . . a few years ago," had become by the 1850's "a kind of whirlpool" for railroads.[33]

The traveler departing from Georgia for the West encountered some of the raw frontier that existed in Alabama before the Civil War. Cotton and slavery were frequently discussed by railroad passengers who could see ample evidence of these aspects of Southern economy from the windows of their car. George Featherstonhaugh reported the plantations near Tuscumbia looked "like potato-fields before they go into blossom." The fields were populated by "a great number of slaves, particularly children," who were weeding them.[34] Some of the flora of the state was recorded by Amelia Murray in the 1850's. Near Montgomery, she observed the railroad was bordered on each side with

Cherokee roses and vivid evergreens with single white blossoms. The foliage was so thick "that it is said not even a snake can get through it."[35]

The half-way point of the "Grand Tour" was frequently reached by traveling on the Lake Pontchartrain Railroad to New Orleans. Of interest to travelers on this line was the rich undergrowth that bordered the rails. One of the early passengers to use the line in the 1830's reported the road passed through groves of cypress trees growing in the swamps. In the evening passengers could hear the serenade of the frogs. Bullfrogs were especially frightening since they "bellowed almost as loudly as oxen." During the spring one could hear "thousands of turtle doves cooing" in their homes in the swamps.[36] Another traveler who used the Louisiana railroad in the 1830's reported the roadbed was lined by drawf trees and a luxuriant undergrowth of tall, coarse grass, and vines. The grass twisted and wound its "long, serpentine folds around the trunks of the trees like huge, loathsome water-snakes."[37] A similar description of the region was offered by Francis and Theresa Pulszky during their brief stay in the South in 1851. The railroad was "adorned by rich oaks, cypress, lilac, water lilies, cactuses and crane, with luxuriant yellow flowers."[38]

Although the railroad offered a smoother ride than the stage coach and faster transportation than waterways, it still remained a very uncomfortable way of travel. Harriet Martineau remarked that she found railroad travel the most fatiguing mode of all. In her opinion, railroads throughout the United States were "fatiguing and noisy" because they were rapidly constructed and put into service as soon as they were built.[39] Captain Marryat believed that fatigue on trains was induced by the "constant coughing of the locomotive" and the "rapidity with which objects are passed." Other irritants were the sparks and ashes that annoyed passengers and burned their clothes. The only consolation afforded travelers on railroads, said Marryat, was "the speed with which you are passing over the ground."[40] Fredrika Bremer complained while traveling through Georgia that the "fatiguing day's journey" by rail sometimes gave her a headache. The cause for her discomfort was cited as the heat of the Southern sun, augmented by the smoke and steam emitted from the locomotive. Such discomforts, according to this traveler, were why she greatly expressed a preference to the steamboat to the railway, for it was not as tiring.[41]

Charles Dickens described traveling on American railroads as consisting of "a great deal of jolting, a great deal of noise, a great deal of wall, not much window, a locomotive engine, a shriek, and a bell."[42] To Charles Mackay, discomforts of rail travel were caused by what he termed mental and physical strains and nuisances in the cars. Mackay added that his experience revealed Northern railroads were better conducted than the "ill served and ill-regulated" ones in the South.[43] The most fatiguing element of rail travel, according to Thomas Nichols, was the "violent motion" of the cars, which was caused by the displacement of the track ties because of frost. In some instances the "dancing" cars swayed so severely on the unaligned rails that passengers were thrown from their seats.[44]

That antebellum railroads were uncomfortable and rough cannot be denied. Yet, for Joseph Biggs and Léon Beauvallet, they had other aspects which offset these disadvantages. Biggs was impressed with how in America one could "travel with such facility and cheapness." On American lines it was unnecessary to "make all those previous enquiries and arrangements" that complicated travel on European lines. People in the United States were inclined to have an "aptitude for locomotion," and expressed so much general intelligence on the subject, that Biggs discovered "almost anyone can give you all the information you require, as to the best mode of proceeding."[45] Léon Beauvallet commented that "perpetual traveling" on American railroads had a special attraction that could not be denied, and "a charm which you cannot help feeling." The "eternal locomotion" and "intoxication" caused by the train obliterated seasons and all meaning of time. "I have to refer to my almanac" to determine the month and day, said Beauvallet, concluding that railroad travelers could "go mad very easily in this country!"[46]

The passenger's trip was sometimes interrupted by having to detrain along sections of road which had not yet been constructed. In 1849, William Cullen Bryant, traveling from Richmond to Charleston, remarked that the passengers had to leave their cars at Blakely, North Carolina on the Roanoke River. For a quarter of a mile they were led by a Negro carrying a "blazing pine torch" to the banks of the river. Other Negroes followed the procession with their baggage. A steamer was boarded at the river which transported the passengers two and one-half miles to Weldon in an hour, where the train was boarded for Wilmington.[47] Similar experiences greeted Charles Lanman and Léon Beauvallet. Lanman had to leave his car for a dozen miles and travel by coach in the eastern part of South Carolina, because the line was incomplete.[48] Beauvallet complained that even on completed lines passengers had to "grope about" in the middle of the night to find cars, with "not a man to tell you the way or show you" your waiting train.[49] Similar discomforts were caused by washouts and wrecks.[50]

Olmsted also witnessed the effect of American impatience on railroad travel. During his Southern tour, he passed through "long stretches of cypress swamps" with "occasional intervals of either pine-barrens or clear water ponds." In the midst of the forest Olmsted reported the train had reached the end of the line. Before continuing by stage coach, the author observed a camp, with a small tent for the "hands engaged in laying the rails."[51]

To relieve the monotony of delays, passengers found various activities at stations and in the cars to pass the time while traveling by train. Bishop Henry Whipple was amused observing "crackers" at a Georgia depot, while Amelia Murray passed the time collecting "specimens of a very curious water-plant" and "flint fossils" along the roadbed.[52] Harriet Martineau reported in March, 1835, that when her train broke down in South Carolina the "men occupied themselves by frog-hunting" and by raiding the dinner table of a nearby "comfortable-looking house," taking an entire chicken and part of a turkey. Others undertook botanical explorations or, if possible, decided to pass the time by walking to the next station.[53]

A traveler's lot was improved somewhat by stewards passing through the cars supplying water for thirsty passengers. The practice of "watering the passengers" was novel to Charles Weld, who said it was another of the "peculiar" features incorporated on American lines. Usually a Negro man or boy walked through the coaches carrying a tin can and glasses in a frame. Without charge to the passengers, a drink of water was procured by simply indicating one's thirst. During the summer months this feature was very popular and considered "indispensible."[54]

Several other passengers familiar with the policy included Lillian Foster, Thomas Nichols and Eyre Crowe. Miss Foster observed in the cars a "stewardess to attend to the wants of the passengers" in South Carolina.[55] Nichols noted a water attendant while traveling between Cleveland, Ohio and Memphis, Tennessee. In this instance the steward was a Negro who supplied passengers with water "when that luxury is not kept in well-iced reservoirs in every car."[56] According to Eyre Crowe the service on some lines was continued during the winter months as well. This traveler reported the Negro fireman passing through the cars relieved the passengers' sensation of being parched from the heat of the coach stove by providing thirsty passengers with "a large bucket full of water and a huge wooden long handled ladle."[57]

Occasional stops at water stations along the lines furnished another diversion. Henry Tanner, in the 1830's, stated that those in Georgia were usually erected at ten-mile intervals "or as near this distance as the circumstances will permit." Besides providing provisions for taking on water, each station featured a turn-out about 800 feet in length, to allow two trains to pass. Storehouses could be found at some of the water-stations for the "accommodation of the local business" and for "dwellings for the persons entrusted with the supervision of the road."[58] A much more exciting diversion was provided by frantic rides in the mountains. Fredrika Bremer traveled on one of these mountain railroads which followed the "romantic banks of a little river" during a trip from Baltimore to Harper's Ferry, Virginia. The train's abruptness and irregularity along the winding road reminded her of a "terrified cow" that might at any moment plunge into the river.[59]

Indeed, "the art of flying without wings" had made great advances from the time the Baltimore & Ohio railroad ran its first cars from that city to Ellicott's Mills. Yet, despite these advances, many continued to regard railroad travel in America by 1860 as a special type of trial, to be endured only by those willing to suffer discomfort for the sake of convenience. Perhaps the journey of Salomon de Rothschild, enroute to Baltimore in 1860, best warned the fledgling traveler of the ordeal in store:

> I cannot admire the way Americans travel. Their railroads are in a deplorable state, and no one cares a rap. To get to Washington, you must change lines six times, take a steamboat—called a "ferry"—three times, and pile into a great omnibus containing all kinds of people any number of times. Here, too, is the great American pleasure of American railroads: there is only one class, in which everyone travels indiscriminately. You should see what fine traveling companions one collects! Let us ignore those that one only sees, though it is true they spit outrageously and do all sorts

of obnoxious things. But there are some who follow you in spite of all you can do, and who, finding themselves comfortable in your company, multiply without limit! . . . As for the degree of comfort of the coaches, nothing need be said: they are first-class coaches for the use of sixty people, who, upon entering, [have] the right to do everything except rest; for when you have finally fallen asleep you never fail to be jolted awake, rudely shoved by the vigorous hand of the conductor who asks for one of your many tickets, or summoned back to reality by the shrill voice of the "boy" who offers you newspapers and the latest publications.[60]

The growing pains of the railroad industry were far from over by 1860. As de Rothschild's description indicates, provisions for passenger safety and comfort still left much to be desired, and as the first shots were fired at Fort Sumter the military potential of the industry had hardly been touched at all.[61] In both the North and the South, the giddy speed of railroad expansion had left little time for reflection on the latter score, yet it was the inferior state of Southern railways which was shortly to become a matter of decisive importance in determining the course of the Civil War.

Epilogue

Southerners, by the time the nation entered the Civil War, had come to boast proudly of their pioneering efforts with railroads. With the new miles of track now dotting their agricultural landscape came the hope of a broadened and self-sustaining economy. As the section's railroad development linked the hinterlands to the seaboard, centers of trade had been tapped from as far away as Richmond, Memphis, and parts of Florida, and passengers were traveling faster and farther than ever before. Advancements in road construction were exemplified by the use on some lines of the efficient "T-rail." Efforts to eliminate sharp curves and steep grades were an important contribution of several companies, while others replaced older and worn out rolling stock with shiny new cars and engines. However, in spite of the merriment of opening celebrations and cries of Southern nationalism and scorn for the North, the Southern railway system by 1861 left much to be desired. The network was severely handicapped by the failure to develop any real system of trunk lines. By the time of the clash at Fort Sumter, most of the section's railroads were concentrated east of the Mississippi River and not in the West where the fortunes of war were early to go against the Confederacy. Some fringe areas of the South were in fact nearly isolated. In more settled areas problems were almost as severe. Between Danville, Virginia, and Greensboro, North Carolina "a potential route through the Piedmont was broken sharply by a fifty-mile intermission." South of Charlotte "no direct line to Atlanta existed." A lack of uniform gauge and inadequately financed companies also added to the weakness of the Southern system.[1]

Once the war erupted, the South found her railroads "insufficient in number" and too "poorly furnished with rolling stock" to supply adequately troops awaiting munitions and supplies.[2] Over-burdened coaches, the pride of companies in peaceful times, were ravaged by the rigors of war and the demands of the soldiers. Troops mutilated cars by kicking out the sides for better ventilation. Seats were often removed to provide more room. The demands of the war were equally hard on the locomotives and tracks, which became difficult to repair as Confederate iron works at Richmond, Nashville, Augusta, and Atlanta were threatened or captured by Federal troops. By summer, 1865, "twisted rails, burnt ties, destroyed bridges, gutted depots, and dilapidated or lost rolling stock scattered from Virginia to Louisiana was the heritage of the typical southern railway."[3] According to one other authority on the subject, "that many Southern carriers remained in operation as long as they did reflects an ingenuity of a high order."[4]

The destruction of the Southern rails was substantiated by the accounts of visitors traveling on the war-torn roads. Sidney Andrews discovered the railroads around Columbia, South Carolina were so devastated that it was almost impossible to enter or leave the city by rail. Englishman John H. Kennaway found that rails south of Weldon, North Carolina were so badly worn from over-use that he was "awakened time and time again, thinking the train was off the track." Whitelaw Reid encountered a war-scarred locomotive "which had only the battered remains of a stack, no headlight and a broken bell." This traveler noted, however, that the best cars were still reserved for the ladies.[5] Similar stories were told by other travelers.[6]

That passenger service in the South was disrupted because of the war is obvious from the accounts of passengers and troops describing the railroads. However, once the Federal armies gained control of certain pacified areas, some service, under military control, was restored. In fact, close examination of some of the railroad guidebooks of the 1860's scarcely reveals that there was then a war in progress.[7] One guide printed in 1864 reminded passengers to observe the proper habits of travel as though one were traveling in times of peace. Passengers were instructed that they could save ten cents by purchasing tickets at the depot, that an article in a seat was *prima facie* evidence the seat had been taken, and carried articles and poems in its pages such as "Give Me the Hand That Is Warm, Kind, and Ready," "The Blindfold Marriage," and a tale of Alexander II of Russia entitled "The Emperor and the Mother."[8]

At war's end the railroad slowly returned to the antebellum pattern, as guidebooks began advising passengers of fares, hack rates and hotel costs. Fashion was still of concern to many passengers, who were advised to have a "traveling suit equal to rude usage." The proper colors, according to *Appleton's Companion Hand-Book* in 1866, were gray or brown, which did not show the dust encountered on a stage or in a railway car. The guidebook also advised passengers to "don a felt hat,—it does not crush itself on your head in car or carriage, or blow overboard on steamboats." Ladies were instructed to travel in "*stout calf-skin*" boots, leaving the lighter ones at home. For the most fashionable the *Guide* suggested: "In mountain tramps, a generous sized flask, filled with most excellent brandy, may be swung over the shoulder with very picturesque effect."[9]

As the troubled 1860's yielded to the post-war era, ever greater refinements came to the railroad, making travel both safer and more comfortable. But as the streamlining process took place, there were those who remembered nostalgically the colorful and exciting days of the railroad's first attempts to conquer speed and distance. For those who had ridden the trains of the Old South, the account Charles Dickens penned would forever leave a picture of travel on antebellum Southern railroads. In the passenger's memory:

> Tears the mad dragon of an engine with its train of cars; scattering in all directions a shower of burning sparks from its wood fire; screeching, hissing, yelling, panting, until at last the thirsty monster stops beneath a covered way to drink, the people cluster round, and you have time to breathe again.[10]

Appendix

DATES OF TRAVEL

Although visitors to the South often failed to record the dates of their journey the following table lists as well as can be determined the period of time that travelers visited America and the Southern states. Specific dates of tours in the South have been listed where they can be determined.

Abbott, John *December, 1859*
Alexander, James Edward *1831*
An Anonymous Immigrant *1831–?*
Arese, Francesco *1837–1838*
Beauvallet, Léon *August, 1855 to January, 1856*
Biggs, Joseph *May, 1837–?*
Bremer, Fredrika *October, 1849 to September, 1851*
Bryant, William Cullen *1834 to 1850. In the South from March 1 to April 28, 1843, and from March to April, 1849.*
Buckingham, James Silk *September, 1837 to 1840. In the South from January to August, 1839*
Cather, Thomas *1836*
Chambers, William *September, 1853 to December, 1853*
Chevalier, Michel *December, 1833 to October, 1835*
Cobden, Richard *1835 and 1859*
Combe, George *September, 1838 to June, 1840*
Crockett, David *1834*
Crowe, Eyre *November, 1852 to April, 1853*
Davidson, James D. *1836*
Davies, Ebenezer *January to April, 1848 (?) In the South from January to February, 1848*
Dickens, Charles *January to June, 1842*
Featherstonhaugh, George *August, 1834 to February, 1835 and July to October, 1836*
Foster, Lillian *July, 1853 to July, 1859*

Godley, John Robert *July to November, 1842*
Hall, Abraham Oakey *1846 to 1847 (?)*
Hall, Basil & Margaret *1827–1828*
Hall, Frederick *May to October, 1837 and July to August, 1838*
Hamilton, Thomas *February to April, 1831*
Hundley, Daniel Robinson *About 1850 to 1860*
Ingraham, Joseph Holt *About 1830 to 1835*
Kemble, Frances Anne *Winter of 1838–1839*
Kingsford, William *November to December, 1858*
Lanman, Charles *1846 (?) to 1856*
Lardner, Dionysius *Early 1840's*
Latrobe, Charles Joseph *1832 to 1834*
Lewis, George *February to July, 1844*
Lyell, Charles *1841 to 1846. In the South from August, 1841 to August, 1842; December, 1841 to January, 1842; December, 1845 to June, 1846*
Mackay, Alexander *January, 1846 to January, 1847. In the South from May, 1846 to early fall, 1846*
Mackay, Charles *October, 1857 to May, 1858*
Marryat, C. B. *May, 1837 through 1838*
Martineau, Harriet *September, 1834 to August, 1836. In the South from December, 1834 to July, 1835*
Maxwell, Archibald M. *August to October, 1840*
Mendell, Sarah *One early short visit to the South in 1833 and another in the summer of 1853 or 1854*
Mitchell, David W. *1848 to 1858*
Murat, Achille *1826 to 1832*
Murray, Amelia Matilda *July, 1854 to October, 1855*
Murray, Charles Augustus *1834 to 1836*
Murray, Henry A. *1852 to 1853 (?)*
Nichols, Thomas Low *In the South from November, 1845 to March, 1859*
Olmsted, Frederick Law *1853 to 1854*
Parsons, Charles G. *1852 to 1853*
Pierce, George F. *September, 1855 to December, 1856*
Pingree, Enoch M. *About 1840 to 1849*
Pollard, Edward A. *1858*
Power, Tyrone *1834 to 1835*
Pulszky, Francis *December 5, 1851 to June, 1852. In the South from March 4 to April 15, 1851*
Raeder, Munch *1847 to 1848. In the South, November, 1847*
Robinson, Solon *1825 to 1851. In the South August, 1841; January to April, 1845; November 14, 1848 to June, 1849; November, 1849 to June, 1850; December, 1850 to May, 1851*
Rogers, Carlton H. *February to May, 1856*
Rogers, George *December, 1836 to April, 1844*
Rothchild, Salomon de *1859 to 1861*
Schliemann, Henry *1850 to 1851*

Shaw, John *August, 1845 to April (?), 1846. In South, January 1–24, 1846*
Stevenson, David *1837*
Stirling, James *August, 1856 to May, 1857*
Sturge, Joseph *April to July, 1841*
Summer, Henry *1837*
Thomson, William *August, 1840 to May, 1842*
Tower, Philo *1853 to 1854*
Tremenheere, Hugh S. *August to December, 1851*
Tudor, Henry *1831 to 1832*
Waylen, Edward *June, 1834 to June, 1845*
Weld, Charles Richard *Either 1854 or 1855*
Wells, William H. *1840*
Whipple, Henry B. *October, 1843 to May, 1844*
Williams, John Lee *Sometime before 1837*
Willis, Nathaniel Parker *Spring and summer, 1852. In the South May to June, 1852*
Wortley, Emmeline Charlotte Stuart *1849 to 1850. Probably in the South from November, 1849 to January, 1850*

CANAL MILEAGE BY DECADES, 1830–1850

State	1830	1840	1850
New York	546	640	803
Pennsylvania	230	954	954
Ohio	245	744	792
Virginia	—	216	216
Tennessee	—	—	—
Kentucky	2	2	2
North Carolina	—	13	13
Massachusetts	74	89	89
Georgia	16	28	28
Indiana	—	150	214
South Carolina	52	52	52
Alabama	—	52	52
Maine	21	21	29
Illinois	—	—	100
Maryland	10	136	136
Missouri	—	—	—
Mississippi	—	—	—
New Jersey	20	142	142
Louisiana	—	14	14
Connecticut	34	36	36
Vermont	—	1	1
New Hampshire	—	11	—
Michigan	—	—	—
Rhode Island	11	11	11
Arkansas	—	—	—
Delaware	14	14	14
Florida	—	—	—
Iowa	—	—	—
Wisconsin	—	—	—
Texas	—	—	—
California	—	—	—
Total	1,277	3,326	3,698

These sources are from Freeman Hunt, ed., *Hunt's Merchants' Magazine*, XXV (September, 1851), 381–382. For conflicting accounts of mileage see Caroline E. MacGill, *History of Transportation in the United States Before 1860,* 573.

RAILROAD MILEAGE CHART BY DECADES, 1830–1860

State	1830	1840	1850	1860
New York	—	453	1,409	2,682
Pennsylvania	70	576	900	2,598
Ohio	—	39	590	2,946
Virginia	—	341	341	1,731
Tennessee	—	—	48	1,253
Kentucky	—	32	80	534
North Carolina	—	247	249	937
Massachusetts	3	270	1,042	1,264
Georgia	—	212	666	1,420
Indiana	—	20	226	2,163
South Carolina	—	136	270	973
Alabama	—	51	112	743
Maine	—	10	257	472
Illinois	—	26	118	2,799
Maryland	—	273	315	386
Missouri	—	—	4	817
Mississippi	—	50	60	862
New Jersey	—	192	332	560
Louisiana	—	62	89	335
Connecticut	—	94	436	601
Vermont	—	—	366	554
New Hampshire	—	15	471	661
Michigan	—	114	349	779
Rhode Island	—	47	61	108
Arkansas	—	—	—	38
Delaware	—	16	16	127
Florida	—	52	52	402
Iowa	—	—	—	655
Wisconsin	—	—	20	905
Texas	—	—	—	307
California	—	—	—	23
Total	73	3,328	8,879	30,635

These sources are from Freeman Hunt, ed., *Hunt's Merchants' Magazine*, XXV (September, 1851), 381–382 for the years 1830, 1840, and 1850; and Henry V. Poor, *Manual of the Railroads of the United States for 1868–69* (New York: H. V. and H. W. Poor, 1868), 20–21. For conflicting accounts of railroad mileage see, Caroline E. MacGill, *History of Transportation in the United States Before 1860,* 573.

THE RAILWAY CAR
Charles P. Shiras

No more we sing as they sang of old,
  To the tones of the lute and lyre,
For lo! we live in an Iron Age—
  In the age of Steam and Fire!
The world is too busy for dreaming,
  And hath grown too wise for War;
So, to-day, for the glory of Science,
  Let us sing of the Railway Car!

The golden chariots of ancient kings
  Would dazzle the wondering eye,
And the heads of a million slaves might bow
  As the glittering toy rolled by;
But this is the *Car of the People*,
  And before it shall bow all kings—
Be they warned when they hear the shrieking
  Of the dragon with iron wings!

The blood-stained Car of the Juggernaut,
  Oe'r millions of necks hath rolled,
And its priests have cried, 'Such a triumph as ours,
  The world shall never behold!'
But wo! when this harnessed Dragon,
  Comes vomiting smoke and fire,
For the Priests, with their Car and Idols,
  Shall perish beneath his ire!

And wo to all who uphold the wrong—
  Love darkness rather than light—
For Science hath opened a broad highway
  For Knowledge and Truth and Right.
And he sends forth his Car to gather
  The people of many lands,
Until the uttermost nations
  Are grasping each other's hands!

And thus, when the people as one are joined,
  And each to his fellow is known,
Incention, and Art, and Skill shall work
  At the bidding of Science alone.
And who can tell of the greatness
  The world may hope for then!
For the Faith that moveth mountains
  Hath entered the souls of men!

Then sing no more, as they sang of old,
  To the tones of the lute and lyre,
But sound the praise of the Iron Age—
  Of the age of Steam and Fire.
And sing to the glory of Science—
  Exult in the downfall of War—
And shout for the fiery Dragon,
  As he flies with the Railway Car.

From Freeman Hunt, ed., *Hunt's Merchants' Magazine and Commercial Review*, XXVI (April, 1852), 497.

Northeast and Southwest Alabama R.R. Train

THE STEAM ENGINE

"Whizz———whip!
I must not slip"———
And the steam-king buckles, and holds his breath,
And braces his sinews for life or death,
And clinches his bands,
Like a pair of hands,
To the long iron rail stretched out before;
While his elbows bend and his body shakes,
And out of his nostrils the black clouds pour—
And says he, "we're off if nothing breaks."
So he clears his throat with a terrible scream,
And tries his wheels;
And like some huge monster we see in a dream—
A cyclops, a hydra, a comet at play—
Through city and country he gallops away,
With his long train switching behind at his heels....*

'Singing through the forests,
  Rattling over ridges,
Shooting under arches,
  Rumbling over bridges,
Whizzing through the mountains
  Buzzing o'er the vale,
Bless me! this is pleasant,
  Riding on the Rail!†

*Putnam's Monthly: A Magazine of American Literature, Science, and Art, V (April, 1855), 365–368.
†The Knickerbocker or New York Monthly Magazine, XLIII (April, 1854), 395.

Notes

CHAPTER 1

1. According to the plan of General Edmund P. Gaines in an article carried in the *North American Review,* "Good roads, canals, and above all, rail-roads, augment the capability of troops to defend a country many fold." *North American Review,* LII (January, 1841), 21–22.

2. For a study of the transportation revolution during the antebellum years see, George Rogers Taylor, *The Transportation Revolution, 1815–1860* (New York, 1951).

3. Charles Richard Weld, *A Vacation Tour in the United States and Canada* (London, 1855), 394; Thomas Yoseloff, ed., *Voyage to America: The Journals of Thomas Cather* (New York, 1961), 21.

4. Robert Edgar Riegel, *Young America, 1830–1840* (Norman, Oklahoma, 1949), 11.

5. Taylor, *Transportation Revolution,* 52–55. According to one estimate one mile of railroad cost $5,000 less than one mile of canal. *Hunt's Merchants Magazine,* XXVIII (January, 1853), 507.

6. Canal Traffic did not decrease on important waterways such as the Erie Canal. For instance, in 1840, 4,071 boats used the canal as compared to 7,184 in 1850. *American Railroad Journal,* XXIV (January 4, 1851), 18. See Appendix (herein) for canal mileage statistics. For a general treatment on canals see, J. L. Ringwalt, *Development of Transportation Systems in the United States* (Philadelphia, 1888), 41–54, 108–111.

7. *The Museum of Foreign Literature and Science,* VI (January–June, 1825), 282, 286.

8. Savings from the use of railroads according to one account were described as follows. "By the canal, the cost of a ton from Pittsburg to Baltimore, at one cent and a half a mile, would be five dollars and eighty five cents; and at the same rate, it would be but three dollars and seventy five cents by the railroad." *North American Review,* XXV (July, 1827), 65, 67–68.

9. *Niles' Weekly Register,* XXXV (September, 27, 1828), 67; *Ibid.,* (January 3, 1829), 299; *Ibid.,* XXXVII (January 16, 1830), 338. Another periodical stated that, "For passengers, the railroad has no rival in the canal; and for the transportation of most kinds of heavy freight, the canal is not less pre-eminent over the railroad." *Hunt's Merchants Magazine,* XXXI (July, 1854), 123.

10. Michel Chevalier, *Society, Manners, and Politics in the United States: Letters on North America* (New York, 1961), 250–251.

11. Herbert A. Kellar, "A Journey Through the South in 1836: Diary of James D. Davidson," *Journal of Southern History,* I (August, 1935), 374. *Niles' Weekly Register* in 1834 also doubted the ability of stage lines to stand-up against railroads as indicated by the following items. "The other day, not withstanding a heavy fall of snow, the mail car arrived from Frederick, 60 miles, on the rail road, in six hours; but on the same day, passengers in one of the stages from Washington, were sixteen hours on the road—distance 36 miles." *Niles' Weekly Register,* XLV (January 25, 1834), 366; *Ibid.,* LI (January 28, 1837), 352.

12. John Lee Williams, *The Territory of Florida: Or Sketches of the Topography, Civil, and Natural History, of the Country, the Climate, and the Indian Tribes, from the First Discovery to the Present Time, with a Map, Views, etc.* (New York, 1839), 146.

13. *North American Review,* XXV (July, 1827), 65, 66. Another mode of transportation considered besides railroads and canals was the plank road. See *DeBow's Review,* VII (December, 1849), 534–536; *Ibid.,* IX (September, 1850), 334–336).

14. Franklin M. Reck, *The Romance of American Transportation* (New York, 1962), 76. For a brief account of the early applications of steam to American roads see James Truslow Adams, "Railroads," *Dictionary of American History,* IV, 406–409.

15. *The Museum,* (January–June, 1825), 286.

16. Dionysius Lardner, *Railway Economy; A treatise on the New Art of Transport, Its Management, Prospects, and Relations, Commercial, Financial, and Social, with an Exposition of the Practical Results of the Railways in Operation in the United Kingdom, on the Continent, and in America* (New York, 1850), 327. Also see Henry Anthony Murray, *Lands of the Slave and the Free; Or, Cuba, the United States, and Canada,* II (London, 1855), 143.

17. Ulrich Bonnell Phillips, *Life and Labor in the Old South* (Boston, 1946), 146. Michel Chevalier said of the Charleston & Hamburg Railroad, "This road was undertaken with the purpose of diverting to Charleston part of the cotton which descended the river Savannah to the town of the same name. It has fully answered the expectations of its projectors." Chevalier, *Society, Manners, and Politics,* 247.

18. Samuel Augustus Mitchell, *An Accompaniment to Mitchell's Reference and Distance Map of the United States* (Philadelphia, 1835), 251.

19. Edward Hungerford, *The Story of the Baltimore & Ohio Railroad, 1827–1927* (New York, 1928), 77.

20. *Niles' Weekly Register,* XXXV (September 27, 1828), 40. The *Register* added that, "Hundreds of thousands of persons, in the repeated journeys of citizens and strangers, will travel upon it, from curiosity or for amusement."

21. Reck, *American Transportation,* 78. William Henry Harrison was the first president-elect to arrive in Washington on the Baltimore & Ohio

Railroad on February 9, 1841. Joseph Nathan Kane, *Facts About the Presidents* (New York, 1964), 112.

22. Henry Tudor, *Narrative of a Tour in North America; Comprising Mexico, the Mines of Real del Monte, the United States, and the British Colonies; With an Excursion to the Island of Cuba*, I (London, 1834), 79, 80.

23. Francesco Arese, *A Trip to the Prairies and in the Interior of North America (1837–1838)*. Translated by Andrew Evans. (New York, 1934), 14.

24. Ulrich Bonnell Phillips, *A History of Transportation in the Eastern Cotton Belt to 1860* (New York, 1908), 140.

25. Samuel Melanchthon Derrick, *Centennial History of the South Carolina Railroad* (Columbia, South Carolina, 1930), 112.

26. Seymour Dunbar, *A History of Travel in America*, III (Indianapolis, 1915), 963. An antebellum account of the famous explosion of the *Best Friend* can be found in *DeBow's Review*, XXIV (June, 1858), 567–568, and in *Niles' Weekly Register*, XL (June 25, 1831), 291.

27. *Niles' Weekly Register*, XXXV (September 27, 1828), 40.

28. Charles Joseph Latrobe, *The Rambler in North America, 1832–1833*, I, (London, 1836), 34.

29. *Niles' Weekly Register*, XLII (April 17, 1832), 93. *Ibid.*, XLIV (July 27, 1833), 354. *Ibid.*, XLVIII (April 25, 1835), 133. Also see Chevalier, *Society, Manners, and Politics*, 247.

30. Rosser H. Taylor, "Hamburg: An Experiment in Town Promotion," *North Carolina Historical Review*, XI (January, 1934), 28–29.

31. Joseph Biggs, *To America in Thirty-nine Days Before Steamships Crossed the Atlantic* (Idbury, England, 1927), 10–11.

32. Charles Lyell, *A Second Visit to the United States of North America*, II (New York, 1849), 264.

33. *Niles' Weekly Register*, LI (October 29, 1836), 136.

34. Grenville Mellen, *A Book of the United States: Exhibiting Its Geography, Divisions, Constitution and Government, and Presenting a View of the Republic Generally, and of the Individual States* (Hartford, 1839), 791.

35. *Hunt's Merchants Magazine*, IX (July, 1843), 95. *Ibid.*, XII (February, 1845), 158.

36. *DeBow's Review*, XVI (February, 1854), 205. *Ibid.*, I (March, 1846), 285. *Ibid.*, XVIII (February, 1855), 264.

37. Reports on rail mileage are often conflicting. Some tables only list track in operation, while others include track under construction. Differences are also found on lines using draft power, or both. For a discussion concerning the rapid growth of American railroads, see Emory R. Johnson and Thurman W. Van Metre, *Principles of Railroad Transportation* (New York, 1922), 26–37. See Appendix (herein) for mileage tables.

38. Chevalier, *Society, Manners, and Politics*, 75.

39. Phillips, *Transportation in the Eastern Cotton Belt*, 12, 13, states that "nowhere was their acceptance more eager than in the staple regions of the South."

40. *DeBow's Review*, XV (December, 1853), 642. *Ibid.*, XXVIII (May, 1860) 592.

41. John F. Stover, *The Railroads of the South, 1865–1900* (Chapel Hill, 1955), 13.

42. *DeBow's Review*, XXVIII (April, 1860), 593–594.

43. Chevalier, *Society, Manners, and Politics*, 72. *Ibid.*, 297. *Ibid.*, 72–74.

44. Tudor, *A Tour in North America*, I, 79–80.

45. Latrobe, *The Rambler in North America*, I, 33.

46. Arese, *A Trip to the Prairies and in the Interior of North America*, 15.

47. Frances Anne Kemble, *Journal of a Residence on a Georgian Plantation in 1838–1839* (New York, 1961), 13.

48. Léon Beauvallet, *Rachel and the New World: A Trip to the United States and Cuba* (New York, 1856), 295.

49. Quoted in Chevalier, 270.

50. *DeBow's Review*, XXIV (May, 1858), 394.

CHAPTER 2

1. *DeBow's Review*, XII (June, 1852), 671.

2. Joseph Holt Ingraham, *The Southwest. By A Yankee* (New York, 1835), I, 171, 176–178. For a study of New Orleans and the railroad see Merl E. Reed, *New Orleans and the Railroads: The Struggle for Commercial Empire, 1830–1860* (Baton Rouge, 1966).

3. Wilton P. Ledet, "The History of the City of Carrollton," *Louisiana Historical Quarterly*, XXI (January, 1938), 235.

4. *DeBow's Review*, XVI (June, 1854), 650.

5. Philo Tower, *Slavery Unmasked: Being a Truthful Narrative of a Three Years' Residence and Journeying in Eleven Southern States* (Rochester, 1856), 194.

6. Amelia Matilda Murray, *Letters From the United States, Cuba and Canada* (New York, 1856), 194.

7. Thomas D. Clark, *A Pioneer Southern Railroad from New Orleans to Cairo* (Chapel Hill, 1936), 20, 21.

8. Phillips, *Transportation in the Eastern Cotton Belt*, 13.

9. *DeBow's Review*, VII (December, 1849), 532-533.

10. *Ibid.*, V (May–June, 1848), 454.

11. *The Atlantic Monthly. A Magazine of Literature, Art, and Politics*, II (November, 1858), 643.

12. Yoseloff, *Journal of Thomas Cather*, 51–52.

13. *Hunt's Merchants Magazine*, XVIII (January, 1848), 98.

14. Lardner, *Railway Economy*, 384.

15. Frederick Hall, *Letters from the East and from the West* (Washington, 1840), 128.

16. James Silk Buckingham, *The Eastern and Western States of America*, III (London, 1842), 2.

17. Lester B. Shippee, ed., *Bishop Whipple's Southern Diary, 1843–1844* (Minneapolis, 1937), 76.

18. *American Railroad Journal,* XXVI (June 25, 1853), 401.
19. David Crockett, *An Account of Col. Crockett's Tour to the North and Down East* (New York, 1845), 15, 16.
20. Derrick, *South Carolina Railroad,* 34, 118.
21. N. P. Renfro, Jr., *The Beginning of Railroads in Alabama* (Auburn, 1910), 4. For additional information on the Tuscumbia & Decatur Railroad see, Ernest F. Patterson, "Alabama's First Railroads," *Alabama Review,* IX (January, 1956), 33–45.
22. George W. Pettengill, Jr., "The Story of the Florida Railroads," *The Railway and Locomotive Historical Society,* XXCVI (July, 1952), 23.
23. Murray, *Letters From the United States,* 186.
24. Derrick, *South Carolina Railroad,* 126, 127, 217–219.
25. *Niles' Weekly Register,* XXXIV (June 7, 1828), 233.
26. *Ibid.,* (July 12, 1828), 325, 327–328. Riegel, *Young America,* 12.
27. *Ibid.,* 316, 317–325.
28. Derrick, *South Carolina Railroad,* 94, 95.
29. *Niles' Weekly Register,* XLV (September 14, 1833), 36.
30. *DeBow's Review,* XXIII (July, 1857), 94.
31. *American Railroad Journal,* XXX (May 16, 1857), 312.
32. Champion McDowell Davis, *"Atlantic Coast Line," Fragments of its History During Over a Century* (New York, 1950), 11.
33. Kincaid Herr, *The L & N Railroad, 1850–1963* (Louisville, 1964), 23.
34. *American Railroad Journal,* XXIV (May 31, 1851), 343.
35. Robert C. Black, *The Railroads of the Confederacy* (Chapel Hill, 1952), 2. For information on Northern railroads during the Civil War see Thomas Weber, *The Northern Railroads in the Civil War, 1861–1865* (New York, 1952). For opening ceremonies and celebrations on other lines see *New England Magazine,* I (December, 1831), 530; *Ibid.,* II (January, 1832), 79; Clark, *A Pioneer Southern Railroad,* 33, 87, 88, 76–79; *Niles' Weekly Register,* LVIII (June 20, 1840), 245; Derrick, *South Carolina Railroad,* 187–189; *DeBow's Review,* XVI (February, 1854), 205–207.
36. A negative approach to railroads in the cotton belt is offered by U. B. Phillips in *Transportation in the Eastern Cotton Belt,* 388. An opposing argument is taken by Robert Spencer Cotterill, "Southern Railroads, 1850–1860," *Mississippi Valley Historical Review,* X (March, 1924), 396–405.
37. The spreading of news and opinions in the South sometimes had the reverse effect. For instance, Francis and Theresa Pulszky, touring the South in 1851, made the following comments about secessionists. "They have been defeated in their scheme of political secession, they continue the strife in another form by endeavoring to sever the feeling of the moral unity of the North Americans; they wish to teach the youth of the South to look upon those who do not belong to planter States as foreigners. This spirit would be dangerous could it ever pervade all the slave States, but in these days of steamboats, railways and telegraphs, every attempt to isolate a country, and to break up its intellectual connection

with its neighbors, will always prove a failure." Francis and Theresa Pulszky, *White, Red, Black: Sketches of Society in the United States* (New York, 1853), II, 122–123.

CHAPTER 3

1. *Niles' Weekly Register*, XXXVII (December 5, 1829), 230. For an excellent selection of drawings and photographs of antebellum engines see Reed Kinert, *Early American Steam Locomotives*, 1830–1900 (New York, 1962).

2. *Ibid.*, XXXVIII (May 15, 1830), 214., *Ibid.*, XXXVII (January 16, 1830), 337.

3. Thomas *Hamilton, Men and Manners in America*, II (London, 1834), 158. James Edward Alexander, *Transatlantic Sketches, Comprising Visits to the Most Interesting Scenes in North and South America, and the West Indies* (London, 1833), III, 257. Also see Buckingham, *The Eastern and Western States of America*, III, 1, 2.

4. David Stevenson, "Railways in America in 1837," *The Railway Library, 1915* (Chicago, 1916), 15.

5. Lardner, *Railway Economy*, 338.

6. Murray, *Lands of the Slave and the Free*, I, 384. In this account Murray commented that Petersborough, Virginia (?) was "so far behind the American age, that they would not allow a railroad to pass through their town."

7. *Niles' Weekly Register*, XL (June 25, 1831), 291.

8. Dunbar, *A History of Travel in America*, III, 784.

9. *Niles' Weekly Register*, XL (July 16, 1831), 339.

10. Dunbar, *A History of Travel in America*, III, 779.

11. *Niles' Weekly Register*, XXXVII (January 2, 1830), 294.

12. *Ibid.*, LI (December 3, 1836), 224.

13. *Ibid.*, XXXVII (January 2, 1830), 294.

14. It should be noted that other railroads made similar experiments with horses and wind. On one instance the Baltimore & Ohio Railroad reported that one of its horse-drawn cars pulled forty-one persons ten to eleven miles per hour for more than five miles.

15. Nathaniel Parker Willis, *Health Trip to the Tropics* (New York, 1853), 326. Willis was concerned over how the railroads in Savannah would destroy the old charms of the Georgia city.

16. Charles Dickens, *American Notes* (New York, 1961), 83.

17. Weld, *A Vacation Tour in the United States*, 65, 66.

18. Carlton H. Rogers, *Incidents of Travel in the Southern States With A Description of the Mammoth Cave* (New York, 1852), 45.

19. Ingraham, *The Southwest*, I, 172–173.

20. William H. Wills, "A Southern Traveler's Diary in 1840," *Publications of the Southern History Association* (September, 1903), VII, 350.

21. Abraham Oakey Hall, *The Manhattaner in New Orleans: Or, Phases of "Crescent City" Life* (New York, 1851), 113.

22. Tower, *Slavery Unmasked*, 35.

23. Crockett, *Col. Crockett's Exploits*, 15.

24. *Harper's New Monthly Magazine*, II (January, 1851), 194.

25. *The Knickerbocker or New York Monthly Magazine*, XLIII (New York, 1854), 395.

'26. Clark, *A Pioneer Southern Railroad*, 31–33.

27. Johnson and Van Metre, *Principles of Transportation*, 59. In 1850 a locomotive weighing 50,000 pounds was considered large.

28. The engine *Gowan* and *Marx* of the Philadelphia & Reading Railroad pulled one hundred and one loaded cars for 54½ miles in five hours and thirty-three minutes. *United States Commercial & Statistical Register*, II (March 18, 1840), 181.

29. *Hunt's Merchants Magazine*, XXIX (October, 1853), 503–504. Also see *American Railroad Journal*, XXXII (September 24, 1859), 610–611.

30. *American Railroad Journal*, XXIII (February 23, 1850), 119.

31. Chevalier, *Society, Manners, and Politics*, 256.

32. *American Railroad Journal*, XXII (June 9, 1849), 361; *Ibid.*, XXII (February 24, 1849), 120; *Ibid.*, XXII (June 16, 1849), 373.

33. Articles carried in American magazines confirm the faster speeds of European trains. "The improvements making in England seem almost past belief. They now talk of travelling 20 or 30 miles an hour on a common road, and think that *one hundred* is practicable on a rail-way." *Niles' Weekly Register*, XXXVII (January 16, 1830), 337. An engine on the English Great Western Railroad was cited as achieving a speed of one hundred miles per hour for twenty eight miles in 1839. *United States Commercial & Statistical Register*, I (August 21, 1839), 391. *Ibid.*, I (August 14, 1839), 121–122.

34. *American Railroad Journal*, XXXI (May 22, 1858), 325.

35. Edwin P. Alexander, *Iron Horses: American Locomotives, 1829–1900* (New York, 1941), 64.

36. *DeBow's Review*, XVI (January–June, 1854), 678.

37. Charles Augustus Murray, *Travel in North America During the Years 1834, 1835, & 1836. Including a Summer Residence with the Pawnee Tribe of Indians, in the Remote Prairies of the Missouri, and a Visit to Cuba and the Azore Islands*, II (New York, 1839), 195.

38. Tower, *Slavery Unmasked*, 157.

39. Pulszky, *Sketches of Society in the United States*, II, 332.

40. Frederick Law Olmstead, *The Cotton Kingdom: A Traveller's Observations on Cotton and Slavery in the American Slave States* (New York, 1953), 44. Edited by Arthur M. Schlesinger, Jr.

41. Chevalier, *Society, Manners, and Politics*, 257.

42. Kellar, "A Journey Through the South in 1836," 373. Also see *Niles' Weekly Register*, LI (October 29, 1836), 135–136.

43. Stevenson, "Railways in America in 1837," 15.

44. Chambers, *Things As They Are in America*, 334.

45. *North American Review*, XXVIII (January, 1829), 185. Herbert A. Kellar, ed., *Solon Robinson, Pioneer and Agriculturist* (Indianapolis, 1936), II, 387.

46. *American Railroad Journal,* XXXI (June 19, 1858), 392–393.

47. *Ibid.,* XXXII (February, 12, 19, 1859), 109, 121.

48. *Ibid.,* XXXII (April 9, 1859), 229. Also see *Hunt's Merchants Magazine,* XXXIII (November, 1855), 638.

49. *Hunt's Merchants Magazine,* XXXVII (September, 1857), 379.

50. *United States Commercial & Statistical Register,* II (February 19, 1840), 116.

51. Harriet Martineau, *Society in America* (New York, 1837), II, 8.

52. Stevenson, "Railways in America in 1837," 17.

53. Buckingham, James Silk, *The Slave States of America,* II (London, 1842), 412.

54. Alexander Mackay, *The Western World or Travels in the United States* (London, 1849), II, 146.

55. Dickens, *American Notes,* 89.

56. *Hunt's Merchants Magazine,* XVII (October, 1847), 428.

57. Chambers, *Things As They Are in America,* 334.

58. *North American Review,* XXVIII (January, 1829), 177.

59. Phillips, *Transportation in the Eastern Cotton Belt,* 249.

60. Derrick, *South Carolina Railroad,* 124.

61. Elizabeth Hoon Cawley, ed., *The American Diaries of Richard Cobden* (Princeton, 1952), 154. For an interesting article concerning slaves in skilled occupations in the Old South, see John Hebron Moore, "Simon Gray, Riverman: A Slave Who Was Almost Free," *Mississippi Valley Historical Review,* XLIX (December, 1962), 472–484.

62. Charles Lanman, *Adventures in the Wilds of the United States and British American Provinces* (Philadelphia, 1856), II, 97.

63. Derrick, *South Carolina Railroad,* 124.

64. John Hope Franklin, *Reconstruction After the Civil War* (Chicago, 1962), 223, 224.

65. Tower, *Slavery Unmasked,* 157.

66. John Stevens Cabot Abbott, *South and North; Or Impressions Received During a Trip to Cuba and the South* (New York, 1860), 228.

67. Olmsted, *The Cotton Kingdom,* 64–65.

68. Shippee, *Bishop Whipple's Diary,* 76.

69. *American Railroad Journal,* XXII (September 8, 1849), 572.

70. Dunbar, *A History of Travel in America,* III, 1029–1030.

71. Englishman Henry Murray took special notice of cabs on American locomotives during his visit to America in 1852–1853. "But the point to which I wish to call especial attention, is the very sensible provision made for the comfort of the engineer and stokers, who are throughly protected by a weather-proof compartment, the sides whereof, being made of glass, enable them to exercise more effective vigilance than they possibly could do if they were exposed in the heartless manner prevalent in this country." Murray, *Lands of the Slave,* I, 49.

72. Dunbar, *A History of Travel in America,* III, 1032–1033.

73. Abbott, *South and North,* 343.

74. *American Railroad Journal,* XXXI (September 11, 1858), 585.

75. Black, *Railroads of the Confederacy,* 17.

76. *Niles' Weekly Register*, XLV (September 28, 1833), 70.
77. *Ibid.*, XLVIII (August 29, 1835), 451–452.
78. Beauvallet, *Rachel and the New World*, 200.
79. Stevenson, "Railways in America in 1837," 17.
80. Weld, *A Vacation Tour in the United States*, 65.
81. Captain Frederick Marryat, *A Diary in America, With Remarks on its Institutions* (Philadelphia, 1840), 9.
82. Mackay, *The Western World*, I, 162.
83. *Ibid.*, 161–162.

CHAPTER 4

1. A study of the American passenger coach, complete with pictures and plans, is offered in August Mencken, *The Railroad Passenger Car* (Baltimore, 1957).
2. *New England Magazine*, II (January, 1832), 80.
3. Stevenson, "Railways in America in 1837," 7.
4. Hamilton, *Manners in America*, II, 158.
5. Chambers, *Things As They Are in America*, 334.
6. Buckingham, *The Eastern and Western States of America*, III, 1, 2.
7. Dunbar, *A History of Travel in America*, III, 1017.
8. Derrick, *South Carolina Railroad*, 109–110. Although the "barrel car" was used almost exclusively by the South Carolina Railroad, Lady Stuart-Wortley mentioned "waiting in a curious circular sort of car" while traveling on the Lake Pontchartrain Railroad in Louisiana. Lady Emmeline Stuart-Wortley, *Travels in the United States, etc., During 1849 and 1850.* (New York, 1868), 130.
9. *Niles' Weekly Register*, XXXVIII (May 15, 1830), 214.
10. *New England Magazine*, II (January, 1832), 80.
11. Ebenezer Davies, *American Scenes—and Christian Slavery: A Recent Tour of Four Thousand Miles in the United States* (London, 1849), 187.
12. Murray, *Lands of the Slave and the Free*, I, 46.
13. Weld, *A Vacation Tour in the United States*, 65.
14. Dickens, *American Notes*, 80.
15. Beauvallet, *Rachel and the New World*, 203.
16. Lardner, *Railway Economy*, 337.
17. Chambers, *Things As They Are in America*, 335.
18. James Buckingham in the 1830's made reference to a coach holding as many as eighty passengers. James Silk Buckingham, *America, Historical, Statistical, and Descriptical* (London, 1841), I, 257. *Niles' Weekly Register* carried an article in 1831 that reported the Baltimore & Ohio Railroad owned a car named the *Columbus* that could hold as many as 150 passengers. It was stated this was the largest car on rails, and had a promenade on top surrounded by iron railings, ornamented rails, and was equipped with numerous comfortable settees both above and below. *Niles' Weekly Register*, XL (July 2, 1831), 308.

19. Chambers, *Things As They Are in America*, 335.

20. Weld, *A Vacation Tour in the United States*, 65. *Atlantic Monthly*, II (November, 1858), 646.

21. Mencken, *The Railroad Passenger Car*, 18.

22. George Foster Pierce, *Incidents of Western Travel* (Nashville, 1859), 136.

23. Ingraham, *The Southwest*, I, 173.

24. Charles F. Adams, *Railroads: Their Origins and Problems* (New York, 1878), 49.

25. Murray, *Lands of the Slave and the Free*, I, 47.

26. Reck, *American Transportation*, 91.

27. R. R. Russel, "Revaluation of the Period Before the Civil War: Railroads," *Mississippi Valley Historical Review*, XV (December, 1928), 344.

28. Marryat, *A Diary in America*, 8.

29. Kemble, *Georgian Plantation*, 14.

30. Thomas Low Nichols, *Forty Years of American Life, 1821–1861* (New York, 1937), 75.

31. Chambers, *Things As They Are in America*, 335.

32. Mencken, *The Railroad Passenger Car*, 13.

33. Hall, *The Manhattaner in New Orleans*, 113.

34. Beauvallet, *Rachel and the New World*, 203.

35. Mencken, *The Railroad Passenger Car*, 24.

36. A typical description of this arrangement can be found in Shirley H. Weber, ed., *Schliemann's First Visit to America, 1850–1851* (Cambridge, Massachusetts, 1942), 25. "The seats are on both sides, and on each bank sit 2 persons. The leaning can be turned over, so that 4 can sit together if they choose proper."

37. *Ibid.*

38. Mencken, *The Railroad Passenger Car*, 24.

39. Wortley, *Travels in the United States*, 80, 81.

40. Kemble, *Georgian Plantation*, 13, 14.

41. *Ibid.*, 43. Also see *Hunt's Merchants Magazine*, XV (December, 1846), 609–610.

42. *American Railroad Journal*, XXXII (May 14, 1859), 313.

43. *Ibid.*, XXIII (March 30, 1850), 153. A dust proof car tested on the Vermont Central Railroad was described as being kept completely free of cinders and dust by a system that forced air in the car from scoops on the top of the coach, and then forced it through a screen filter of fine wires. The windows in the car were permanently closed and were designed to admit light into the car. The air was let out of the car through blinds on the sides of the car that were arranged so as to not interfere with the passage of the air. See *Hunt's Merchant's Magazine*, XXVI (January, 1852), 109–110.

44. In 1852 the *American Railroad Journal* carried an advertisement for one company which offered $800 to any inventor who could build an apparatus that would clear dust from passenger cars. *American Railroad Journal*, XXV (January 31, 1852), 79.

45. Nichols, *Forty Years of American Life*, 159.
46. Mencken, *The Railroad Passenger Car*, 53.
47. Shippee, *Bishop Whipple's Diary*, 74.
48. Dickens, *American Notes*, 79–80.
49. Daniel Robinson Hundley, *Social Relations in Our Southern States* (New York, 1860), 47.
50. Murray, *Lands of the Slave and the Free*, I, 136, 145.
51. William Cullen Bryant, *Letters of a Traveller; Or, Notes of Things Seen in Europe and America* (New York, 1850), 78.
52. Davies, *American Scenes*, 187.
53. Lyell, *A Second Visit to the United States*, I, 178.
54. Mackay, Charles, *Life and Liberty in America; Or, Sketches of a Tour in the United States and Canada, in 1857–8* (London, 1859), 218.
55. Mencken, *The Railroad Passenger Car*, 54.
56. *Ibid.*
57. *American Railroad Journal*, XXXII (June 11, 1859), 377–378.
58. Kemble, *Georgian Plantation*, 22.
59. Lardner, *Railway Economy*, 337.
60. Mencken, *The Railroad Passenger Car*, 55.
61. Olmsted, *The Cotton Kingdom*, 133.
62. Mackay, *Life and Liberty in America*, 218.
63. Eyre Crowe, *With Thackeray in America* (New York, 1893), 141–142.
64. Mackay, *Life and Liberty in America*, 218.
65. Mencken, *The Railroad Passenger Car*, 56.
66. *Ibid.*, 56–68.
67. George Lewis, *Impressions of America and the American Churches* (Edinburgh, 1845), 145.
68. Nichols, *Forty Years of American Life*, 75.
69. John Shaw, *A Ramble Through the United States, Canada, and the West Indies* (London, 1856), 206.
70. Crockett, *Col. Crockett's Exploits*, 15.
71. Dunbar, *A History of Travel in America*, III, 807, 1043–1044.
72. Nichols, *Forty Years of American Life*, 75.
73. Rogers, *Incidents of Travel*, 262.

CHAPTER 5

1. Williams, *Appleton's Railroad and Steamboat Companion*, 26.
2. Pulszky, *Sketches of Society in the United States*, II, 327. Also see *United States Commercial & Statistical Register*, I (August 14, 1839), 122; Clark, *A Pioneer Southern Railroad*, 153; *Hunt's Merchants Magazine*, XXIII (August, 1850), 237.
3. Mitchell, *Mitchell's Reference Map of the United States*, 252.
4. *Ibid.*, 269.
5. Clark, *A Pioneer Southern Railroad*, 62.
6. Pettengill, "Florida Railroads," 5–6.

7. Several travelers who mentioned this practice were Henry Murray and Michel Chevalier. "Owing to the usual recklessness of American habits, we had to cross a railroad which runs for some way along the side of the road." Murray, *Letters from the United States*, 204. "The Petersburg and Roanoke railroad, which is shorter than the post road follows with very little deviation an old Indian trail." Chevalier, *Society, Manners, and Politics*, 246.

8. Cross ties and sleepers were defined as "pieces of timber laid at intervals of two or three feet, across the road-way, upon which the string pieces and rails are placed. They are intended to keep the rails in their proper position." Henry Schenck Tanner, *A Description of the Canals and Railroads of the United States, Comprehending Notices of All the Works of Internal Improvement Throughout the Several States*, (New York, 1840), 150, 244. Also see "Stevenson, Railways in America in 1837," 12.

9. *Ibid.*, 150.

10. Derrick, *South Carolina Railroad*, 42.

11. *Hunt's Merchants Magazine*, XXXVIII (March, 1858), 384. It was added that unless more trees were planted for use on railroads that "the forests of our country will not always support the heavy drain upon them required to keep up nearly 30,000 miles of railroads." Wooden rails on the Wilmington & Raleigh Railroad decayed so rapidly that the mail service from Raleigh to Gaston was shifted from daily deliveries to a tri-weekly basis. A. R. Newsome, "Simeon Colton's Railroad Report, 1840," *North Carolina Historical Review*, XI (July, 1934), 234. Also see Tanner, *A Description of the Canals and Railroads of the United States*, 170.

12. Lardner, *Railway Economy*, 337. Lardner said, however, he had "never met with a well authenticated case of this kind."

13. Shippee, *Bishop Whipple's Diary*, 76.

14. Pettengill, "Florida Railroads," 5–6.

15. Emory R. Johnson, *American Railway Transportation* (New York, 1908), 34–38. Included in these pages are excellent sketches of wooden, U and T-rails. Also see Max Dixon, "Building the Central Railroad of Georgia," *Georgia Historical Quarterly*, XLV (March, 1961), 1–21; Olmsted, *Cotton Kingdom*, 133.

16. Dunbar, *A History of Travel in America*, III 1041–1042.

17. Caroline E. MacGill, *History of Transportation in the United States Before 1860* (Washington, 1917), 313–314.

18. Dunbar, *A History of Travel in America*, IV, 1349.

19. The Louisville & Nashville Railroad, in making the change, used 8,000 men to convert its 2,000 miles of track, and adjusted the wheels of 300 locomotives and 10,000 pieces of rolling stock to conform to the standard gauge. C. Van Woodward, *Origins of the New South* (Baton Rouge, 1951), 123–124. Also see *Harper's Weekly*, XXX (June 5, 1886), 364; Phillips, *Transportation in the Eastern Cotton Belt*, 383; Herr, *The L & N Railroad*, 45–49.

20. Chevalier, *Society, Manners, and Politics*, 256.

21. Beauvallet, *Rachel and the New World*, 200–201.

22. Davies, *American Scenes*, 188.

23. *Ibid.*

24. Chambers, *Things As They Are in America*, 324.

25. Chevalier, *Society, Manners, and Politics*, 246.

26. Stevenson, "Railways in America in 1837," 14.

27. Kemble, *Georgian Plantation*, 13.

28. Weber, *Schliemann's First Visit*, 24.

29. *Niles' Weekly Register*, XLVIII (May 30, 1835), 218. Also see Tanner, *A Description of the Canals and Railroads of the United States*, 150.

30. Chevalier, *Society, Manners, and Politics*, 258. Also see Tudor, *A Tour in North America*, I, 79–80.

31. *North American Review*, XXVIII (January, 1829), 182.

32. *Atlantic Monthly*, II (November, 1858), 647, 648. Lardner, *Railway Economy*, 334.

33. Chevalier, *Society, Manners, and Politics*, 247.

34. Martineau, *Society in America*, II, 10.

35. Kellar, "A Journey Through the South in 1836," 373.

36. Stevenson, "Railways in America in 1837," 12. Also see Tanner, *A Description of the Canals and Railroads of the United States*, 169.

37. Lewis, *Impressions of America*, 146. A Mississippi bridge over the Big Black River, twelve miles from Vicksburg, was used during the travels of Sir Charles Lyell during the 1840's. Lyell described the structure as "a long wooden bridge and viaduct built on piles, nearly a mile in length." Further South in Louisiana he traveled on the Lake Pontchartrain Railroad, which was another railroad constructed on piles. Lyell, *A Second Visit to the United States*, II, 90, 160.

38. Murray, *Letters from the United States*, 194.

39. Chambers, *Things As They Are in America*, 325.

40. Mackay, *The Western World*, II, 151. Also see Crowe, *With Thackeray in America*, 130.

41. Pierce, *Incidents of Western Travel*, 140.

42. *Ibid.*, 139–140, 251.

43. Abbott, *South and North*, 127.

44. Beauvallet, *Rachel and the New World*, 296. Also see Dunbar, *A History of Travel in America*, III, 1053, for a vivid drawing of the results of poorly constructed bridges.

45. *Niles' Weekly Register*, XXXV (January 3, 1829), 299.

46. *The Museum*, XXII (January–June, 1833), 670.

47. *Atlantic Monthly*, II (November, 1858), 645, 646.

48. Dunbar, *A History of Travel in America*, III, 790–792, 796, 920.

49. *Niles' Weekly Register*, XL (November 19, 1831), 219. Also see *North American Review*, XXVIII (January, 1829), 178.

50. Derrick, *South Carolina Railroad*, 104–105. For descriptions of other inclines see Dunbar, *A History of Travel in America*, III, 790–792, 796, 920.

51. Chevalier, *Society, Manners, and Politics*, 76.

52. Crowe, *With Thackeray in America*, 126.

53. Tanner, *A Description of the Canals and Railroads of the United States,* 258.

54. William Couper, "Claudius Crozet, Soldier-Scholar-Educator-Engineer," *Southern Sketches,* VIII (1936), 140–141.

55. Chambers, *Things As They Are in America,* 324.

CHAPTER 6

1. Dunbar, *A History of Travel in America,* III, 1051.

2. The *American Railroad Journal* in 1858 stated that accidents were not necessarily caused by high speeds, but by inferior rail joints and weakened tracks that could not sustain the weight and stresses of speeding trains. In 1859 the *Journal* reported that with adequate tracks, trains could safely run at thirty miles per hour. *American Railroad Journal,* XXXI (August 7, 1858), 505; *Ibid.,* XXXII (March 5, 1859), 147.

3. Beauvallet, *Rachel and the New World,* 200.

4. *Hunt's Merchants Magazine,* XXXVIII (February, 1858), 240. *Ibid.,* XL (February, 1860), 252; *Ibid.,* XXXIII (August, 1855), 247–248. *American Railroad Journal,* XXVIII (October 27, 1855), 680, demanded that trespassing laws be enacted to keep persons off tracks, and stated that in 1855 more fatalities occurred on railroads by people being hit on the roadway than from any other cause. *Ibid.,* XXXI (September 11, 1858), 584–585.

5. *Hunt's Merchants Magazine,* XXI (December, 1849), 685. "We should like to see a careful estimate of the casualties on roads in the United States. They are not, we believe, any greater than those in England; while in that country the guards set up against danger are much more complete than in our own."

6. *American Railroad Journal,* XXXI (June 5, 1858), 355.

7. Black, *Railroads of the Confederacy,* 32. For a sampling of other numerous safety surveys of the 1850's see, *Hunt's Merchants Magazine,* XXXVII (November, 1857), 629; *Ibid.,* XXXIX (October, 1858), 504; *American Railroad Journal,* XXXI (May–June, 1858), 328, 355; *Atlantic Monthly,* II (November, 1858), 643.

8. By 1848 steamboats "were being blown up, burned, sunk by snags or otherwise destroyed at the rate of a hundred or more a year [which] . . . caused many people to avoid them altogether." Dunbar, *A History of Travel in America,* III, 1097–1098.

9. *North American Review,* L (January, 1840), 20. Concerning the railroads the *Review* portentously added that the "scene of danger and or risk to the traveller is about to be removed from the water to the land." 41.

10. *DeBow's Review,* VII (August, 1849), 183–189.

11. *Niles' Weekly Register,* LIV (May 5, 1838), 160. It was estimated that 125 lives were lost on the *Moselle,* included was the captain who was blamed for the accident by racing his ship. For another graphic account

of an explosion see George Rogers, *Memoranda of the Experience, Labors, and Travels of a Universalist Preacher* (Cincinnati, 1845), 288.

12. Leading guidebooks and magazines of the day often carried accounts of rail disasters such as the following. "Boilers are bursting all over the country—rail-road bridges breaking and rails snapping—human life is sadly and foolishly squandered—but nobody is to blame. Boilers burst themselves. Rails break themselves. And it may be questioned whether the consequent slaughter of men, women and children is not really suicide. Cited in Dunbar, *A History of Travel in America*, III, 1057.

13. Wellington Williams, *Williams Traveller's Guide Through the United States and Canada* (Philadelphia, 1858), 199.

14. *Hunt's Merchants Magazine*, XXXIII (August, 1855), 247–248.

15. *American Railroad Journal*, XXV (September 11, 1852), 584. The most disastrous steamboat explosion in the United States occurred on April 27, 1865, when the *Sultana* exploded on the Mississippi River near Memphis, taking 1,450 lives.

16. William Kingsford, *Impressions of the West and South* (Toronto, 1858), 42.

17. Rogers, *Travels of a Universalist Preacher*, 263.

18. *DeBow's Review*, XXIV (June, 1858), 567–568, and Dunbar, *A History of Travel in America*, III, 963. The Negro fireman died from the injury received. See Derrick, *South Carolina Railroad*, 83–84.

19. Dunbar, *A History of Travel in America*, III, 964.

20. *American Railroad Journal*, XXIII (March 30, 1850), 197.

21. *Ibid.*, XXII (April 7, 1849), 209–212.

22. *Ibid.*, XXII (November 17, 1849), 725.

23. *Ibid.*, XXVI (September 3, 1853), 567.

24. Henry Jewell, *Life and Writings of Reverend Enoch M. Pingree* (Cincinnati, 1850), 74.

25. *American Railroad Journal*, XXVI (July 2, 1853), 426.

26. Dunbar, *A History of Travel in America*, III, 992.

27. Stewart H. Holbrook, *The Story of American Railroads* (New York, 1947), 8. Also see *Niles' Weekly Register*, XLIV (April 20, 1833), 115; *Ibid.*, XLV (September 28, 1833), 70.

28. Dunbar, *A History of Travel in America*, III, 1042.

29. Holbrook, *The Story of American Railroads*, 34.

30. Biggs, *To America in Thirty-nine Days*, 11.

31. *Niles' Weekly Register*, XLVIII (May 23, 1835), 204.

32. Murray, *Letters from the United States*, 188. Cattlemen were often indifferent to their cattle being "smashed now and then," since the railroad paid for the animals. This arrangement to the *American Railroad Journal* was the most expedient, since the companies were likely to lose a law suit in the local courts. *American Railroad Journal*, XI (January 15, 1843), 45.

33. Murray, *Lands of the Slave and the Free*, I, 61.

34. Murray, *Letters From the United States*, 277.

35. Lyell, *A Second Visit to the United States,* I, 218–219.

36. Murray, *Letters From the United States,* 276–277.

37. Charles Heartman, ed., *An Immigrant of A Hundred Years Ago: A Story of Someone's Ancestor* (Hattiesburg, Mississippi, 1941), 32. Livestock often stood or laid on roadbeds, because the gravel roads provided dry places to rest. Charles Weld related that he once heard of a flock of 180 sheep lying on a track, of which the greater portion "were summarily converted into mutton." Weld, *A Vacation Tour in the United States,* 65, 66.

38. Ingraham, *The Southwest,* I, 175.

39. Gunnar J. Malmin, trans., *America in the Forties; The Letters of Ole Munch Raeder* (Minneapolis, 1929), 159–161.

40. John Hammond Moore, "A South Carolina Lawyer Visits St. Augustine—1837," *The Florida Historical Quarterly,* XLIII (April, 1965), 362.

41. Cited in Phillips, *Transportation in the Eastern Cotton Belt,* 236. The *American Railroad Journal* in 1858 advised that it was unsafe for two engines to pull one train, since the second engineer cannot see signals of danger. *American Railroad Journal,* XXXI (September 18, 1858), 600–601.

42. Clark, *A Pioneer Southern Railroad,* 131–132. A similar accident was reported in *Niles' Weekly Register* in 1834. "It is stated in the *Louisiana Advertiser* of the 10th ult, that 'yesterday the *Creole,* of the rail road, being ready to start for the city, with several cars attached, having been left by the engineer for a few moments, started backwards with full steam, and safely deposited itself and cars in twelve feet of water at the end of the wharf.' " *Niles' Weekly Register,* XLVII (October 11, 1834), 83.

43. Weld, *A Vacation Tour in the United States,* 246–252.

44. Murray, *Lands of the Slave and the Free,* I, 382–383.

45. Murray, *Letters From the United States,* 275.

46. Davies, *American Scenes,* 188–189.

47. Pierce, *Incidents of Western Travel,* 16, 136.

48. Concerning this accident, and with reference to the Baltimore & Ohio Railroad, *Niles' Weekly Register* commented: "It is now about three years and a half since the travelling on the Baltimore and Ohio rail road was commenced, and more than three hundred thousand passengers have since travelled on it without a single instance of serious injury, to life or limb, having occurred to any one of them." *Niles' Weekly Register,* XLV (November 16, 1833), 179. *Ibid.,* XLV (November 23, 1833), 204–205.

49. For a photograph of Mrs. Pierce and her nine year old son Bennie in 1850, see *Life,* July 5, 1968, 68. An account of the disaster may be found in the *New York Daily Times* (January 7, 1853), 1. After the inauguration of President Garfield in 1881, the former President, Hayes, departed Washington in a special car of the Baltimore & Potomac Railroad, and when a few miles out of the city his train colided with another. The former President was thrown from his chair, and two passengers were killed. Kane, *Facts About the Presidents,* 222, 223.

50. *Niles' Weekly Register*, XLVII (February 14, 1835), 413.

51. George Combe, *Notes on the United States of North America, During a Phrenological Visit in 1838–9–40* (Philadelphia, 1841), I, 281.

52. Tyrone Power, *Impressions of America, During the Years 1833, 1834, 1835* (London, 1836), I, 131–133.

53. *American Railroad Journal*, XXVIII (December 15, 1855), 796.

54. Derrick, *South Carolina Railroad*, 88, 89.

55. *Ibid.*, 309–311.

56. Dunbar, *A History of Travel in America*, III, 1059–1060.

57. Phillips, *Transportation in the Eastern Cotton Belt*, 154.

58. Lanman, *Adventures in the United States*, II, 98.

59. Dunbar, *A History of Travel in America*, III, 1059–1060.

60. The first telegraph was installed in service in 1844, but not used by a railroad as an aid to traffic until 1851. *Ibid.*, 1045.

61. *Ibid.*, 1026–1027.

62. *American Railroad Journal*, XXXI (September 25, 1858), 616.

63. Chambers, *Things As They Are in America*, 335–336. These signs were also mentioned by other travelers. See Weld, *A Vacation Tour in the United States*, 66–67, and Dickens, *American Notes*, 82. Dickens' description read: "It rushes across the turnpike road, where there is no gate, no policeman, no signal: nothing but a rough wooden arch, on which is painted, 'WHEN THE BELL RINGS, LOOK OUT FOR THE LOCOMOTIVE.' "

64. *Hunt's Merchants Magazine*, XXXII (March, 1855), 380.

65. Dunbar, *A History of Travel in America*, III, 934–935.

66. *American Railroad Journal*, XXVI (August 27, 1853), 555.

67. *Ibid.*, (May 9, 1857), 292. *Hunt's Merchants Magazine*, XXXVIII (May, 1858), 633.

68. *Hunt's Merchants Magazine*, XXXII (March, 1855), 380; *Ibid.*, XXXVIII (April, 1858), 491.

69. Charles A. Goodrich, *The Universal Traveller: Designed to Introduce Readers at Home to an Acquaintance with the Arts, Customs, and Manners, of the Principal Modern Nations of the Globe* (Hartford, 1838), 33, 34.

70. Lardner, *Railway Economy*, 337. At approximately the same time, in 1838, Fanny Kemble offered the following comments concerning the safety of passengers on railroads. "It is a curious fact enough, that half the routes that are traveled in America are either temporary or unfinished—one reason, among several, for the multitudinous accidents which befall wayfarers." Kemble, *Georgian Plantation*, 12.

71. Dunbar, *A History of Travel in America*, III, 1056.

CHAPTER 7

1. For instance, the first depot in the nation's capitol was built of brick and opened in 1835. The terminal was a renovated three-story house purchased by the Baltimore & Ohio Railroad. See Carroll Louis Vander-

slice Meeks, *The Railroad Station, An Architectural History* (New Haven, 1956), 49, 50.

2. One example of this is that American stations were never attracted to installing "carriage docks." These were private stalls used in the days of horse-cars where the "lordly" boarded their train in privacy. *Ibid.*, 33.

3. *Ibid.*, 51.

4. *American Railroad Journal*, XXV (August 28, 1852), 549.

5. Ledet, "History of Carrollton," 240.

6. *American Railroad Journal*, XXVIII (September 15, 1855), 587–588. In 1856 Carlton Rogers described the Macon depot as "one of the finest depots that I had seen since I left the North." Rogers, *Incidents of Travel*, 235.

7. Herr, *The L & N Railroad*, 19.

8. Meeks, *The Railroad Station*, 50, 51.

9. Lanman, *Adventures in the United States*, II, 96. Other travelers, such as James Stirling, also mentioned the isolation of some stations. "Few towns or villages are to be seen even at the stations of the railway. James Stirling, *Letters From the Slave States* (London, 1857), 178.

10. Mackay, *Life and Liberty in America*, 284–285. Lardner, *Railway Economy*, 334.

11. Cited in Jack K. Williams, "Travel in Ante-Bellum Georgia as Recorded by English Visitors," *Georgia Historical Quarterly*, XXXIII (September, 1949), 201.

12. Chambers, *Things As They Are in America*, 327.

13. Dickens, *American Notes*, 82.

14. Kemble, *Georgian Plantation*, 19.

15. Lillian Foster, *Way-Side Glimpses North and South* (New York, 1860), 92, 181. Over-hanging eaves were extended much further than in Europe, and became an identifying characteristic of American stations. Meeks, *The Railroad Station*, 48–49.

16. Charles Grandison Parsons, *Inside View of Slavery: Or A Tour Among the Planters* (Cleveland, 1855), 21–23, 28.

17. Mackay, *Life and Liberty in America*, 202. Also see Fredrika Bremer, *The Homes of the New World; Impressions of America*, III (London, 1853), 358.

18. Murray, *Lands of the Slave and the Free*, II, 146.

19. Mackay, *The Western World*, I, 157.

20. Murray, *Lands of the Slave and the Free*, II, 146.

21. Hundley, *Social Relations in Our Southern States*, 178.

22. Lyell, *A Second Visit to the United States*, II, 264.

23. Chambers, *Things As They Are in America*, 326–327.

24. Weber, *Schliemann's First Visit*, 24.

25. Mackay, *Life and Liberty in America*, 284.

26. *American Railroad Journal*, XXVII (July 1, 1854), 405.

27. Kellar, "A Journey Through the South in 1836," 373.

28. Edward Waylen, *Ecclesiastical Reminiscences of the United States* (New York, 1846), 192.

29. Weld, *A Vacation Tour in the United States*, 287. Passenger Weld also added that one was not to trust the porters carrying baggage to the hotel.

30. Shippee, *Bishop Whipple's Diary*, 94.

31. Wellington Williams, *The Traveller's and Tourist's Guide Through the United States, Canada, etc.* (Philadelphia, 1855), 169.

32. John Disturnell, *Disturnell's American and European Railway and Steamship Guide* (Published by the author, 1853), 6.

33. The Lake Pontchartrain Railroad depot was described by Abraham Hall as "hidden away in a labyrinth of dingy houses." Hall, *The Manhattaner in New Orleans*, 112.

34. Mackay, *Life and Liberty in America*, 179.

35. Archibald Maxwell, *A Run Through the United States During the Autumn of 1840* (London, 1841), 183.

36. Yoseloff, *Journal of Thomas Cather*, 142. Of American democracy Cather said, "At present in the United States, democracy is absolutely running to seed and if the popular feeling which at present exists continue for some years longer it will make sad work of the constitution." *Ibid.*, 137.

37. The sexes were separated in the Weldon, North Carolina depot by a large folding door. Kemble, *Georgian Plantation*, 21.

38. Cited in Phillips, *Transportation in the Eastern Cotton Belt*, 156–158. Sub-standard conditions in the South during the early 1830's were also reported in some travel guides. "Persons who travel in the southern states, go chiefly for business or health, for few would travel for pleasure. The three great requisites for agreeable travelling are wanting;—good roads, good vehicles, and good inns. . . . The public vehicles are not often easy or comfortable, and the better way of travelling is on horseback." S. G. Goodrich, *A System of Universal Geography, Popular and Scientific, Comprising A Physical, Political, and Statistical Account of the World and Its Various Divisions; Embracing Numerous Sketches From Recent Travels* (Boston, 1832), 261.

39. Rogers, *Incidents of Travel*, 270.

40. George William Featherstonhaugh, *Excursion Through the Slave States, From Washington on the Potomac to the Frontier of Mexico* (London, 1844), 11. For additional information concerning Barnum's Hotel see Doris Elizabeth King, "The First-Class Hotel and the Age of the Common Man," *Journal of Southern History*, XXIII (May, 1957), 173–188.

41. Several typical advertisements in guidebooks of the 1850's are those in Williams' *Traveller's and Tourist's Guide Through the United States*, 141, 179, 184 and *Disturnell's Guide*, 168. Representative of the numerous patent medicine advertisements placed in stations, cars, and guides was a panacea of the early 1850's called "SANDS SARSAPARILLA." The tonic was sold in quart bottles and was intended "FOR THE REMOVAL and permanent cure of all diseases arising from an impure state of the blood, or habit of the system." The cost for this wonder was listed as one dollar, the price of which would aid "General Prostration of the Vital Powers. . . ." Road and mileage information was terse and specific:

From Atlanta, Ga., 293 miles from Nashville, a place on the above Route, diverges a railroad to Montgomery, Ala., via West Point. This road forms a link in the southern route of travel between the North and South, extending to N. Orleans.

The *Richmond and Danville R. R.* will soon be completed to Greensboro', N.C., where it will connect with the *North Carolina Central R. R.*

42. Chambers, *Things As They Are in America*, 330.

43 Derrick, *South Carolina Railroad*, 93, 217.

44. *DeBow's Review*, XII (June, 1852), 678.

45. Williams, *Traveller's and Tourist's Guide Through the United States*, 188.

46. Disturnell, *Disturnell's Guide*, 15.

47. Quoted in Thomas D. Clark, *A Pioneer Southern Railroad from New Orleans to Cairo* (Chapel Hill, 1936), 133.

48. Mackay, *Life and Liberty in America*, 285. William Chambers stated that some passengers bought the tickets on board the train rather than bother with purchasing them in the stations. Chambers, *Things As They Are in America*, 330–331.

49. Clark, *A Pioneer Southern Railroad*, 133.

50. Ingraham, *The Southwest*, I, 172.

51. Bryant, *Letters of a Traveller*, 80.

52. Stephen L. Massey, *James Traveler's Companion* (Cincinnati, 1851), 68.

53. Dunbar, *A History of Travel in America*, III, 1122–1123.

54. Clark, *A Pioneer Southern Railroad*, 133.

55. Derrick, *South Carolina Railroad*, 309.

56. The nation's railroads did not adopt a standard time-table until October 18, 1883, when four time belts were incorporated. Holbrook, *The Story of American Railroads*, 12, 13.

57. Henry A. Murray stated that each passenger was given a "brass ticket" that had a duplicate. The second plate was used by the passenger. In the event an article was lost the company was held responsible. Murray, *Lands of the Slave and the Free*, I, 48.

58. Chambers, *Things As They Are in America*, 333–334.

59. Davies, *American Scenes*, 187.

60. Nichols, *Forty Years of American Life*, 76. Also see *Hunt's Merchants Magazine*, XIII (December, 1845), 581–582.

61. *United States Commercial & Statistical Register*, I (August 21, 1839), 131.

62. *Hunt's Merchants Magazine*, XVIII (March, 1848), 334.

63. *Ibid.*, XXI (December, 1849), 683.

64. *Ibid.*, XXVII (July, 1852), 75, 76.

65. Lyell, *Second Visit to the United States*, II, 38.

66. *American Railroad Journal*, XXV (December 18, 1852), 811.

67. Hamilton, *Manners in America*, II, 158. Also see Malmin, *The Letters of Ole Munch Raeder*, who listed the price of breakfast at 50 cents. 162.

68. Bremer, *The Homes of the New World,* I, 346.
69. Chambers, *Things As They Are in America,* 324–325. The Charleston & Hamburg Railroad allowed twenty minutes for meals. Derrick, *South Carolina Railroad,* 111. Charles Mackay commented that in 1858 that between ten to fifteen minutes was allowed for breakfast and diner. Mackay, *Life and Liberty in America,* 218.
70. William Thomson, *A Trademan's Travels, in the United States and Canada, in the Years 1840, 41, & 42* (Edinburgh, 1842), 44.
71. Kemble, *Georgian Plantation,* 20.
72. Shaw, *A Ramble Through the United States,* 205.
73. Murray, *Lands of the Slave and the Free,* I, 36.
74. Bryant, *Letters of a Traveller,* 71.
75. Marryat, *A Diary in America,* 9–10.

CHAPTER 8

1. Some passengers referred to cars reserved only for whites as first class cars, whereas those specifically designated for Negroes and slaves were called second and third class cars.
2. Murray, *Lands of the Slave and the Free,* II, 147.
3. Nichols, *Forty Years of American Life,* 79.
4. Cawley, *American Diaries of Richard Cobden,* 208; Lardner, *Railroad Economy,* 337, 346. One reason for the absence of classes in American cars, according to Lardner, was because Americans disliked being relegated to a lower standard, characterized by lower fares and inferior accommodations. This fact generally promoted a classless system in cars with only one fare and one class.
5. Chambers, *Things As They Are in America,* 271.
6. Davies, *American Scenes,* 187. Alexander Mackay reported: "There are no distinctions of class on American railways, all the carriages being first class, or second class carriages, just as the traveller may please to view them." Mackay, *The Western World,* II, 249. Some other arrangements which smacked of class distinction was the designation of smoking cars and reserved sections for ladies. See Carroll H. Quenzel, "The Manufacture of Locomotives and Cars in Alexandria in the 1850's," *Virginia Magazine of History and Biography,* LXII (April, 1954), 189; Angus J. Johnson, "Virginia Railroads in April 1861," *Journal of Southern History,* XXIII (August, 1957), 324.
7. Yoseloff, *Journal of Thomas Cather,* 24, 134, 136, 137, 142.
8. Nichols, *Forty Years of American Life,* 79.
9. George William Featherstonhaugh, *A Canoe Voyage up the Minnay Sotor; With an Account of the Land and Copper Deposits in Wisconsin; of the Gold Region in the Cherokee Country; and Sketches of Popular Manners* (London, 1847), II, 187–188. Another passenger who mentioned cursing in the South was Sir Charles Lyell, *A Second Visit to the United States,* II, 38. An excellent sampling of "cracker talk" can be found in Rogers, *Incidents of Travel,* 260–265.

10. Davies, *American Scenes*, 187.
11. Wortley, *Travels in the United States*, 142–143.
12. Shaw, *A Ramble Through the United States*, 212.
13. Nichols, *Forty Years of American Life*, 78.
14. Dickens, *American Notes*, 80–82.
15. Shippee, *Bishop Whipple's Diary*, 75.
16. Murray, *Lands of the Slave and the Free*, I, 36.
17. Murray, *Letters from the United States*, 186.
18. Lanman, *Adventures in the United States*, II, 96–97.
19. Mackay, *Life and Liberty in America*, 219–220.
20. Combe, *Notes on the United States*, I, 46. Combe added the Germans and French chewed, "although England is happily free from it."
21. Murray, *Lands of the Slave and the Free*, I, 138.
22. Buckingham, *Slave States of America*, II, 123.
23. Biggs, *To America in Thirty-nine Days*, 20. Most travelers reported that chewing was socially unacceptable in the presence of ladies.
24. Nichols, *Forty Years of American Life*, 80.
25. Mackay, *The Western World*, I, 150–151.
26. *Ibid.*, 151–152.
27. Quoted in Williams, "Travel in Ante-Bellum Georgia," 164.
28. Mackay, *The Western World*, I, 152.
29. Lillian Foster proposed regulations against depositing "apple-parings and paw-paws" on the floors as well as "crumbs of bread and cheese." "The human animal has no more right to chew tobacco and strew nuisance upon the floor of a public conveyance, at the expense of other people's comfort, than he has in a public parlor." Foster, *Way-Side Glimpses North and South*, 132.
30. Today in certain sections of the country one can still find signs warning chewers not to spit on courthouse floors.
31. Abbott's comments concerning railroads were very limited. However, he did observe "about one hundred" young male slaves packed in the "negro cars" on their way to South Carolina. Abbott, *South and North*, 227–228.
32. Parsons, *Inside View of Slavery*, 122. Harriet Beecher Stowe asserted Parsons' book was "the simple, straight-forward narrative of an impartial witness."
33. Edward Alfred Pollard, *Black Diamonds Gathered in the Darkey Homes of the South* (New York, 1860), 22.
34. Frederick Law Olmsted, *The Slave States* (New York, 1959), 47, 48. Edited by Harvey Wish.
35. Dickens, *American Notes*, 158.
36. Mackay, *The Western World*, I, 154–155. A strange contrast to this episode was the installment of a Negro sleeping car on the Central of Georgia Railroad in 1858. See Ulrich Bonnell Phillips, *American Negro Slavery* (New York, 1918), 201–202.
37. For the treatment of the antebellum Northern Negro see Leon F. Litwack, *North of Slavery: The Negro in the Free States, 1790–1860* (Chicago, 1961).

38. Dickens, *American Notes*, 79. Pro-slavery remarks concerning the Northern free Negro can be found in *DeBow's Review*, XXVIII (May, 1860), 573–581.

39. Chevalier, *Society, Manners, and Politics*, 349.

40. Nichols, *Forty Years of American Life*, 336.

41. David W. Mitchell, *Ten Years Residence in the United States; Being an Englishman's View of Men and Things in the North and South* (London, 1862), 17.

42. Crowe, *With Thackeray in America*, 104–105.

43. Parsons, *Inside View of Slavery*, 296–299.

44. Biggs, *To America in Thirty-nine Days*, 22.

45. Weld, *A Vacation Tour in the United States*, 245.

46. Lardner, *Railway Economy*, 346. Joseph Ingraham observed, on the Lake Pontchartrain Railroad in Louisiana, that the rear two or three coaches of his train were reserved for "coloured gentlemen and ladies." *The Southwest*, I, 172. Ebenezer Davies reported that Negroes had to sit in the "luggage-van." *American Scenes*, 187. According to Olmsted, the car used for hauling slaves was called the "servant's car." *Cotton Kingdom*, 126.

47. Stirling, *Letters from the Slave States*, 53–54.

48. One Southern lady stated that she did not object to sitting next to a "fat Negro woman" even when the temperature climbed to the 90's, provided her fellow travelers understood the Negro was her property. Samuel Eliot Morison and Henry Steele Commager, *The Growth of the American Republic* (New York, 1962), I, 526.

49. Biggs, *To America in Thirty-nine Days*, 19.

50. Marryat, *A Diary in America*, 8.

51. Dickens, *American Notes*, 79.

52. Nichols, *Forty Years of American Life*, 79. Miss Mendell noted that Southern ladies hardly ever traveled alone over twenty miles from home, unless they were placed under someone's care. *Notes of Travel and Life*, 183. Charles Dickens found that any woman in America could travel alone and expect "the most courteous and considerate treatment everywhere." Dickens, *American Notes*, 80.

53. Charles Dickens commented, "There are no first and second class carriages as with us; but there is a gentlemen's car and a ladies' car; the main distinction between which is, that in the first everybody smokes; and in the second, nobody does." *American Notes*, 79.

54. Weld, *A Vacation Tour in the United States*, 239.

55. Combe, Notes on the United States, I, 263. Fanny Kemble reported a compartment furnished for ladies in a Baltimore & Ohio Railroad car which was of "comfortable dimensions, and without a stove." *Georgian Plantation*, 14.

56. Lardner, *Railway Economy*, 337.

57. Malmin, *The Letters of Ole Munch Raeder*, 159–160.

58. Adams, *Railroads: Their Origin and Problems*, 73, 74.

59. Although the conductor's word was supreme authority on trains, they were not necessarily the highest paid. On the Charlotte & South Carolina Railroad engineers received $45 to $100 per month, while conductors were paid $60 per month. For general work laborers were paid $12.50. *Stockholders Report December 31, 1856,* 28–29.

60. The weekly opposed uniforms for the other crewmen as well. *American Railroad Journal,* XXVIII (September 1, 1855), 395.

61. The conductor's duties were usually determined by the company. According to *Miller's Almanac,* in 1835 the Charleston & Hamburg Railroad established the following rules:

1. All baggage at owner's risk, 75 lbs. allowed
2. Servants not admitted in cars, unless having care of children, without the consent of the passengers.
3. Passengers not allowed to stand on the outside platform.
4. Smoking prohibited.
5. No guns allowed unless examined by the conductor.
6. Feet not to be put on seats, nor cars to be soiled, defaced or injured in any way.
7. Dogs not admitted in the passenger cars.
8. At the sound of the bell passengers will be allowed one minute to take their places.
9. Seats must be claimed fifteen minutes before departure.
10. Conductors will insure good conduct of the passengers.
Cited from Phillips, *Transportation in the Eastern Cotton Belt,* 165.

62. Chambers, *Things As They Are in America,* 331–332.

63. Mendell, *Notes of Travel and Life,* 157.

64. Foster, *Way-Side Glimpses North and South,* 104.

65. Kellar, *Solon Robinson, Pioneer and Agriculturist,* II, 387.

66. Dickens, *American Notes,* 80.

67. Weld, *A Vacation Tour in the United States,* 246.

68. Mackay, *Life and Liberty in America,* 285.

69. Lyell, *A Second Visit to the United States,* II, 38.

70. Pierce, *Incidents of Western Travel,* 137–138.

71. Shaw, *A Ramble Through the United States,* 206.

72. Olmsted, *Slave States,* 44–45.

73. Mitchell, *Ten Years in the United States,* 8.

74. John Robert Godley, *Letters from America* (London, 1844), I, 30, II, 188.

75. Chambers, *Things As They Are in America,* 270. Raeder and Lyell reported that spitting was not as common in the United States as generally believed. Tremenheere stated that travelers remember annoyances more than favorable observations.

76. The traveler reported that "A great decency is observable among the people. I did not in all my travels see an individual obeying the call of nature in any corner however secluded. Was told by a person to whom I mentioned this that it would not be permitted by the police." Cawley, *American Diaries of Richard Cobden,* 208–209.

77. Harriet Martineau, *Retrospect of Western Travel* (London, 1838), I, 234, II, 37.

78. Kellar, "A Journey Through the South in 1836," 367.

79. Hamilton, *Manners in America*, II, 4.

CHAPTER 9

1. Nichols, *Forty Years of American Life*, 71.

2. Chevalier, *Society, Manners, and Politics*, 297.

3. See Thomas D. Clark, *Travels in the Old South* (Norman, Oklahoma, 1959), III, 3–11.

4. Crowe, *With Thackeray in America*, 136.

5. Kemble, *Georgian Plantation*, 17.

6. At another point along the road Olmsted reported, "At a way-station a trader had ready a company of negroes intended to be shipped South; but the 'servant's car' being quite full already, they were obliged to be left for another train." Olmsted, *Cotton Kingdom*, 31, 126.

7. Shaw, *A Ramble Through the United States*, 207.

8. Olmsted, *Cotton Kingdom*, 133.

9. Kemble, *Georgian Plantation*, 18.

10. Shaw, *A Ramble Through the United States*, 200.

11. Bremer, *The Homes of the New World*, III, 312.

12. Mackay, *Life and Liberty in America*, 208.

13. Stirling, *Letters from the Slave States*, 264.

14. Lewis, *Impressions of America*, 113–114.

15. Margaret Hall, *The Aristocratic Journey; Being the Outspoken Letters of Mrs. Basil Hall Written During a Fourteen Months' Sojourn in America, 1827–1828* (New York, 1931), 208. Edited by Una Pope-Hennessy.

16. Basil Hall, *Travels in North America in the Years 1827 and 1828* (Edinburg, 1829), III, 172–173.

17. Hall, *The Aristocratic Journey*, 213.

18. Achille Murat, *America and the Americans*, trans. W. H. Graham (New York, 1849), 17. James D. Davidson wrote in 1836: "I am now in this Southern City of Aristocrats. But it is not objectionable on that account. The true aristocrat is a plain generous man. The people of Charleston move in high style, but their manners are plain and generous." Kellar, "A Journey Through the South in 1836," 373.

19. Rogers, *Incidents of Travel*, 50–51.

20. Bremer, *The Homes of the New World*, I, 329.

21. Buckingham, *Slave States of America*, II, 2.

22. Foster, *Way-Side Glimpses North and South*, 89.

23. Abbott, *South and North*, 206.

24. Stirling, *Letters from the Slave States*, 200.

25. *Ibid.*, 205.

26. Olmsted, *Cotton Kingdom*, 212.

27. Rogers, *Incidents of Travel*, 236.

28. Foster, *Way-Side Glimpses North and South*, 99.

29. Kellar, *Solon Robinson, Pioneer and Agriculturist*, II, 468.
30. Shippee, *Bishop Whipple's Diary*, 76.
31. *Ibid.*, 74.
32. Shaw, *A Ramble Through the United States*, 207.
33. Lanman, *Adventures in the United States*, II, 150.
34. Featherstonhaugh, *A Canoe Voyage Up the Minnay Sotor*, II, 186.
35. Murray, *Letters from the United States*, 310.
36. Heartman, *An Immigrant of A Hundred Years Ago*, 32–33.
37. Ingraham, *The Southwest*, I, 173.
38. Pulszky, *Sketches of Society in the United States*, II, 110.
39. Martineau, *Society in America*, II, 8.
40. Marryat, *A Diary in America*, 9.
41. Bremer, *The Homes of the New World*, I, 346.
42. Dickens, *American Notes*, 79.
43. Mackay, *Life and Liberty in America*, 224, 237.
44. Nichols, *Forty Years of American Life*, 161.
45. Biggs, *To America in Thirty-nine Days*, 12, 15.
46. Beauvallet, *Rachel and the New World*, 298.
47. Bryant, *Letters of a Traveller*, 77–78.
48. Lanman, *Adventures in the United States*, II, 96.
49. Beauvallet, *Rachel and the New World*, 296. Olmsted was informed by the conductor he would haye to cross eighty miles in South Carolina by coach. To inform him of the arrival of the carriage the conductor told him a signal would be sounded on the locomotive whistle. Olmsted, *Cotton Kingdom*, 155.
50. Harriet Martineau's journey was delayed by a ruptured engine boiler. "At half-past four, our boiler sprang a leak, and there was an end of our prosperity. In two hours, we hungry passengers were consoled with the news that it was mended. But the same thing happened, again and again; and always in the middle of a swamp, where we could do nothing but sit still." Martineau, *Society in America*, II, 10.
51. Olmsted, *Cotton Kingdom*, 155.
52. Murray, *Letters from the United States*, 275–276.
53. Martineau, *Society in America*, II, 10.
54. Weld, *A Vacation Tour in the United States*, 67.
55. Foster, *Way-Side Glimpses North and South*, 89.
56. Nichols, *Forty Years of American Life*, 160.
57. Crowe, *With Thackeray in America*, 141–142.
58. Tanner, *A Description of the Canals and Railroads of the United States*, 176.
59. Bremer, *The Homes of the New World*, III, 353. Passengers who sought diversion within the cars were given some sage advice by the *Merchant's Almanac* in 1855. Lest insomnia should lead to bad manners, the *Almanac* admonished, "If you cannot sleep, don't prevent others from doing so by whistling." The magazine also warned passengers not to sit beside a traveler with an ear trumpet, since it "may be clogged, forcing unusual exertions upon your lungs and larynx when you attempt

conversation, thus also upsetting your fellow passengers." As a final bit of practical wisdom, the *Almanac* cautioned that one should "never sit in a seat, in warm weather, with a man weighing 244 pounds."

60. Sigmund Diamond, ed., *A Casual View of America: The Home Letters of Salomon de Rothschild, 1859–1861* (Stanford, California, 1961), 32.

61. See E. G. Campbell, "Railroads in National Defense, 1829–1848," *Mississippi Valley Historical Review,* XXVII (December, 1940), 361–378.

EPILOGUE

1. See Black, *Railroads of the Confederacy,* 1–11, 294–295, and Charles W. Ramsdell, "The Confederate Government and the Railroads," *American Historical Review,* XXII (July, 1917), 795.

2. Jefferson Davis, *The Rise and Fall of the Confederate Government* (New York, 1958), I, 315.

3. John F. Stover, "The Ruined Railroads of the Confederacy," *Georgia Historical Quarterly,* XLII (December, 1958), 376.

4. Black, "Railroads of the Confederacy," 236.

5. Stover, "Ruined Railroads of the Confederacy," 376–388. Four travelers who visited the South in 1865 and recorded their observations were: Sidney Andrews, *The South Since the War* (Boston, 1866); Whitelaw Reid, *After the War: A Southern Tour* (Cincinnati, 1866); John T. Trowbridge, *The South: A Tour of its Battlefields and Ruined Cities* (Hartford, 1866), and John H. Kennaway, *On Sherman's Track: Or the South After the War* (London, 1867).

6. Such dim views are refuted by some writers who maintain the roads were not as bad as commonly believed. James F. Doster, for instance, maintains that while it is commonly accepted that "the bankruptcies of the Southern railroads grew out of the military damage of the Civil War, these bankruptcies actually occurred from five to fifteen years after the war ended." James F. Doster, "Were the Southern Railroads Destroyed by the Civil War?" *Civil War History,* VII (September, 1961), 320.

7. Sometimes these guidebooks carried humorous anecdotes about the war. One was entitled "The Practical Soldier." "A soldier in one of the late battles, sitting very cooly behind one of his guns, where the shot was falling fast, being asked by the chaplain whether he was supported by Divine Providence, replied, 'No Sir; I am supported by the Ninth New Jersey.' " G. F. Thomas, *Appletons' Illustrated Railway and Steam Navigation Guide* (New York, August, 1864), 63.

8. *Ibid.,* 41, 58–61.

9. R. T. Addison, ed., *Appleton's Companion Handbook* (New York, 1866), 6–8.

10. Dickens, *American Notes,* 83.

Bibliography

BOOKS

Primary Sources

Abbott, John S. C., *South and North; Or Impressions Received During a Trip to Cuba and the South*. New York: Abbey & Abbott, 1860.

Alexander, James Edward, *Transatlantic Sketches, Comprising Visits to the Most Interesting Scenes in North and South America, and the West Indies. With Notes on Negro Slavery and Canadian Emigration*. 2 vols. London: R. Bentley, 1833.

Arese, Francesco Conte, *A Trip to the Prairies and in the Interior of North America (1837–1838)*. Translated by Andrew Evans. New York: The Harbor Press, 1934.

Beauvallet, Léon, *Rachel and the New World. A Trip to the United States and Cuba*. New York: Dix, Edwards & Company, 1856.

Biggs, Joseph, *To America in Thirty-nine Days Before Steamships Crossed the Atlantic*. Idbury, England: The Village Press, 1927.

Bremer, Fredrika, *The Homes of the New World; Impressions of America*. 3 vols. Translated by Mary Howitt. London: Arthur Hall, Virtue, & Company, 1853.

Bryant, William Cullen, *Letters of a Traveller; Or, Notes of Things Seen in Europe and America*. New York: George P. Putnam, 1850.

Buckingham, James Silk, *America, Historical, Statistical and Descriptical*. 3 vols. London: Fisher, Son & Company, 1842.

———, *The Eastern and Western States of America*. 3 vols. London: Fisher, Son, & Company, 1842.

———, *The Slave States of America*. 2 vols. London: Fisher, Son, & Company, 1842.

Cawley, Elizabeth Hoon, ed., *The American Diaries of Richard Cobden*. Princeton University Press, 1952.

Chambers, William, *Things as They Are in America*. Philadelphia: Lippincott, Grambo & Company, 1854.

Chapin, William, *A Complete Reference Gazetteer of the United States of North America*. New York: William Chapin and J. B. Taylor, 1839.

Chevalier, Michael, *Society, Manners, and Politics in the United States: Letters on North America*. Translated after the Thomas G. Bradford edition. New York: Doubleday & Company, Inc., 1961.

Colton, Joseph Hutchins, *Colton's Traveler and Tourist's Guide Book Through the United States of America and the Canadas: Containing the Routes and Distances on the Great Lines of Travel by Railroads, Canals, Stageroads, and Steamboats; Together with Descriptions of the Several States, and of the Principal Cities, Towns, and Villages in Each.* New York: J. H. Colton, 1856.

Combe, George, *Notes on the United States of North America, During a Phrenological Visit in 1838–9–40.* 2 vols. Philadelphia: Carey & Hart, 1841.

Crockett, David, *An Account of Col. Crockett's Tour to the North and Down East.* New York: Nafis & Cornish, 1845.

Crowe, Eyre, *With Thackeray in America.* New York: Charles Scribner's Sons, 1893.

Davies, Ebenezer, *American Scenes and Christian Slavery: A Recent Tour of Four Thousand Miles in the United States.* London: John Snow, 1849.

Davis, Jefferson, *The Rise and Fall of the Confederate Government.* 2 vols. New York: Thomas Yoseloff, 1958.

Diamond, Sigmund, ed., *A Casual View of America: The Home Letters of Salomon de Rothschild, 1859–1861.* Stanford, California: Stanford University Press, 1961.

Dickens, Charles, *American Notes.* Greenwich, Connecticut: Fawcett Publications, Inc., 1961.

Disturnell, John, *Disturnell's American and European Railway and Steamship Guide, Giving the Arrangement on All the Great Lines of Travel Through the United States and Canada, Across the Atlantic Ocean, and Throughout Central Europe. Also Containing a Brief Description of the Principal Places in England, France, Etc.* New York: Published by Disturnell, 1853.

Featherstonhaugh, George William, *A Canoe Voyage up the Minnay Sotor; With an Account of the Lead and Copper Deposits in Wisconsin; of the Gold Region in the Cherokee Country; and Sketches of Popular Manners; &c., &c.* 2 vols. London: Richard Bentley, 1847.

————, *Excursion Through the Slave States, from Washington on the Potomac to the Frontier of Mexico; With Sketches of Popular Manners and Geological Notices.* 2 vols. New York: Harper & Brothers, 1844.

Foster, Lillian, *Way-Side Glimpses, North and South.* New York: Rudd & Carleton, 1860.

Godley, John Robert, *Letters from America.* 2 vols. London: J. Murray, 1844.

Goodrich, Charles A., *The Universal Traveller: Designed to Introduce Readers at Home to an Acquaintance with the Arts, Customs, and Manners, of the Principal Modern Nations on the Globe.* Hartford: Canfield & Robins, 1838.

Goodrich, Samuel Griswold, *A System of Universal Geography, Popular and Scientific, Comprising a Physical, Political, and Statistical Account of the World and its Various Divisions.* Boston: Carter, Handee & Company, 1832.

Hall, Abraham Oakey, *The Manhattaner in New Orleans; Or, Phases of "Crescent City" Life.* New York: J. S. Redfield; New Orleans, J. C. Morgan, 1851.

Hall, Basil, *Travels in North America in the Years 1827 and 1828.* 3 vols. London: Simpkin and Marshall, 1829.

Hall, Frederick, *Letters from the East and from the West.* Washington: F. Taylor and W. M. Morrison; Baltimore, F. Lucas, Jr., 1840.

Hall, Margaret, *The Aristocratic Journey: Being the Outspoken Letters of Mrs. Basil Hall Written During a Fourteen Months' Sojurn in America, 1827–1828.* New York: G. P. Putnam's Sons, 1931. Edited by Una Pope-Hennessy.

Hamilton, Thomas, *Men and Manners in America.* 2 vols. London: T. Cadell, Strand, 1834.

Haskel, Daniel and J. Calvin Smith, *A Complete Descriptive and Statistical Gazetteer of the United States of America, Containing a Particular Description of the States, Territories, Counties, Districts, Parishes, Cities, Towns, and Villages—Mountains, Rivers, Lakes, Canals, and Railroads: With an Abstract of the Census and Statistics for 1840, Exhibiting A Complete View of the Agricultural, Commercial, Manufacturing, and Literary Condition and Resources of the Country.* New York: Sherman & Smith, 1843.

Heartman, Charles, ed., *An Immigrant of A Hundred Years Ago: A Story of Someone's Ancestor, Translated and Retold by an Old Hand.* Hattiesburg, Mississippi: The Book Farm, 1941.

Hundley, Daniel Robinson, *Social Relations in Our Southern States.* New York: Henry B. Price, 1860.

Ingraham, Joseph Holt, *The South-West. By a Yankee.* 2 vols. New York: Harper & Brothers, 1835.

Jewell, Henry, *Life and Writings of Reverend Enoch M. Pingree, Who Died in Louisville, Kentucky, January 6, 1849. Aged 32 Years.* Cincinnati: Longlay & Brother, 1850.

Kellar, Herbert A., ed., *Solon Robinson, Pioneer and Agriculturist.* 2 vols. Indianapolis, Indiana: Indiana Historical Bureau, 1936.

Kemble, Frances Anne, *Journal of a Residence on a Georgian Plantation in 1838-1839.* New York: Alfred A. Knopf, 1961. Edited by John A Scott.

Kingford, William, *Impressions of the West and South During a Six Weeks' Holiday.* Toronto: A. H. Armour and Company, 1858.

Lanman, Charles, *Adventures in the Wilds of the United States and British American Provinces.* 2 vols. Philadelphia: John W. Moore, 1856.

Lardner, Dionysius, *Railway Economy; A Treatise on the New Art of Transport, Its Management, Prospects, and Relations, Commercial, Financial, and Social, with an Exposition of the Practical Results of the Railways in Operation in the United Kingdom, on the Continent, and in America.* New York: Harper & Brothers, 1850.

Latrobe, Charles Joseph, *The Rambler in North America; 1832–1833.* 2 vols. London: R. B. Seeley & W. Burnside, 1836.

Latrobe, J. H. B., *The Baltimore and Ohio Railroad: Personal Recollections.* Baltimore: Sun Printing Establishment, 1868.

Lewis, George, *Impressions of America and the American Churches.* Edinburgh: W. P. Kennedy, 1845.

Lyell, Charles, *A Second Visit to the United States of North America.* 2 vols. New York: Harper & Brothers, 1849.

———, *Travels in North America, in the Years 1841–2; With Geological*

Observations on the United States, Canada, and Nova Scotia. 2 vols. New York: Wiley and Putnam, 1845.

Mackay, Alexander, *The Western World; Or Travels in the United States in 1846-47: Exhibiting Them in Their Latest Development, Social, Political and Industrial.* 3 vols. London: R. Bentley, 1849.

Mackay, Charles, *Life and Liberty in America; Or, Sketches of a Tour in the United States and Canada, in 1857-8.* New York: Harper & Brothers, 1859.

Malmin, Gunnar J., trans., *America in the Forties: The Letters of Ole Munch Raeder.* Minneapolis: University of Minnesota Press, 1929.

Marryat, Frederick, *A Diary in America, with Remarks on its Institutions.* Philadelphia: T. K. & P. G. Collins, 1840.

Martineau, Harriet, *Retrospect of Western Travel.* 3 vols. London: Saunders and Otley, 1838.

——, *Society in America.* 2 vols. New York: Saunders and Otley, 1837.

Massey, Stephen L., *James Traveler's Companion. Being a Complete Guide Through the Western States, to the Gulf of Mexico and the Pacific, via the Great Lakes, Rivers, Canals, Etc. Giving Full and Accurate Descriptions of All Places on, and in the Vicinity of, the Western Waters; Interspersed with Historical Notes and Statistical Tables; Together with a Vast Amount of General Information Not Found in Other Works of a Similar Character with Numerous Maps and Illustrations. Also, Containing All of the Principal State, Steamboat, and Railroad Routes in the West, and the Chief Routes to Oregon and California, with Their Respective Distances. The Whole Brought Down to the Present Time.* Cincinnati: J. A. and U. P. James, 1851.

Maxwell, Archibald Montgomery, *A Run Through the United States, During the Autumn of 1840.* 2 vols. London: H. Colburn, 1841.

Mellen, Grenville, ed., *A Book of the United States: Exhibiting Its Geography, Divisions, Constitution and Government, and Presenting a View of the Republic Generally, and of the Individual States; Together with a Condensed History of the Land, from Its First Discovery to the Present Time. The Biography of About Three Hundred of the Leading Men. A Description of the Principal Cities and Towns; With Statistical Tables, Relating to the Religion, Commerce, Manufactures, and Various Other Topics.* Hartford: H. F. Sumner & Company, 1839.

Mendell, Sarah, *Notes of Travel and Life. By Two Ladies—Misses Mendell and Hosmer.* New York: For the Authors, 1854.

Mitchell, David W., *Ten Years Residence in the United States.* London: Smith, Elder and Company, 1862.

Mitchell, Samuel Augustus, *An Accompaniment to Mitchell's Reference and Distance Map of the United States; Containing an Index of All the Counties, Districts, Townships, Towns, &c., in the Union; Together with an Index of the Rivers; by Which Any County, District, Township, &c., or River, May Be Found on the Map, Without Difficulty: Also, a General View of the United States, and the Several States and Territories; With an Account of the Actual and Prospective Internal Improvements Throughout the Union.* Philadelphia: Mitchell and Hinman, 1835.

Murat, Achille, *America and the Americans*. Translated by W. H. Graham. New York: William H. Graham, 1849.

Murray, Amelia Matilda, *Letters from the United States, Cuba and Canada*. New York: G. P. Putnam & Company, 1856.

Murray, Charles Augustus, *Travels in North America During the Years 1834, 1835, & 1836. Including a Summer Residence With the Pawnee Tribe of Indians, in the Remote Prairies of the Missouri, and a Visit to Cuba and the Azore Islands*. 2 vols. New York: Harper & Brothers, 1839.

Murray, Henry Anthony, *Lands of the Slave and the Free; Or, Cuba, the United States, and Canada*. 2 vols. London: John W. Parker and Son, 1855.

Nichols, Thomas Low, *Forty Years of American Life, 1821–1861*. New York: Stackpole Sons, 1937.

Olmsted, Frederick Law, *The Cotton Kingdom: A Traveller's Observations on Cotton and Slavery in the American Slave States*. New York: Alfred A. Knopf, 1953. Edited by Arthur M. Schlesinger.

————, *The Slave States Before the Civil War*. New York: G. P. Putnam's Sons, 1959. Edited by Harvey Wish.

Parsons, Charles Grandison, *Inside View of Slavery: Or a Tour Among the Planters*. Cleveland, Ohio: Jewett, Proctor and Worthington, 1855.

Phelps' Hundred Cities and Large Towns of America: With Railroad Distances Throughout the United States, Maps of Fourteen Cities, and Other Embellishments. New York: Phelps, Fanning & Company, 1853.

Pierce, George Foster, *Incidents of Western Travel: In a Series of Letters*. Nashville: Southern Methodist Publishing House, 1859. Edited by Thomas O. Summers.

Pollard, Edward Alfred, *Black Diamonds Gathered in the Darkey Homes of the South*. New York: Pudney & Russell, Publishers, 1860.

Power, Tyrone, *Impressions of America, During the Years 1833, 1834, 1835*. 2 vols. London: Richard Bentley, 1836.

Pulszky, Francis and Theresa, *White, Red, Black: Sketches of American Society in the United States During the Visit of their Guest*. 2 vols. New York: Redfield, 1853.

Richards, Thomas Addison, ed., *Appletons' Companion Hand-Book of Travel*. New York: D. Appleton & Company, 1866.

————, *Appletons' Illustrated Hand-Book of American Travel*. New York: D. Appleton & Company, 1857.

Rogers, Carlton H., *Incidents of Travel in the Southern States and Cuba. With a Description of the Mammoth Cave*. New York: R. Craighead, 1862.

Rogers, George, *Memoranda of the Experience, Labors, and Travels of a Universalist Preacher*. Cincinnati: J. S. Gurley, 1845.

Shaw, John, *A Ramble Through the United States, Canada, and the West Indies*. London: J. F. Hope, 1856.

Shippee, Lester B., ed., *Bishop Whipple's Southern Diary, 1843–1844*. Minneapolis: University of Minnesota Press, 1937.

Smith, William Prescott, *Great Railway Celebrations of 1857*. New York: D. Appleton & Company, 1858.

Stevenson, David, "Railways in America in 1837," *The Railway Library, 1915.* Chicago: Stromberg, Allen & Company, 1916.

Stirling, James, *Letters from the Slave States.* London: John W. Parker and Son, 1857.

Stuart-Wortley, Lady Emmeline Charlotte, *Travels in the United States, Etc., During 1849 and 1850.* New York: Harper & Brothers, 1868.

Sturge, Joseph, *A Visit to the United States in 1841.* Boston: Dexter S. King, 1842.

Tanner, Henry Schenck, *A Description of the Canals and Railroads of the United States, Comprehending Notices of All the Works of Internal Improvements Throughout the Several States.* New York: T. R. Tanner & J. Disturnell, 1840.

————, *Memoirs on the Recent Surveys, Observations, and Internal Improvements in the United States.* Philadelphia: Published by the Author, 1829.

Thomas, G. F., *Appletons' Illustrated Railway and Steam Navigation Guide.* New York: D. Appleton & Company, 1864.

Thomson, William, *A Trademan's Travels, in the United States and Canada, in the Years 1840, 41, & 42.* Edinburgh: Oliver & Boyd, 1842.

Tower, Philo, *Slavery Unmasked: Being a Truthful Narrative of A Three Years' Residence and Journeying in Eleven Southern States: To Which is Added the Invasion of Kansas, Including the Last Chapter of Her Wrongs.* Rochester: E. Darrow & Brother, 1856.

Tremenheere, Hugh Seymour, *Notes on Public Subjects, Made During a Tour in the United States and in Canada.* London: John Murray, 1852.

Tudor, Henry, *Narrative of a Tour in North America; Comprising Mexico, the Mines of Real del Monte, the United States, and the British Colonies, with an Excursion to the Island of Cuba.* 2 vols. London: James Duncan, Paternoster Row, 1834.

Warner, I. W., *The Immigrant's Guide, and Citizen's Manual: A Work for Immigrants of All Classes to the United States of North America; With Directions and Valuable Information for Travellers.* New York: C. M. Saxton, 1848.

Waylen, Edward, *Ecclesiastical Reminscences of the United States.* New York: Wiley and Putnam, 1846.

Weber, Shirley H., ed., *Schliemann's First Visit to America, 1850–1851.* Cambridge, Massachusetts: Harvard University Press, 1942.

Weld, Charles Richard, *A Vacation Tour in the United States and Canada.* London: Longman, Brown, Green, and Longmans, 1855.

Williams, John Lee, *The Territory of Florida: Or Sketches of the Topography, Civil, and Natural History, of the Country, Climate, and the Indian Tribes, from the First Discovery to the Present Time, With a Map, Views, Etc.* New York: A. T. Goodrich, 1839.

————, *The Traveller's and Tourist's Guide Through the United States, Canada, Etc. Exhibiting the Various Routes of Travel, with Explanatory Notes, and Other Useful Information, Together with Descriptions of, and Routes to, the Prominent Places of Fashionable and Healthful Resort.* Philadelphia: Lippincott, Grambo and Company, 1855.

Williams, Wellington, *Appleton's Railroad and Steamboat Companion.*

Being a Traveller's Guide Through the Northern, Eastern, and Middle States, Canada, New Brunswick, and Nova Scotia. New York: D. Appleton and Company, 1849.

Willis, Nathaniel Parker, *Health Trip to the Tropics.* New York: C. Scribner, 1853.

Yoseloff, Thomas, ed., *Voyage to America: The Journals of Thomas Cather.* New York: Thomas Yoseloff, 1961.

Secondary Sources

Adams, Charles F., *Railroads: Their Origin and Problems.* New York: G. P. Putnam & Company, 1878.

Adams, James Truslow, ed., *Dictionary of American History*, IV, New York: Charles Scribner's Sons, 1940.

Alexander, Edwin P., *American Locomotives, 1829–1900.* New York: W. W. Norton & Company, Inc., 1941.

Alexander, Edwin P., *Down at the Depot: American Railroad Stations From 1831–1920.* New York: Bramhall House, 1970.

Berger, Max, *The British Traveller in America, 1836–1860.* New York: Columbia University Press, 1943.

Black, Robert C., *The Railroads of the Confederacy.* Chapel Hill: The University of North Carolina Press, 1952.

Brown, William H., *The History of the First Locomotives in America.* New York: D. Appleton and Company, 1874.

Catalogue of the Centenary Exhibition of the Baltimore & Ohio Railroad, 1827–1927. Baltimore: Published by the Baltimore & Ohio Railroad, 1927.

Clark, Thomas D., *A Pioneer Southern Railroad from New Orleans to Cairo.* Chapel Hill: The University of North Carolina Press, 1936.

————, *Travels in the Old South.* 4 vols. Norman, Oklahoma: University of Oklahoma Press, 1959.

Clark, William H., *Railroads and Rivers.* Boston: L. C. Page & Company, 1939.

Clarke, Thomas Curtis, *The American Railway, Its Construction, Development, Management, and Appliances.* New York: Charles Scribner's Sons, 1892.

Commager, Henry S., *America in Perspective: The United States Through Foreign Eyes.* New York: Random House, Inc., 1947.

Coulter, E. Merton, *Travels in the Confederate States.* Norman, Oklahoma: University of Oklahoma Press, 1948.

Couper, William, "Claudius Crozet Soldier-Scholar-Educator-Engineer," *Southern Sketches*, VIII (1936), 127–173.

Davis, Champion McDowell, *"Atlantic Coast Line," Fragments of Its History During Over a Century.* New York: The Newcomen Society in North America, 1950.

Derrick, Samuel Melanchthon, *Centennial History of the South Carolina Railroad.* Columbia, South Carolina: The State Company, 1930.

Dick, Everett, *The Dixie Frontier: A Social History of the Southern Frontier from the First Transmontane Beginnings to the Civil War.* New York: Alfred A. Knopf, 1948.

Dunbar, Seymour, *A History of Travel in America.* 4 vols. Indianapolis: The Bobbs-Merrill Company, 1915.

Fish, Carl Russell, *The Rise of the Common Man.* New York: Macmillan Company, 1929.

Herr, Kincaid, *The L & N Railroad, 1850–1963.* Louisville: Public Relations Department, Louisville & Nashville Railroad, 1964.

Holbrook, Stewart H., *The Story of American Railroads.* New York: Crown Publishers, 1947.

Hungerford, Edward, *The American Railroad in Laboratory.* Washington: American Railway Association, 1933.

———, *The Story of the Baltimore & Ohio Railroad, 1827–1927.* 2 vols. New York: G. Putnam's Sons, 1928.

Hunter, Louis C., *Steamboats on the Western Rivers: An Economic and Technological History.* Cambridge: Harvard University Press, 1949.

Johnson, Emory R., *American Railway Transportation.* New York: D. Appleton & Company, 1908.

———, *Principles of Railroad Transportation.* D. Appleton & Co., 1916.

Kane, Joseph Nathan, *Facts About the Presidents.* New York: Pocket Books, Inc., 1964.

Kinert, Reed, *Early American Steam Locomotives, 1830–1900.* New York: Crown Publishing Company, 1962.

Klein, Maury, *History of the Louisville & Nashville Railroad.* New York: The Macmillan Company, 1972.

Kohn, David, ed., *Internal Improvement in South Carolina, 1817–1828.* Washington: Privately Printed, 1938.

Laut, Agnes C., *The Romance of the Rails.* New York: Tudor Publishing Company, 1936.

Litwack, Leon F., *North of Slavery: The Negro in the Free States, 1790–1860.* Chicago: University of Chicago Press, 1961.

Luxon, Norval N., *Niles' Weekly Register, News Magazine of the Nineteenth Century.* Baton Rouge: Louisiana State University Press, 1947.

MacGill, Caroline E., *History of Transportation in the United States Before 1860.* Washington: Carnegie Institution of Washington, 1917.

Meeks, Carroll Louis Vanderslice, *The Railroad Station. An Architectural History.* New Haven: Yale University Press, 1956.

Mencken, August, *The Railroad Passenger Car.* Baltimore: The Johns Hopkins Press, 1957.

Monaghan, Frank, *French Travellers in the United States, 1765–1932.* New York: Antiquarian Press Ltd., 1961.

Morison, Samuel Eliot and Henry Steele Commager, *The Growth of the American Republic.* 2 vols. New York: Oxford University Press, 1962.

Nevins, Allan, *American Social History as Recorded by British Travellers.* New York: H. Holt, 1923.

Phillips, Lance, *Yonder Comes the Train.* New York: A. S. Barnes, 1965.

Phillips, Ulrich Bonnell, *A History of Transportation in the Eastern Cotton Belt to 1860*. New York: The Columbia University Press, 1908.

―――, *American Negro Slavery. A Survey of the Supply, Employment and Control of Negro Labor as Determined by the Plantation Regime*. New York: D. Appleton and Company, 1918.

―――, *Life and Labor in the Old South*. Boston: Little, Brown, & Company, 1946.

Reck, Franklin M., *The Romance of American Transportation*. New York: Thomas Y. Crowell Company, 1962.

Reed, Merl E., *New Orleans and the Railroads. The Struggle For Commercial Empire, 1830–1860*. Baton Rouge: Louisiana State University Press, 1966.

Renfro, N. P., Jr., *The Beginning of Railroads in Alabama*. Auburn: Alabama Polytechnic Institute of Historical Studies, 1910.

Riegel, Robert Edgar, *Young America, 1830–1840*. Norman: University of Oklahoma Press, 1949.

Ringwalt, J. L., *Development of Transportation Systems in the United States*. Philadelphia: Published by the author, 1888.

Schwaab, Eugene L., ed., *Travels in the Old South, 1783–1860*. Lexington: University of Kentucky Press, 1974.

Stover, John F., *The Railroads of the South, 1865–1900. A Study in Finance and Control*. Chapel Hill: University of North Carolina Press, 1955.

Taylor, George Rogers and Irene D. Neu, *The American Railroad Network, 1861–1890*. Cambridge: Harvard University Press, 1956.

―――, *The Transportation Revolution, 1815–1860*. New York: Rinehart & Company, 1951.

Thomson, Thomas Richard, *Check List of Publications on American Railroads Before 1841. A Union List of Printed Books and Pamphlets, Including State and Federal Documents, Dealing With Charters, By-Laws, Legislative Acts, Speeches, Debates, Land Grants, Officers and Engineers' Reports, Travel Guides, Maps, etc.* New York: The New York Public Library, 1942.

Tuckerman, Henry T., *America and Her Commentators. With a Critical Sketch of Travel in the United States*. New York: Antiquarian Press, Ltd., 1961.

Turner, George Edgar, *Victory Rode the Rails. The Strategic Place of the Railroads in the Civil War*. New York: The Bobbs-Merrill Company, Inc., 1953.

Van Metre, Thurman William, *Transportation in the United States*. Chicago: The Foundation Press, Inc., 1939.

Weber, Thomas, *The Northern Railroads in the Civil War, 1861–1865*. New York: King's Crown Press, 1952.

White, John H., *Cincinnati Locomotive Builders, 1845-1868*. Washington: U. S. Government Printing Office, 1965.

―――, *James Millholland and Early Railroad Engineering*. Washington: Smithsonian Press, 1967.

―――, *The "Pioneer" Light Passenger Locomotive of 1851*. Washington: Smithsonian Institution, 1964.

Wiltse, Charles M., *The New Nation 1800–1845*. New York: Hill and Wong, 1961.

Winther, Oscar Osburn, *The Transportation Frontier: Trans-Mississippi West, 1865–1900*. New York: Holt, Rinehart and Winston, 1964.

Woodward, C. Van, *Origins of the New South, 1877–1913*. Baton Rouge: Louisiana State University Press, 1951.

PERIODICALS

(Periodicals used are from the years 1827–1861.)

Primary Sources

American Railroad Journal
The Atlantic Monthly
Cotterill, R. S., "Southern Railroads and Western Trade, 1840–1850," *Mississippi Valley Historical Review*, III (March, 1917), 427–441.
DeBow's Review
Harper's Weekly Magazine
Hoyt, William D., Jr., "Journey to the Springs, 1846," *Virginia Magazine of History*, LIV (April, 1946), 119–136.
Hunt's Merchants Magazine and Commercial Review
Illustrated London News
Kellar, Herbert A., ed., "A Journey Through the South in 1836: Diary of James D. Davidson, *Journal of Southern History*, I (August, 1935), 345–377.
The Knickerbocker or *New York Monthly Magazine*
Literary World
More, John Hammond, ed., "A South Carolina Lawyer Visits St. Augustine—1837," *The Florida Historical Quarterly*, XLIII (April, 1965), 361–378.
Museum of Foreign Literature and Science
Newsome, A. R., ed., "Simeon Colton's Railroad Report, 1840," *North Carolina Historical Review*, XI (July, 1934), 205–238.
New York Times
Niles' Weekly Register
North American Review
Poor, H. V. & H. W., *Manual of the Railroads of the United States for 1868–1869*. New York: H. V. & H. W. Poor, 1868
The Port Folio
Putnams Magazine
Taylor, Rosser H., "Hamburg: An Experiment in Town Promotion," *North Carolina Historical Review*, XI (January, 1934), 20–38.
Wills, William H., "A Southern Traveler's Diary in 1840," *Publications of the Southern History Association*, VII-VIII, (September, 1903–March, 1904), 349–352.

Secondary Sources

Black, Robert C., "Railroads in the Confederacy," *Civil War History*, VII (September, 1961), 231–238.

Brewster, Lawrence Fay, "Ante-Bellum Planters and their Means of Transportation," *Proceedings of the South Carolina Historical Association*, XVII (1948), 15–25.

Campbell, E. G., "Railroads in National Defense, 1829–1848," *Mississippi Valley Historical Review*, XXVII (December, 1940), 361–378.

Clark, Thomas D., "The Montgomery and West Point Railroad Company," *Georgia Historical Quarterly*, XVII (December, 1933), 293–298.

Cotterill, Robert Spencer, "Southern Railroads," *Mississippi Valley Historical Review*, X (March, 1924), 396–405.

Dixon, Max, "Building the Central Railroad of Georgia," *Georgia Historical Review*, XLV (March, 1961), 1–21.

Doster, James F., "Were the Southern Railroads Destroyed by the Civil War?" *Civil War History*, VII (September, 1961), 310–320.

Johnston, Angus J., "Virginia Railroads in April 1861," *Journal of Southern History*, XXIII (August, 1957), 307–330.

King, Elizabeth Doris, "The First-Class Hotel and the Age of the Common Man," *Journal of Southern History*, XXIII (May, 1957), 173–188.

Ledet, Wilton P., "The History of the City of Carrollton," *Louisiana Historical Quarterly*, XXI (January, 1938), 220–281.

Livingood, James W., "Chattanooga: A Rail Junction of the Old South," *Tennessee Historical Quarterly*, VI (September, 1947), 230–250.

McGuire, Peter S., "Athens and the Railroads: The Georgia and the Northeastern," *Georgia Historical Quarterly*, XVIII (March, 1934), 1–27.

Moore, John Hebron, "Simon Gray, Riverman: A Slave Who Was Almost Free," *Mississippi Valley Historical Review*, XLIX (December, 1962), 472–484.

Patterson, Ernest F., "Alabama's First Railroad," *Alabama Review*, IX (January, 1956), 33–45.

Pelzer, Louis, "Pioneer Stage-Coach Travel," *The Mississippi Valley Historical Review*, XXIII (June, 1936), 1–26.

Pettengill, George W., "The Story of the Florida Railroads," *The Railway and Locomotive Historical Society*, XXCVI (July, 1952).

Quenzel, Carroll H., "The Manufacture of Locomotives and Cars in Alexandria in the 1850's," *Virginia Magazine of History and Biography*, LXII (April, 1954), 181–189.

Ramsdell, Charles W., "The Confederate Government and the Railroads," *American Historical Review*, XXII (July, 1917), 794–810.

Russel, R. R., "A Revaluation of the Period Before the Civil War: Railroads," *Mississippi Valley Historical Review*, XV (December, 1928), 341–354.

Stover, John F., "The Ruined Railroads of the Confederacy," *Georgia Historical Quarterly*, XLII (December, 1958), 376–388.

Taylor, Rosser H., "Hamburg: An Experiment in Town Promotion," *North Carolina Historical Review*, XI (January, 1934), 20–38.

Turner, Charles W., "The Louisa Railroad, 1836–1850," *North Carolina Historical Review*, XXIV (January, 1947), 35–57.

Ward, James A., "A New Look at Antebellum Southern Railroad Development," *Journal of Southern History*, XXXIX (August, 1973), 409–420.

Whitman, Alice, "Transportation in Territorial Florida," *Florida Historical Quarterly*, XVII (July, 1938), 25–53.

Williams, Jack K., "Travel in Ante-Bellum Georgia as Recorded by English Visitors," *Georgia Historical Quarterly*, XXXIII (September, 1949), 191–205.

Index

Abbott, John, 41, 42, 76, 133, 155
Abolitionists, 133, 151
Accidents, 72, 81ff
Acquia Creek, Va., 129
Adams, Charles F., 140
Adams, John Quincy, 21, 22, 98
Aiken, S. C., 74, 78, 94, 113, 124
Air Conditioning, 57ff, 60
Alabama, 19, 112, 128, 157
Allen, Horatio, 42
Alligators, 155
Altonna, 87
American Railroad Journal, 17, 34, 37,
    41, 59, 62, 82, 84, 85, 87, 102, 103,
    104, 112, 113, 123, 141
Andrews, Sidney, 165
Appleton's Companion Handbook, 166
Appleton's Railroad and Steamboat Companion, 68
Appleton's Railway Guide, 118, 119
Arese, Francesco, 7, 12
Aroostook War, 115
Athens, Ga., 40
Atlanta, Ga., 16, 66, 118, 133, 157, 165
Atlantic Monthly, 16, 74
Augusta, Ga., 7, 18, 22, 65, 75, 76, 111,
    124, 148, 151, 156, 165
Augusta, Georgia *Chronicle and Sentinel*, 94
Availability of construction material,
    10, 11
Axle breakage, 98, 99

Baggage and baggage cars, 64, 121,
    122, 137, 139; liability for baggage,
    122
Baltimore, Md., 6, 21, 27, 35, 45, 50,
    72, 97, 99, 100, 114, 116, 119, 120,
    122, 128, 131, 136, 139, 148, 151,
    162
Baltimore & Ohio Railroad, 5, 6, 7, 8,
    21, 22, 27, 34, 37, 39, 44, 48, 49, 60,
    64, 69, 73, 93, 123, 162
Barnesville, Ga., 157
Barnum's Hotel, 116, 117, 128
Barnwell, S. C., 18
Barrel Car, 49
Barrier Car, 86
Baton Rouge, La., 151
Baxter, William, 110
Beauvallet, Léon, 12, 13, 44, 51, 56, 72,
    76, 82, 159, 160
Bells, 42, 101, 125
Best Friend of Charleston, 33, 37, 86, 100
Biggs, Joseph, 8, 36, 89, 131, 136, 137,
    138, 139, 159
Blackville, S. C., 18, 115, 116
Blue Mountain Railroad, 79
Boardman Locomotive Boiler Company, 37
Boiler Plugs for locomotives, 87
Boston & Lowell Railroad, 35
Bowling Green, Ky., 24
Brakes, 42, 49, 50, 53, 54, 79
Branchville, S. C., 155
Bremer, Fredrika, 123, 152, 153, 154,
    155, 159, 162
Bridges, 73ff, 82

Brown, Barney, 18
Bryant, William Cullen, 61, 119, 124, 160
Buckingham, James Silk, 17, 38, 48, 130, 155
Burden Cars, 99
Burford, S. H., 19

Cairo & New Orleans Railroad, 40, 119
Camden & Amboy Railroad, 44, 88, 89, 98
Camden Journal, 19
Canals, 3ff, 171
Carroll, Charles, 21
Carrollton, La., 14, 109
Carrollton, Louisiana Star, 108
Carrollton Railroad, 108
Cather, Thomas, 16, 115, 127, 128
Celebrations of railroads, 20ff
Center aisle of American coaches, 54ff
Center posts, 103
Chambers, William, 36, 39, 45, 48, 51, 55, 75, 103, 110, 112, 117, 118, 121, 122, 123, 124, 127, 141, 142, 143, 147
Charleston, S. C., 10, 18, 22, 23, 31, 38, 74, 94, 113, 118, 119, 120, 124, 148, 151, 153, 155, 160
Charleston & Hamburg Railroad, 5, 7, 8, 22, 28, 32, 35, 37, 40, 41, 42, 69, 74, 75, 78, 86, 94, 100, 115, 118, 132
Charlotte, N. C., 165
Charlottesville, Va., 91
Chattahoochee River, 76
Chattanooga, 16, 97, 111, 116
Chehaw, Ala., 122
Chesapeake & Ohio Canal, 21
Chevalier, Michel, 4, 10, 11, 12, 33, 35, 72, 73, 74, 135, 150
Civil War, 24, 72, 163, 164
Class accommodations, 126, 127ff
Clemens, George, 79
Clermont, 2
Cobden, Richard, 40, 126, 147, 148
Coles, Governor of Indiana, 21

Columbia, S. C., 35, 148, 151, 153, 165
Columbia & Philadelphia Railroad, 37
Columbus, Ga., 76, 151
Collisions, 85, 88, 90ff
Combe, George, 99, 130, 139
Comparison of European and American Railroads, 33, 34, 42, 43, 52, 83, 91, 95, 107, 110, 112, 114, 115, 121, 152, 154
Commercial & Statistical Register, 122
Communications between the engineer and conductor, 102
Conductors, 40, 41, 55, 119, 120, 140ff, 163; dress of, 141; equipment, 142; negligence of duties, 143, 144
Corinth, Miss., 16
Cotton, 111, 153, 156, 157
Couplings, 52, 53
Covington, Ga., 120
Cowcatcher, 43ff, 88, 89, 90
"Crackers," 161
Crockett, David, 18, 31, 32, 66
Crossings, 102, 103
Crowe, Eyre, 64, 79, 136, 152, 161
Cumberland, Md., 93
Cumberland Valley Railroad, 63, 64
Curves, 33

Danville, Va., 165
Darrell, Nicholas, 86
Davidson, James D., 4, 36, 74, 113, 148
Davies, Ebenezer, 50, 61, 72, 73, 97, 122, 127
Davis, Jefferson, 24
Deaths on American railroads, 81ff
DeBow, J. D. B., 14
DeBow's Review, 9, 10, 11, 13, 118
Decorations, 48
Depots, 23, 27, 28, 101, 107, 112, 160, 161
Derailments, 69, 82, 85, 92
Destruction of Southern railroads, 165ff
Dickens, Charles, 30, 39, 51, 61, 110, 129, 134, 143, 159, 167

Dining Car, 123
Disturnell's Guide, 114, 118
Dress of passengers, 58, 166
Dripps, Issac, 88
Drunks, 64, 132, 144

Eating accommodations, 108, 109, 112, 116, 122, 123, 124
Egalitarian spirit of American railroads, 54, 67, 97, 98, 107, 115, 125, 126ff 162, 163, 173
Ellicott's Mills, 6, 27, 123, 162
Engineers, 41, 82, 100, 104, 120
Erie Canal, 2, 3, 6
Explosions, 19, 86
Explosions of steamboats, 83, 84, 85
Express trains, 102

F. *Harris*, 79
Fares, 6, 113, 118, 120, 159
Featherstonhaugh, George, 128, 157
Fitzhugh, George, 133
Firemen, 64, 86, 161
Flags, 102
Florida, 4, 19, 151
Forests, 152, 153, 156, 158, 160
Forsyth, Ga., 41
Foster, Lillian, 111, 143, 155, 156, 161
Frankfort, Ky., 17, 24, 48
Fredericksburg, Va., 79, 120, 124
Freedom of speech, 155
Freight, 15, 16, 35, 36
Freight cars and trains, 15, 40, 49, 66, 78, 134
French Academy of Medicine, 104
Fulton, Robert, 2

Gaston, N. C., 63, 152
Georgia, 11, 17, 75, 110, 129, 136, 155, 157, 159, 161, 162
Georgia, 94
Georgia Central Railroad, 43, 111, 155, 156
Georgia Railroad Company, 40, 87, 94
Godley, John Robert, 147
Goodrich, Charles A., 105

"Grand Tour," 151, 154, 155, 158
Greensboro, N. C., 165

Hacker, S. S., 49
Hall, Abraham Oakey, 31, 56
Hall, Basil and Margaret, 154
Hall, Frederick, 17
Hamburg, S. C., 7, 8, 22
Hamilton, Thomas, 48, 123, 149
Harper's Ferry, Va., 162
Harper's Monthly, 32
Hazards, 34, 42, 44, 53, 68, 70, 76, 77, 80
Headrest, 56
Headlights, 41, 42
Health and entertainment, 16
Heating stoves, 51, 58, 60, 61, 62, 64, 161
Holly Springs, Miss., 40, 118
Horse path for pulling engines, 70
Hospitality, 154
Hotels, 113, 114, 115, 116, 117, 124, 136
Hundley, Daniel Robinson, 61, 112
Hunt's Merchants Magazine, 9, 16, 39, 82, 103, 104, 122

Imlay, Richard, 49
Immigrants, 137, 140
Inclines, 33, 77ff, 164
Ingraham, Joseph Holt, 14, 31, 92, 119
Insurance, 104

Jackson, Miss., 15
James River, 75
John Bull, 88

Kemble, Frances Anne, 12, 54, 58, 63, 73, 110, 124, 152
Kennaway, John H., 165, 166
Kentucky, 11
Kingsford, William, 85

Lake Pontchartrain Railroad, 14, 31, 56, 92, 158; depot, 114, 119

Lanman, Charles, 40, 101, 109, 130, 157, 160
Lardner, Dionysius, 5, 17, 27, 51, 63, 70, 105, 126, 137, 139
Latrobe, Charles Joseph, 7, 12
Lewis, George, 65, 75, 153
Lexington, Ky., 17, 48, 99
Lighting in cars, 62, 63
Lincoln, Abraham, 71
Locomotives: cabs, 42; coal fuel, 31, 33, 36ff; compared to animals, 31ff, 38, 39, 167, 175; cost of, 33; decorations, 43; names, 43; size, 33; smokestacks, 31, 39; wood fuel, 31, 33, 36ff
Locomotive power: dogs, 29; horses, 6, 26, 27, 29, 48, 50, 69; horse tread, 28; sails, 6, 29; springs, 29; steam, 6, 7, 26ff, 30ff 175
London *Morning Chronicle,* 131
Louisiana, 75, 115
Louisville & Nashville Railroad, 24, 109
Louisville, Ky., 24, 108, 109
Luggage train, 97
Lyell, Charles, 8, 17, 61, 62, 91, 112, 124, 144, 145, 147

Mackay, Alexander, 38, 45, 75, 112, 131, 132, 133, 134, 135
Mackay, Charles, 64, 111, 114, 119, 130, 144, 153, 159
Macon, Ga., 17, 70, 76, 108, 109, 111, 151, 155, 156
Madison, Ga., 65, 75
Mail, 7
Mammoth Cave, Ky., 151
Marietta, Ga., 87
Marion, 94
Marryat, C. B., 45, 46, 54, 124, 125, 158
Martineau, Harriet, 38, 74, 148, 161
Maryland, 5, 6
Maxwell, Archibald, 114, 115
Mellen, Grenville, 9
Memphis, Tenn., 60, 118, 147, 151, 161, 164

Mendell, Sarah, 143
Mercury, 34
Miles, William P., 23
Military weakness of Sourthern railroads, 164ff
Mississippi, 75, 97
Mississippi Central Railroad, 24
Mississippi Free Trader, 32
Missouri, 11
Mitchell, David W., 136, 147
Mitchell's Guidebook, 6
Mobile, Ala., 120, 133, 151
Mobile & Ohio Railroad, 84
Montgomery & West Point Railroad, 24
Montgomery, Ala., 24, 76, 120, 148, 151, 155, 157
Murat, Achille, 154
Murray, Amelia Matilda, 15, 19, 75, 91, 97, 129, 130, 157, 158, 161
Murray, Charles Augustus, 35
Murray, Henry A., 50, 61, 91, 96, 111, 112, 124, 129, 130
Museum of Foreign Literature and Science, 5

Nashville, Tenn., 24, 97, 109, 165
Natchez & Jackson Railroad, 32
Natchez, Miss., 151
Natchez Trace, 15
National Convention of Railroad Engineers, 100
Negroes, 69, 71, 86, 101, 113, 114, 118, 124, 126, 128, 129, 130, 134, 135, 136, 137, 146, 160, 161
Newspapers, 104, 118, 129; reporting accidents, 104, 105
New England Magazine, 47, 50
New Orleans, La., 31, 94, 114, 116, 119, 120, 133, 148, 151, 154, 155, 158
New Orleans & Great Northern Railroad, 15
New Orleans & Jackson Railroad, 69
New York Monthly, 32

Nichols, Thomas Low, 55, 60, 65, 122, 126, 129, 131
Night travel, 39, 63, 64, 81, 101, 115
"Nigger Car," 133, 135, 137
Niles, J. M., 16
Niles' Weekly Register, 3, 7, 8, 9, 21, 22, 23, 26, 29, 44, 49, 78, 90
Noise, 67, 158, 159
North American Review, 3, 39
North Carolina, 17, 23, 91, 109, 110, 152
Northern railroads, 11, 35, 68, 71, 155, 159, 163

Odell, Engineer, 95
Ohio River, 151
Olmsted, Frederick Law, 35, 40, 41, 63, 134, 146, 147, 152, 156, 160
Opelika, Ala., 76
Orange & Alexandria Railroad, 61

Parsons, Charles G., 111, 113
Passenger cars, 27, 28, 47, 48, 173, 174
Patapsco River bridge, 73, 74
Pedee, River, 130
Petersburg, Va., 10, 96
Phoenix, 86
Pierce, Franklin, 98, 99
Pierce, George F., 52, 76, 97, 145
Pingree, Enoch M., 87, 88
Platforms on cars, 55
Pollard, Edward A., 134
Porters, 111, 114, 148
Potomac River, 151
Power, Tyrone, 99
Preservation of ties, tracks, 70
Private cars, 66
Profanity, 128
Public pressure for safety, 100ff
Pullman, George, 65
Pulszky, Francis, 35, 158

Raeder, Munch, 93, 139, 140, 147
Railroads: advantages of, 4, 24, 52; construction reasons, 5ff; criticism of, 18, 19, 20; expansion, 3ff, 85; mania for, 5ff, 82, 150
Railroad guidebooks, 117, 166
Rails, 69ff, 159
Reid, Whitelaw, 166
Rex, Dr., 98
Richmond, Va., 61, 79, 110, 129, 134, 136, 148, 151, 152, 153, 154, 155, 156, 160, 164, 165
Right-of-way, 103
Roadbeds, 69, 70
Roanoke, River, 160
Robinson, Solon, 36, 143, 156
Rogers, Carlton H., 31, 67, 156
Rogers, George, 85, 116, 154
Rothschild Salomon de, 162, 163
Ruffin, Edmund, 133
Runners, 113, 117

Safest section of trains, 88
Safety car, 79
Safety cords in cars, 56
Safety regulations, 100, 101
Savannah, 2
Savannah, Ga., 40, 111, 118, 123, 130, 133, 143, 151, 153, 154, 156
Schedules, 91, 101, 120, 121
Schwats, Mrs., 124
Seats and seating arrangements, size of cars, 50ff, 56ff, 65
Segregation in the North, 135, 136, 137
Shaw, John, 66, 124, 129, 145, 146, 157
Sidings, 73, 162
Slaves and slavery, 15, 18, 40, 95, 113, 127, 133, 148, 151, 152, 153, 156, 157
Sleeping cars, 63, 64, 65, 66, 67, 75, 146
Smith, Whitefoord, 20
Smoking, 129, 130
Smoking cars, 66
"Snakeheads," 70, 71
Snakes, 152, 158
Southern Railroad, 119

South Carolina, 5, 18, 19, 22, 23, 209, 111, 130, 132, 153, 154, 155, 160, 161
South Carolina Railroad, 40, 101, 120
Sparks, 30, 37ff, 48ff, 59, 85, 158, 167
Speed, 6, 26ff, 34ff, 66, 82
St. Augustine, Fla., 94, 151
St. Charles Hotel, 114, 116
St. Marks Railroad, 69
Stagecoaches, 53, 120, 158, 160
Standardization, 47, 48
Steamboats, 16, 83ff, 120, 130, 136, 137, 159
Stedman, J. C., 98
Stevens, John, 5
Stevens, Robert L., 71
Stevenson, David, 36, 38, 44, 73, 74
Stirling, James, 137, 153, 155, 156
Suffolk, Va., 152
Summer, Henry, 94
Sunday travel, 19, 20, 81
Suspension systems, 52

T Rail, 71, 164
Tanner, Henry, 162
Tarpley, Colonel, 15, 16
Taxi cabs and fares, 113ff
Tenders, 66
Tennessee, 11
The Mississippian, 16
Thomson, William, 124
Tickets, 108, 109, 117, 118, 142
Ties, 69, 70, 77
Time, lack of standardization, 103, 104, 120
Tobacco chewing, 55, 58, 62, 64, 127, 128, 130ff, 147, 162
Toilets, 56, 66
Tower, Philo, 15, 31, 32, 35, 40, 41
Townsend Horizontal Smoke Pipe, 59, 60
Track: beds, 69, 70; construction cost, 68, 69, 70; fencing, 44, 91ff; gauge, 71, 165; miles of, 7, 9, 10, 11, 23, 172; single track and criticism of, 72, 73, 103; watchmen, 101

Tremenheere, Hugh S., 147
Trevithick, Richard, 5
Tudor, Henry, 6, 12
Turpentine, 153, 160
Tuscumbia & Decatur Railroad, 19
Tuscumbia, Ala., 157

U Rail, 71

Vendors, 124, 163
Vicksburg, Miss., 15, 151
Virginia, 11, 23, 75, 151, 152
Virginia & Tennessee Railroad, 43

Waiting rooms, 108, 109
Warner, I. W., 13
Warning systems, 19
Washington, D. C., 32, 35, 40, 45, 60, 61, 64, 89, 99, 108, 109, 112, 113, 120, 131, 137, 139, 151, 162
Wash-outs and landslides, 76, 160
Waterboys, 161
Water stations, 162
Waylen, Edward, 113
Waynesborough & Georgia Railroad, 156
Weld, Charles Richard, 31, 45, 51, 52, 95, 96, 113, 137, 139, 143, 144, 161
Weldon, N. C., 17, 109, 110, 124, 151, 160, 165
Wells, Mr., 98
West Point, 32
West Point Foundry Works, 32, 33
West Point, Ga., 120
Western & Atlantic Railroad, 43
Westinghouse, George, 54
Wheel arrangements on passenger cars, 51, 52
Whipple, Henry B., 17, 41, 61, 70, 129, 157, 161
Whistle, 101
Wilmington, N. C., 15, 17, 64, 91, 96, 120, 131, 133, 160
Wilmington & Raleigh Railroad, 15
Wilmington & Weldon Railroad, 23, 61, 63, 152

Williams, John Lee, 4
William's Traveller's Guide, 84, 114, 118
Women, segregation of, 65, 126, 132,
   133, 137, 138, 166

Wood saws, 41
Wortley, Emmeline Charlotte Stuart,
   58, 128, 129